Praise for
Selling Your Business

I found this book to be provocative and informative. Louis Crosier lends expertise on complex topics in a non-threating way that allows us all to be more productive as legal, tax and investment advisors. We believe that the more our clients understand the complexity of wealth management, the better we can assist them in meeting their needs.

—Leslie White Allen, President
Family Wealth Management Services

An excellent handbook for corporate insiders or anyone whose wealth is concentrated in a single company. Read this before you sell a share. Well done!

—David Southwell, Chief Financial Officer
Sepracor, Inc. (SEPR)

Founding and making a company grow is fun. Trying to invest the money you make selling a company is not always fun, and this book will help you avoid making the same mistakes that many have made who came before you. Beware of your new-found friends! If you are considering selling your business or have recently done so, read this book.

—William James, Founding Partner
Rockport Capital Partners

An important resource for anyone running a family office. I have used this book to bring family members up to speed on multiple topics related to managing family wealth.

—Russell F. Shappy, Jr., Treasurer
Berwind LLC

This book is right on target. If you are a family business owner considering selling a portion or all of your company, I recommend this book to you highly. In my 18 years of acquiring and investing in family-owned companies I have never come across a better resource than this book for helping the business owner on personal financial issues. It will help you effectively shift focus from running your business to harvesting your life's work.

—Peter Z. Hermann, Founding Partner
Heritage Partners

SELLING YOUR BUSINESS

The Transition from Entrepreneur to Investor

Edited by Louis P. Crosier

WILEY

John Wiley & Sons, Inc.

Published by John Wiley & Sons, Inc., Hoboken, New Jersey
Published simultaneously in Canada

For general information on our other products and services, or technical support, please contact our Customer Care Department within the United States at 800-762-2974, outside the United States at 317-572-3993 or fax 317-572-4002.

Wiley also publishes its books in a variety of electronic formats. Some content that appears in print may not be available in electronic books.

ISBN 0-471-48623-X

Printed in the United States of America

10 9 8 7 6 5 4 3 2 1

For Hope, Catherine, and Wilder,
with all my love.

Contents

Foreword

In the last 20 years, entrepreneurs have created liquid (or semiliquid) wealth to a staggering degree. In general, while they were running and owning their businesses, they were very comfortable with the daily risks they were taking. Now, with cash or stock in an acquiring company, life has become more difficult. Who do they go to for help? What kind of help do they need? How do taxes, estate planning, asset allocation, and charitable issues fit into the equation? What about intergenerational considerations? This book answers many of these questions. Although there are plenty of firms eager to help with complex wealth management issues, few are truly equipped to provide a world-class platform that integrates all aspects of an entrepreneur's financial life. In searching for the right firm, it is helpful to have a broad perspective on the industry and its evolution over the past few decades.

In the late 1960s, the wealth management service providers were trust departments of large banks, accounting firms, family offices, a few financial planning firms, and investment advisors. A few firms offered an integrated wealth advisory business, but this was a new model for managing money for individuals, particularly entrepreneurs who had achieved liquidity through the sale of a business, an IPO, or some other means. As an estate planning lawyer, I had seen how major family wealth was managed by family offices, in which coordinated planning and management were practiced for the super wealthy, but more newly minted millionaires were not being provided with anything like this type of integrated holistic help. Unlike many of the alternatives available to the newly wealthy at the time, very few firms were acutely aware of taxes and the need for comprehensive financial and estate planning, in addition to asset allocation and asset management.

The large banks had departments with estate planning skills, but they were most often separate from the money management group. The brokerage and investment banking businesses were not the best platform for providing wealth management. Their transaction-oriented nature was inconsistent with the need for long-term, tax-efficient planning and investing. Furthermore, the breadth of needs of the entrepreneur was well beyond the scope of what these firms could provide. Even today, few brokers and banks do an excellent job of coordinating an entrepreneur's entire financial life. The incentive structures, cultures, and history of how the large wealth management practices came together have made it difficult to completely align advisor and client interests.

Throughout the 1970s, many new money management companies were getting started, but most were specializing in defined-benefit pension plans. Managing private wealth in a tax-efficient manner was and remains substantially different from the institutional money management business. Of the firms serving the wealthy, from the big money managers to law firms and private trustees, only a few had a reputation of knowing how to deal with the entrepreneur and his or her family—coordinating and integrating estate planning, charitable and generational issues, stock options, taxes, and all aspects of wealth management. Competition in the industry was grouped on both ends of the wealth management spectrum. Either there were money managers whose sole reason for being was to be in the top quartile as compared with their peers (not a bad goal, but there needs to be more), or they were "hand holders" and not very astute investors. It was not easy to find a firm that could "marry" good performance with outstanding coordination and service to fill the role of the trusted advisor.

In the latter part of the 1980s, many firms were beginning to get the idea, and some decided to apply for a trust company charter with the goal of becoming more like a multifamily family office. The trust company was perfect for that objective. It provided the platform for creating many of the wealth-protection and multigenerational wealth-transfer structures integral to a well-thought-out financial plan.

In the 1990s, the wealth management industry began to offer a combination of internal investment management together with what is now popularly known as "open architecture"—meaning that clients had access to investment managers outside of the firm while retaining the coordination under a single roof. For many firms, this began with offering alternative investments to clients by putting together a staff of professionals whose responsibility it was to identify, monitor, and recommend investments that promoted diversification from the more traditional large- and mid-cap growth investing style to which their internal efforts were directed.

In the early 2000s, we went through several years of difficult financial markets, primarily as the markets fell, but, for some, who sold their equities at the wrong time, even as the markets started to rise again. For many people this was a painful period to live through. It has strengthened my conviction that a comprehensive, holistic process to managing wealth is more important than ever. For those who in the mid-1990s believed they could do it themselves, humility has set in and the need for help is clear. Being a fiduciary for families with major wealth is an awesome responsibility. It is my belief that, as this book expertly points out, the seller of a business, in choosing a wealth manager, needs to carefully consider the type of firm, the resources and focus, the track record, the client service staff, and the integrity of the provider.

Furthermore, one needs more than an understanding of modern portfolio theory to successfully manage taxable clients' wealth. One also needs to do more than investment management. There is a requirement to understand taxes, estate planning, philanthropy, and all that goes with providing an integrated service. In the end, the winners will be those who understand, and act upon, the inexorable force that has been at work in advanced economies for centuries: The client rules. Pricing must correspond to value received; meeting your goals is dependent on the clients meeting theirs; and a focused business model must be built around delivering your value proposition.

I anticipate that you will find the following chapters, written by experts in the field, will further enhance your knowledge of the activities and approaches taken by the best and the brightest in our business.

Author Background

Ed Rudman was Co-Founder and Chairman of Pell Rudman, now Atlantic Trust Pell Rudman, and currently serves as a Senior Partner of AMVESCAP. Ed is recognized as a leader in the field of wealth management. He began his career practicing law in New York City, specializing in tax and employee benefit planning. After serving in a variety of senior positions at Laird Capital Management and Estabrook Capital Management, Ed was named President and Chief Executive Officer of The Boston Company Financial Strategies, Inc., a subsidiary of The Boston Company that catered to the needs of wealthy entrepreneurs. He co-founded Pell Rudman & Co. Inc, (now Atlantic Trust Pell Rudman) with Tony Pell in 1980 and has served as a trustee and valued advisor to many families.

Introduction

The idea for putting together *Selling Your Business: The Transition from Entrepreneur to Investor* came from my experience working with entrepreneurs who, leading up to and following a transaction, frequently received incomplete and sometimes flawed advice. "Old money" that has been in families for many generations typically has well-coordinated teams of advisors. But new wealth often seems to flounder, flowing to the hot managers and firms only to be moved from firm to firm through a process of trial and error. Because new wealth comes from a transaction, entrepreneurs often turn to the bankers, lawyers, and others handling the transaction to recommend advisors, or even to manage the money for the entrepreneur following the transaction. Although there is a very broad range of advisory alternatives available to families with substantial wealth, so often families with new wealth begin the search with a small universe of potential alternatives. They do not find out they had better choices available to them until after it is too late.

Thus, I thought it would be helpful to put together in simple terms, all in one place, a set of information specifically tailored to answer the questions entrepreneurs face when thinking about a transaction. *Selling Your Business: The Transition from Entrepreneur to Investor* provides a handbook for entrepreneurs and corporate insiders seeking advice on their personal financial planning prior to selling their business or taking it public. There are multiple books that address business structuring, investing, estate and tax planning, and philanthropy, but these books either target a general audience and are therefore too basic, or they address a single planning issue with such breadth and depth that they fail to distill the key issues for executives contemplating a financial transaction. The goal of this book is to provide an easy-to-read blueprint to help leaders of public and private businesses navigate before and after a transaction, so they are well positioned personally and can avoid costly mistakes.

I have organized the book chronologically, beginning with the issues a business owner should be concerned with prior to a transaction and moving, step by step, through the transaction and into post-transaction diversification, reinvestment, and philanthropy. The book brings together a team of experts whose depth of expertise provides answers to complex questions. It by no means provides comprehensive and personalized answers, but it does help to quickly educate the reader about the kinds of considerations to keep in mind, the questions to ask, and the traps to avoid while interviewing and selecting transaction- and investment-related advice. The information contained in this book should not be acted upon without obtaining specific legal, tax, and investment advice from a licensed professional.

My initial exposure to the industry was in the Private Wealth Management Division of Goldman Sachs. There I focused on planning and investment issues specific to entrepreneurs and corporate insiders. I watched as entrepreneurs repeatedly struggled to get good advice from a variety of service providers and frequently received guidance that led to costly mistakes. The multitude of competing service providers, each with a differing agenda, makes it very difficult to get a clear answer to the many questions facing the business owner looking for liquidity. Some of these questions include:

- When should I exercise stock options, and how does the alternative minimum tax play into the decision?
- What kind of rights do I negotiate for when selling my business in a stock-for-stock transaction?
- What alternatives do I have for protecting wealth in trusts and other structures prior to a transaction?
- How do I select investment advisors—do I work with an investment bank, a consultant, or a multifamily office, or do I manage my own assets?
- What kind of fees should I pay, and how do I evaluate the performance of my managers and hold them accountable?
- How do I make philanthropy a meaningful part of my life, and what are the benefits and drawbacks of the many structures available for giving?

These questions have complex legal, tax-related and investment-related answers. Each service provider competing for an entrepreneur's business cannot give a completely impartial answer because each benefits to a differing degree, depending upon the outcome of the business owner's decisions. In this book, to address the issue of conflict of interest and to try to distill "pure" practical advice, I have combined the deep resources of brand name firms with the independence of boutiques. I have assembled a team of senior professionals from well-known national organizations, including Atlantic Trust Pell Rudman, PricewaterhouseCoopers, Hale & Dorr, Testa, Hurwitz & Thibeault, Harvard University, Russell Investment Group, and State Street Global Advisors among others, and combined them with partners of smaller firms whose independence gives them additional latitude to write candidly about issues such as fees, performance, and firing advisors. My role has been to ask hard questions of the writers. Hopefully, the result is a book with many good ideas and a minimally conflicted agenda. The objective is to help you navigate a complex landscape to find competent advice from firms whose interests are aligned with your own.

As you read through the book, in whole or in part, I would encourage you to come up with lists of questions to use during your interviews with potential service providers. In many cases, I would get the answers to your questions in writing. The best sales people know when and where to be specific and when to be vague. An incorrect answer said with conviction frequently engenders confidence and wins business, while an honest "I'll need to get back to you" can suggest inexperience when in fact it may reflect the professional's desire to be completely accurate. It is a competitive business, so ask the direct questions: What makes you qualified to do this? What are the risks associated with following your suggested approach? Put advisors in competition, even after you have selected them, and hold people accountable.

Generally, my experience suggests that people make the decision to "buy" based on how much they like and trust an advisor and how well the advisor communicates with them, rather than the degree of experience and competence. There are plenty of likable, trustworthy good communicators out there who also are experienced and competent and have fewer conflicts of interest than others. I hope this book helps you understand the industry better and surround yourself with a great team of people.

Louis P. Crosier

I

Before Selling Your Business

Chapter 1

Pre-IPO/Presale Planning

William R. Fleming and Daniel Carbonneau with Richard L. Kohan

SETTING THE STAGE

You have an innovative idea and a solid business plan, so what is next? The obvious tasks are raising money and setting up the business—deciding on business structure and capitalization, choosing advisors, creating an advisory board (graduating to a board of directors), setting up employee benefit plans with maximum value and minimum administration, and determining how, when, and with whom to share equity participation.

Less obvious but perhaps more important is a long-term outlook. What is the planned or potential exit strategy or liquidity event—a sale or a public offering? Should you be sharing wealth with other family members through gifts and trusts? Finally, you should consider the unthinkable—death or disability. Long-term planning involves maximum flexibility and preserving choices. Preserving choices is critical at all stages of the business, especially when drafting shareholder and employee benefit arrangements.

This chapter describes the factors that influence certain activities, practical limitations, and the ability to preserve choices. As with all decisions, there will be tensions between mutually exclusive factors that must be weighed, and some advisors will have preconceived views.

CHOOSING A BUSINESS STRUCTURE

One of the initial steps is to establish the business structure for the new venture. The choices are:

- Sole proprietor
- Partnership (general or limited)
- Limited liability company (LLC; treated like a partnership for tax purposes)
- Corporation (either C corporation or S Corporation)

Usually an attorney or certified public accountant (CPA) is consulted at this stage. The attorney prepares the papers creating the business entity and registers them with the state. The attorney or accountant will consider the nature of the planned activities, the potential future activities, and the need for flexibility in ranking the business forms. The five key factors to consider will be:

1. Need for liability protection
2. Income tax flexibility
3. Management and control over extended periods
4. Current and future capital structure
5. The likely (or least likely) exit strategy

Because businesses tend to graduate *from* the sole proprietor form into the other forms, we will not dwell on the sole proprietor format.

It also is important to consider whether the entrepreneur will be investing in multiple businesses, much like venture capital or equity investors do, or whether the goal is to create and build an operating business. In general, the entrepreneur should *not* mix venture investments with operating businesses in the same entity. The clash of goals is too great.

LIABILITY PROTECTION

The entrepreneur should consider not only the potential for economic reward but also the risks associated with the venture. The attorney or accountant will ask questions about the new venture and the potential for liabilities from either defective products or services or through the actions of employees.

A corporation (either a C corporation or an S corporation) and a limited liability company both provide its owners (the corporate *shareholders* or limited liability company *members*) with liability protection. The shareholder or member's liability will be limited to the capital that he or she has directly invested in the business.

In contrast, the partnership form exposes general partners to unlimited liability for the debts and obligations of the partnership, including liability for defective products or services and any damages caused by employees. This means that a creditor or injured party could look beyond the general partner's business investment and attach to the partner's personal assets, such as other investments, bank accounts, and real estate, to settle a claim. A limited partnership has liability protection for limited partners but not general partners. Limited partners cannot be part of the management of the business.

For liability protection, the corporation or LLC is the preferred structure.

TAX FLEXIBILITY

The income tax treatment of the venture's operations also will be a primary consideration when evaluating the various business entities. Tax features include the choice of year-end for the business, the ability to move assets into and out of the business without tax events, and the determination of who pays tax on income (or saves taxes with losses).

The attorney or accountant will ask whether it is advantageous for a business to use a tax year different from that of its principal owners (based on business cycles or to achieve a deferral of income), whether the business is expected to generate either operating or capital losses, and whether the owners will wish to take cash distributions from the entity.

Only a C corporation is free to choose a tax year totally different from a calendar year. An LLC, partnership, or S corporation may use a noncalendar year with a year-end of September 30, October 31, or November 30 (or a natural business year for seasonal businesses). Fiscal year-end LLCs, partnerships, or S corporations must calculate and make payments on income deferred as a result of the noncalendar year-end.

Some entity structures do not pay tax, but instead the income and loss is reported on the owner's personal tax return. These entities (S corporation, LLC, and partnerships) are known as pass-through entities and are usually the entity of choice for tax purposes. If the business venture will generate operating losses in the early years, a pass-through entity permits those losses to be taken on an individual tax return, offsetting other income. The entity usually makes distributions to the owners for payment of income tax, but it is not required to make distributions. Pass-through entities, especially the LLC and partnership, have a greater ability to move assets into and out of the business without triggering added income taxes. This is important if the business cash flow is to be distributed each year or the business may be sold in whole or in part. The LLC is often the entity of choice for those investing in several businesses, including those involving venture or equity financing arrangements.

In contrast, the C corporation is a taxpaying entity. Income and losses from operations are taxed at the corporate level and do not directly impact the individual shareholders. At times, federal corporate tax rates have been much lower than the individual rates or much higher than individual rates. Today, in 2004, federal corporate rates are similar to individual rates. The difficulty with a C corporation is that distributions from the company to the shareholders (dividends) are subject to a second layer of tax. The shareholder level tax on dividends is 15% until 2009.

Pass-through of losses is important if there are capital losses, particularly sizable ones. For pass-through entities, capital losses are deductible by the owners to the extent of capital gains plus $3,000. Any unused losses can be used in succeeding tax years. The C corporation may deduct capital losses only to the extent of capital gains with any excess carried forward until the company has a capital gain.

In order to go public, a business must be operated as a C corporation. If the time from start-up to public offering is short (months rather than years), the C corporation may be the most efficient entity because no significant reorganizations are required before going public. If there is a significant time from start-up to public offering, the LLC structure may be worthwhile (with a change to the C corporation later). In general, the LLC tends to be the preferred structure for most business entities.

MANAGEMENT

The desired management structure of the venture will have an impact on choosing the appropriate business structure. The attorney and accountant will ask who will be making decisions and taking action on behalf of the business.

In a general partnership, all of the partners have legal authority to act on behalf of the partnership. This would mean that the actions of one partner, as agent for the partnership, could bind the other partners. A limited partnership structure, however, limits management authority to the general partners only. Limited partners have an economic interest but are not permitted to participate in management.

The LLC structure is very flexible because it can allow the LLC owners (known as members) to manage the business as a group or can allow them to appoint a management group, consisting of either some LLC owners, a third party, or some combination, to run the day-to-day affairs of the business. The management group of an LLC is know as *managers* and they have the express authority to act on behalf of the venture.

A corporation (either a C corporation or an S corporation) is managed in a similar fashion. The owners of the corporation (shareholders) appoint a management group consisting of either shareholders or third parties to run the day-to-day affairs of the business.

Anyone dealing with the business (vendors, suppliers, and customers) deals with those specifically authorized to run day-to-day operations and may actually request some proof of the authority.

CAPITALIZATION

Capitalization refers to how a business is financed. Attracting capital may be another factor in determining an appropriate business structure. For example, those making an investment often do not wish to complicate their personal tax situations, thereby making pass-through entity organizations unattractive.

Raising capital for the business venture can be accomplished in two ways—debt or equity. The venture can raise capital by incurring debt or by giving investors a piece of the equity ownership.

Debt can be structured as credit offered by the venture's suppliers or it can be in the form of debt offered to third-party investors. Debt provides an opportunity for the venture to raise needed cash without forgoing any ownership interest in the business. Debt also offers the opportunity to raise cash at a known cost or rate, without sharing an unlimited stake in the equity of the venture.

Equity provides the opportunity for the venture to raise capital without a cash cost. However, equity participation does dilute the interests of existing owners.

Businesses seeking funds from a variety of sources often are organized as a C corporation because traditionally investors request some type of hybrid ownership (a combination of debt and equity participation) via preferred stock. In contrast, ventures making investments in other businesses most often are organized as LLCs.

Founder's Stock and Shareholder Agreements

So-called *founder's stock* is stock issued to the founding individuals of the enterprise. This stock may have certain special tax benefits associated with it and is known as qualified small business stock (QSBS). These special benefits include the ability to roll over gain on sale into another new enterprise without income tax. The special benefits also include a minor reduction in income tax when sold if a series of conditions are met (including a minimum five-year holding period).

Issuing Founder's Stock

The QSBS special tax benefits associated with founder's stock only are available to the original owner. Thus, some shifts of ownership can cause a loss of special tax treatments. QSBS stock can be issued at formation or at a later date. QSBS stock treatment applies to stock issued until the gross assets of the company exceed $50,000,000 on a tax basis.

QSBS stock loses its special treatment if it is contributed to another entity, for example, a contribution to a partnership or LLC. QSBS stock does not lose its special treatment if it is transferred by gift to family members or to trusts for family members. QSBS stock does not lose its special treatment after an initial public offering (IPO) or in a tax-free exchange of stock—a stock purchase or merger.

Founder's stock provides estate and gift planning opportunities because of its relatively low value and the potential for significant and rapid appreciation. In recent years, these potentials have been reduced but not eliminated.

> Sally has founder's stock (QSBS qualified) issued to her directly. She later makes gifts of this stock to her two children and her parents. The QSBS features are *not* lost when she transfers the stock. Her two children and her parents will have QSBS stock tax advantages available to them.

> John exercised his stock options and received QSBS stock. His attorney suggests a family LLC to control and manage investment assets while making gifts to his children and their trusts. John contributes his QSBS stock to the family LLC. The QSBS tax advantages are no longer available. If John had the stock directly issued to the LLC, the QSBS tax advantage would still be available.

When stock is issued, the key is to anticipate future estate planning potential and have the stock issued to the most tax-advantageous entity, especially when using partnerships and LLCs. This requires some forethought.

Shareholder Agreements

Shareholder agreements are designed to control the transfer of stock. They typically apply to all shareholders—founders, employees with vested shares, and venture groups. It is good business practice to restrict the transfer of private company stock so that it does not fall into the hands of "undesirable" shareholders. The restrictions apply to the transfer of stock (sale, resale, or gift). Special shareholder agreements are also put in place at various stages of equity financing by outside parties.

It is important to consider some transfer planning when drafting the shareholder agreements. Any shareholder restrictions should be carefully worded so that transfers for gift and estate planning are permitted (transfers to family members, trusts for family members, and partnerships for family members). Amending shareholder agreements becomes more difficult after venture financing.

> Henry has founded a business called eAutomatic Tools. As part of hard-fought financing requirements, all shareholders must sign an agreement calling for a total prohibition of stock transfers without prior approval from all other shareholders (including the new private equity group). Henry wants to give some stock to his parents for their loyal support (financial and emotional) up to this point. He must obtain permission from a variety of sources. The private equity group insists on further concessions for their approval.

The other issue with shareholder agreements is income tax–related. There are two types of restrictions. The first type, restrictions that pose a risk of forfeiture, has income tax consequences. All other restrictions fall into the second category and have no income tax consequences. Most shareholder agreements require the shareholder, when selling, to first offer the stock to other shareholders or the company (a form of restriction). These agreements restrict who can purchase the stock and at what price. Sometimes these agreements are exceptionally restrictive and the shareholders are advised to make a protective Section 83(b) election (see Restricted Stock below for a complete description of this election). The restrictions may not pose a risk of forfeiture; however, rather than risk a later disagreement with the IRS, the tax election is made. Sometimes the stock issued to founders has forfeiture and transfer restrictions.

> Christine has been issued additional stock as part of her company's initial capitalization. Part of her stock vests monthly over the next four years, and she loses it if she leaves. All of her stock first must be offered to other shareholders

if she wishes to sell. All of her stock is restricted, but only part of the stock is restricted stock for tax purposes.

The best time to formulate an exit plan is before you need it. Some thought should be put into formulating an exit strategy for the entrepreneur even at the early stages of a new venture. Although the entrepreneur's intent may be to exit after an IPO of the company stock, a contingency plan should be adopted. Sometimes founders or early stage management do not continue until IPO or later sale.

Many businesses use life insurance as a means of planning for the premature death of a business owner. If there are multiple founders of the business, insurance typically will be purchased on the lives of each individual and the proceeds of this insurance will be used to buy out that individual's interest upon their death. This is a significant issue in businesses that pass from family member to family member and do not have a sale or IPO to provide liquidity.

BUILDING A PROFESSIONAL SERVICE TEAM

Just as choosing the appropriate business structure for the venture is important, engaging appropriate professional advisors also is important. Early in the development stage of the business, the entrepreneur will rely on an attorney and accountant for services and advice, including choosing a business structure, organizing bookkeeping, and filing any tax elections and registrations. The entrepreneur also should consider additional advisors that will assist with current and future needs of the business.

Building a team of advisors is especially complicated in the current business world because the roles of each advisor are becoming blurred (e.g., some attorneys and accountants can sell life insurance and investments). Further, the team must consist of people who work well with each other (not an easy task). The wise businessman will shop for advice among different advisors and get multiple perspectives before making any significant decisions. As with other aspects of business, those who describe a variety of choices and how they do or do not fit the situation are the best advisors. Advisors with "tunnel vision" must be used with caution.

The services needed by the business and the individual founders are blurred as well. Often the individual founders will have special income tax and legal issues separate from those of the business. Advisors that specialize in business advisory services do not specialize in services to individuals but may be able to speak generally about them. Advisors that specialize in services to the individual do not specialize in services to businesses but may be able to address broad issues. The single lawyer or accountant who can do it all does not exist. Many law firms and accounting firms have special groups for each type of business and individual services and offer a team of advisors.

Another issue is whether the business should pay for individual founders' personal services. Some founder services may relate to the business and are appropriate for payment by the business. Other services may be personal to the founder. The business can pay for these services but should treat this as a taxable benefit to the founder and include the charges in the income of the founder. Advisors should be directed to describe types of services and categorize them as business- or individual-related.

THE CERTIFIED PUBLIC ACCOUNTANT

A CPA typically deals with financial and tax bookkeeping systems and requirements. Many full-service accounting firms also can provide founders with general business advice and personal financial advice concerning estate planning, insurance planning, and investment allocations.

Early on in the venture, the role of the accountant will be to provide the necessary federal and state tax filings for the business. The accountant, however, can assume a broader role that includes getting the appropriate financial systems in place. The accountant may be needed to provide the business with audited financial statements. Although a company may not require audited financials in the initial start-up stage, the audited financial statements provide the business with a formal reporting structure that contains the checks and balances that would be required by an institutional investor (venture capital funds or private equity funds) prior to financing. Further, such a reporting structure is a necessary step for a public offering. The accountant also may be helpful in the overall design of the business, including assistance with processes, internal controls, employee benefit plans, and compensation programs. These are traditional business planning services offered by the accountant.

Another type of accountant can also assist the founders with their personal financial planning needs. These are accountants that specialize in individual planning and are often not skilled in auditing financial statements. Because the business may take a great deal of the entrepreneur's time and resources, he or she will often need help to develop a plan to provide for personal financial planning. Personal planning includes estate planning, asset gifting, retirement planning, education planning, and overall cash flow management.

Many full-service accounting firms also offer benefits and compensation planning advice, as well as assistance with legal documents. The benefits and compensation planning specialists are a different group from the accounting and personal groups. Accounting firms can provide sample documents for discussion, but are not permitted to draft documents for the business. The accounting firm also can provide valuable suggestions and comments on draft documents provided by a law firm.

Many accounting firms deal extensively with business planning and financial reporting needs but are not skilled at individual planning. Before seeking personal planning advice, the entrepreneur should inquire about the accountant's practice and how much experience the accountant has with individual planning concepts. Many large- and medium-sized accounting firms have many nonaccountants (attorneys and certified financial planners) and are well equipped to deal with individual issues and concerns. The entrepreneur should ask to speak to the individual planning specialists at the accounting firm.

> Benjamin's accountant works in a medium-sized accounting firm. His accountant specializes in business functions (auditing and accounting) but claims to be an expert in all the financial and tax aspects of a business and individual. Because the accountant meets with the other business owners and private equity investors, Ben is reluctant to discuss his personal desires concerning the business (family succession with maximum limits on amounts to be received by the children). Ben also is concerned that the accountant is not really interested in him as a person. Ben asks his accountant to bring a personal specialist to the next meeting. Ben meets the personal specialist but excludes his business accountant from the meeting.

An accountant historically could not sell products or take commissions. As a result, the accountant's advice was objective. In the modern business world, accountants can be licensed to sell products and take commissions or referral fees. When selecting an accountant, the entrepreneur may wish to ask about other licenses held by the accountant as well as by his or her accounting firm.

> Sarah's accountant suggests that she create a tax-favored college savings plan for her children and deposit $50,000 into each child's account. Sarah accepts the accountant's suggestion about which state plan to use and deposits a total of $80,000 into the plan. Sarah's accounting fees are about $3,000 each year. Soon after, Sarah's accountant leases an expensive new car using the $2,000 commission he earned. Sarah learns of the commission from the car dealer in casual conversation at a civic function and wonders about the accountant's

advice (since her neighbor made the same investment directly through the state and did not pay a commission).

When selecting an accountant, casually ask about his or her practice, what other licenses the accountant has, and whether the accountant has any referral network. Most states require the accountant to reveal any conflicts that may influence his or her judgment.

THE ATTORNEY

The attorney and his or her law firm typically draft legal documents and make appropriate legal filings with the appropriate state agencies. The attorney serves a vital role in the start-up of the business. The attorney is responsible for organizing the legal structure of the entity, including state filings. Beyond the initial start-up of the business, the attorney also is valuable in the ongoing internal development of the business, including employee rights and responsibilities, benefits programs, and other internal governance concerns.

Another type of attorney also can provide personal planning for the entrepreneur. The personal planning specialist attorney can assist with asset protection, estate planning, and drafting legal documents for family entities (trusts, partnerships, and charitable entities). For most entrepreneurs, their business represents the largest asset they own. As a result, they need to consider steps to share the value of the business with family members and may need to address issues regarding the future control that the family will retain.

As with the CPA, many lawyers specialize in certain legal areas. Before seeking personal planning advice, the entrepreneur should inquire about the lawyer's area of emphasis and how much experience he or she has with individual estate and gift planning concepts. Many large- and medium-sized law firms have many nonlawyers (accountants and certified financial planners) and are equipped to deal with individual issues and concerns.

Like accountants, attorneys historically could not sell products or take commissions. As a result, their advice was objective. In the modern business world, attorneys can be licensed to sell products and take commissions or referral fees. When selecting a lawyer, the entrepreneur may wish to ask about other licenses held by the lawyer, his or her law firm, or any related organizations.

George and Paula have a meeting with their attorney shortly before their company is scheduled to go public. He has prepared new wills and special trusts for both of them. He suggests that they purchase a significant amount of life insurance in order to pay estate taxes. George and Paula have been suspicious of insurance agents (concerned about motive). George takes the attorney's advice and purchases $20,000,000 of life insurance with an annual premium of $70,000 from someone in the attorney's office area. The attorney soon after purchases a new vacation home. George and Paula vacation near the same area and learn about the attorney's share of the insurance commission. They wonder about his advice. Should they have purchased less insurance or a different type?

THE INSURANCE AGENT

Businesses need insurance for a variety of reasons. The business needs property and casualty insurance on business assets and operations. The business also needs liability insurance to cover acts of employees. Business directors may need directors and officers (D&O) liability insurance. The business may need errors and omissions (E&O) insurance.

D&O insurance is designed to protect directors and officers from the actions of the company. Such claims might be brought by customers or other shareholders. Statistically, the greatest number of claims come from employees (discrimination). Directors and officers are personally liable for the actions of the business.

E&O insurance is professional liability coverage. It protects the company against mistakes made by employees or products. Doctors, dentists, and attorneys obtain malpractice insurance, which is a form of E&O coverage.

The business may need employee benefit plans (medical insurance, dental insurance, etc.). In a private business setting, life insurance is a way to protect all the founders against the untimely death of one founder or key employee.

Insurance agents, like accountants and attorneys, specialize in certain types of insurance. The business founders may need a variety of insurance agents for a variety of insurance needs. Business-related insurance needs are met by a property and casualty insurance specialist. The business specialist also can advise on liability insurance (D&O and E&O). In many cases a large business insurance agency can advise on medical insurance and dental insurance.

Life insurance, however, is a specialty area. The life insurance–related risks include liquidity for the business founders at death or disability. The insurance proceeds provide cash to cover potential estate taxes or provide a source of income for surviving family members. For the business, life insurance may provide the necessary cash flow for a buyout agreement or for protection on the life of a key person.

Many insurance agents also are equipped to provide personal planning services to the founders (and therefore compete with accountants and attorneys). When dealing with life insurance agents, always try to determine the agent's financial motivation (how he or she is paid).

Obtaining a second opinion from an objective advisor may be important. Furthermore, there are many estate planning issues associated with life insurance (who should own the policy, who should be the beneficiary, and how premiums are to be paid) that should be reviewed with an attorney and an accountant skilled in individual planning concepts.

> The insurance agent financial planner illustrates the growth of Gail and Paul's assets over 20 years assuming a 10 percent appreciation rate. He also illustrates the estate taxes due and suggests the purchase of a life insurance policy to cover the estate taxes. Gail asks her personal accountant about this plan. The accountant points out that an aggressive gift plan using trusts can cut the estate tax in half. He suggests the purchase of much less insurance using a variety of companies. Paul's personal attorney suggests the use of special trusts for the gift program. Gail and Paul end up with less insurance expense and a simple yet efficient program for making gifts to their three children.

THE INVESTMENT BANKER

Although most of the advisors play some critical role early on in the formation of the new business, the investment banker's role takes place in the period prior to an IPO. At one time the period from organization to IPO was very short (measured in months and days rather than years), and the investment banker was involved in the business from inception (as were venture capital firms). Now that the period from organization to IPO can be years, the investment banker and venture capital firms need not be involved at inception. Typically, it is the venture capital firm that provides investment banker introductions.

The investment banker assists in structuring the business for a debt or equity offering. Usually a company valuation is part of the offering preparation. The investment banker also introduces the business to a broad array of investors and prepares the company executives for investor roadshows.

Investment banking functions are not limited to the major brokerage firms. There are boutique investment bankers as well as investment banking arms of accounting and law firms.

THE INVESTMENT ADVISOR

Most business founders invest the majority of their time and money into their new businesses and ignore other investments [individual retirement accounts (IRAs) and other retirement plans]. Furthermore, if the business founder is successful, he or she will have significant wealth requiring ongoing investment management.

An initial role for the investment advisor might be to design and choose investments for an employee benefit plan [such as a 401(k) plan]. The investment advisor can assist the entrepreneur in designing an investment plan that can be funded as the business grows. The plan can be implemented slowly and will serve an important role when the entrepreneur gains a measure of liquidity.

BUILDING A BOARD OF OPERATIONAL ADVISORS

Business founders often find it helpful to have operational advisors. This group of advisors is knowledgeable about owning and operating a small business. Many times it is a group of owners of other businesses of similar size (either measured by employees or sales). The advisors may be retired.

There is a school of thought that the professional advisors (discussed previously) should be kept separate from the operational advisors. There is a competing school of thought that some, but not all, professional advisors can be of use as operational advisors.

This board can meet on a regular basis (or for special meetings) to discuss general business issues (day-to-day operations and strategic initiatives). The purpose is to provide the business founder with a variety of thoughts and ideas. Potential operational advisors might include large current or potential customers, key service providers, and complementary businesses within the same industry—possible joint venture partners. The operational advisory board might graduate into a formal board of directors or can be kept separate.

OBTAINING FINANCING

There are a variety of sources for start-up business financial assistance that come into play at various stages. The source chosen will depend on the amount of financing and the stage of the business.

SELF-FUNDING, FRIENDS, AND FAMILY

True start-up ventures have a difficult time attracting financing. Often, the founders will finance early stages, including the creation of a business plan and strategy. Founders work without pay during this period and may invest or pledge personal assets (including residences). Family and friends also are possible sources of funding. This seed money is critical in getting to the next stage.

GRANTS AND QUASI-PUBLIC ASSISTANCE

Many states, communities, and large universities will assist start-up businesses that meet certain criteria. This assistance often is targeted at certain communities, technologies, or potential employee populations.

ANGEL INVESTORS

The term *angel investor* generally refers to individuals or groups that have made significant gains in their own business activities and now have turned to help finance other people's emerging companies. Angel investors and angel investment groups typically make small investments in the very early stages of start-up companies.

VENTURE CAPITAL FIRMS

The term *venture capital firm* (or venture capitalist) generally refers to groups that make a living by investing in start-up businesses. Such firms invest in multiple companies (known as *portfolio companies*), knowing that only a select few will produce an investment return. Venture capital firms are often directing funds provided by large institutional investors (pension funds and endowment funds).

Venture capital firms operate in a highly competitive market. In order to generate returns from a few successful investments, they often insist on significant ownership.

Venture funds specialize in companies at different stages of development from seed money stages to near-IPO stages (there are fewer seed money funds). Often, there are several levels of venture financing (known as *rounds* and labeled in alphabetic order) with different venture groups involved. Because of the natural dilution in ownership that takes place at each round of financing, these negotiations can be difficult (especially when several levels of venture groups are involved).

The term *burn rate* refers to the rate at which venture funding is spent. Companies calculate the burn rate (how quickly they will exhaust their current pool of money). After the current pool is exhausted, the company must go back to the market and obtain more.

Many times an attorney or accountant will make introductions to venture firms with an interest in the type of business involved. Business owners can also interact with venture groups at local or regional venture association meetings.

Venture firms usually provide management and human resources assistance to their portfolio group of companies and are active in operational strategy. This approach may sometimes appear intrusive. However, for the fledgling business, such assistance can be invaluable.

PRIVATE EQUITY FIRMS

The term *private equity firm* generally refers to groups that invest in profitable operating businesses. The private equity firm assists such businesses in growth to a new stage. Because the business is already operating, the risk involved is thought to be less than with venture investments. Likewise, the equity position required by the private equity firm is smaller.

CAPITAL FINANCING

Commercial lenders, especially capital financing organizations, usually are not interested in start-up businesses until they have gotten at least one round of venture financing. Capital financing groups take a secured lien on equipment purchases when a company has some tangible assets and an operating track record.

SHARING OWNERSHIP WITH EMPLOYEES

Sharing ownership with employees is a way of motivating them and permitting them to share in the ultimate profit from the venture (perhaps at favorable tax rates). The best part is that sharing equity is not a current cash cost.

There are a variety of ways to share equity with employees. Historically, the financial statement implications of the various choices have tended to influence which techniques were most popular. However, the financial standards boards (in the United States and abroad) have been adjusting the financial statement implications. Furthermore, the administrative burden associated with certain types of equity sharing is greater than others. Early-stage companies are most often interested in arrangements with little administrative activity.

For planning purposes, the most important aspects of sharing ownership include providing employees with long-term capital gain treatment on part of their compensation and the ability to transfer value to family members through trusts and partnerships.

In general, the two most popular ways to share ownership with employees are restricted stock and stock options. Other potential methods include phantom stock and stock appreciation rights (SARs).

RESTRICTED STOCK

The term *restricted stock* generally is an income tax term. Restricted stock has conditions that must be met before it is "vested," that is, before the employee is entitled to keep it. Failure to meet the restrictions results in the employee forfeiting the stock. Employees may or may not be required to purchase the restricted stock.

Restricted stock is relatively simple to track (a key consideration in companies with constrained employee benefit capabilities). It is the first choice for most emerging-stage businesses. A restricted stock grant or award is often part of the initial hiring package.

The restrictions on restricted stock most often are tied to a time period (time-restricted stock) but can be tied to achieving certain goals (performance-restricted stock). Once the required target is met (time or performance goal), the stock "vests," the restrictions are released, and the stock belongs to the employee. Once in the hands of the employee, the private company stock will still have transfer restrictions.

Because the employee might have to forfeit the stock, it is not subject to income tax until it is vested. At the date of vesting the employee recognizes compensation income equal to the current fair market value of the stock.

However, the employee can make a special election to be taxed on the value of the stock when it is issued but prior to its vesting. If the employee makes the Section 83(b) election, he or she pays tax on the value when received (usually a nominal value in an early-stage company). Any gain on the stock when it is later sold is then subject to capital gains tax.

Restricted stock also is easy for an employee to understand: Stay and you get to keep it. Most employees appreciate the opportunity to save taxes by making a Section 83(b) election. The employee also may be able to gift stock to family members, if the restricted stock plan permits it.

For the companies issuing it, the difficulty with restricted stock is the financial statement charge (annual expense) that must be taken over the life of the restrictions. Historically, the early-stage company becomes concerned with the cumulative financial statement expense at some point and moves to another equity reward alternative (typically stock options). The move away from restricted stock due to financial statement impact may no longer be as pronounced due to the changing financial statement treatment of options.

A key feature in drafting a restricted stock plan is to permit transfers to a select class (family, trusts for family, or partnerships for family). The other key is to make sure the employee has the opportunity to consider the Section 83(b) election by putting the employee on notice of the possibility (since the election must be made within 30 days of receiving the stock).

STOCK OPTIONS

Stock options permit the employee to purchase the company's stock at a set price for a set period of time. If the company prospers, the employee profits by buying the stock at the option price and selling at a much higher price. The employee chooses when to purchase the stock and trigger income tax issues.

There are two types of stock options: incentive stock options (ISOs) and nonqualified options (NQOs). Stock options have no tax effect on grant or issuance unless the option is freely transferable. The major difference between the two types is the income tax consequence at exercise, that is, when the employee purchases the stock. ISOs have no regular income tax at exercise. However, there is an alternative minimum tax complication. NQOs trigger compensation income when exercised. ISOs are thought to provide a greater employee benefit.

ISOs also are known as *qualified options* or *statutory stock options* because the governing rules associated with the option are set by statute. ISOs must be issued to employees only, must be priced at the market value of the stock on the date it is granted, and the option can be for no more than 10 years. There are a variety of other technical restrictions as well. Employees like ISOs because there is a great potential for capital gain on sale if certain holding periods are met. The company gets *no* income tax deduction when an ISO is exercised (unless the employee holding periods are not met).

NQOs also are known as *nonstatutory stock options* because they have no particular governing rules. NQOs can be issued to consultants and vendors, can be issued at a price *below* the market price on the date of grant, and have no restrictions on how long they may last. Employers like NQOs because they get an income tax deduction when the option is exercised. Employees have little opportunity to get long-term capital gain treatment.

Historically, stock options were very popular with early-stage companies because there was no cash cost and, if properly structured, no financial statement impact. The financial standards boards in the United States and abroad are making changes to the treatment of stock options, and it is likely that the financial statement advantage will be significantly reduced.

Stock options do require some administrative effort (tracking grants, prices, and exercises). There are several low-cost software programs available to manage this process and provide the required employee notifications at exercise.

Key Option Plan Features

Key features in a stock option plan include (1) the ability to transfer NQOs (but not ISOs) to certain family members or entities, (2) the ability to exercise early and receive restricted stock, and (3) the ability to pay for the option price using current stock or by loan from the employer. Each of these features enhances the flexibility of the basic plan.

Employee Stock Option Planning

There are multiple approaches to employee stock option planning. All of the strategies revolve around future stock prices. Some advisors, most often accountants, place too much emphasis on income tax results and lose the basic economic benefit of a stock option. This is especially true of NQOs. A stock option is a free ride on the company stock. It costs nothing, that is, requires no capital commitment until it is exercised.

Option strategies for the emerging-stage company are much different than strategies for an established company. The level of economic commitment is often less in the emerging-stage company, although the risk is greater. Balancing the advantage of capital gains tax (rather than regular income tax) against the risk that the investment could be lost is a delicate task in the start-up business world. As you move from start-up to established business, this balance shifts away from an exercise-and-hold strategy to a wait-and-see strategy because of the greater capital commitment with less potential capital gain.

ISOs require special attention. The exercise of an ISO is regular income tax–free. If holding periods are met following exercise (two years from date of grant and one year from date of exercise), all the gain on the stock is capital gain. Unfortunately, the exercise of an ISO triggers an item of income for alternative minimum tax (AMT), and this can have a very big impact on your tax bill.

The strategy for ISOs is to carefully monitor the AMT impact. Payment of AMT on an ISO exercise will create another cash cost that must be planned.

Fortunately, payment of AMT on an ISO will generate a tax credit that may be used in future years. However, because of the limitation on the use of the credit (only available to reduce regular tax to the level of AMT), the credit use will likely be spread over many years. It is critical to monitor AMT application and potential use of credits in future years as part of an ISO strategy.

Sharon has an incentive option for 1 million shares at $1 per share. Her company goes public and the stock shoots from $15 to $110 in the opening days. Sharon is subject to a lockup agreement (see Lockup Agreements, below) and cannot sell stock for 175 more days (originally 180 days). A broker friend of hers suggests that she buy the stock immediately because there is no regular tax at exercise. She purchases the stock for $1 when the market price hits $125 in October. Her plan is to hold the stock for a year and get capital gains treatment on her $125 million. There is no regular income tax, but she has a $125 million preference income item for AMT. When doing her taxes in March the next year, her accountant informs her that her AMT (a flat tax at a 28 percent rate) will be $35 million. He also points out that she is entitled to a credit against her regular tax for this amount. He projects that it will take her 350 years to use up the credit. If, in the period between when she exercises her options and when she is allowed to sell the stock, its price drops substantially, she may ultimately pay more in tax than she gains on the sale of the stock. This was a common problem for entrepreneurs during the Internet bubble and caused a good many to go bankrupt.

The key strategy points for ISOs are:

- ISO exercises must be carefully monitored to avoid excessive AMT.
- Sometimes strategic disqualifying dispositions (i.e., selling ISO stock too soon) is a good idea.
- An exercise when you are forbidden to sell (lockup, blackout, or affiliates) can be an invitation to disaster

The key strategy points for NQOs are:

- NQOs are a free ride on the stock with no capital commitment.
- Waiting until close to expiration is usually a good idea.
- Exercising early to get capital gains may not make any economic sense (Why not buy the stock in the market instead?)
- An exercise when you are forbidden to sell (lockup, blackout, or affiliates) can be an invitation to disaster

PHANTOM STOCK

Phantom stock is pretend stock used to measure future compensation. Because the stock is not really issued, there is little dilution effect and the participants are not shareholders with legal rights.

Employees receive units of phantom stock and are credited with appreciation (or depreciation) in the shares from year to year. At some future date (retirement, termination, or a trigger date) the company pays cash or stock based on the appreciation in value from grant date to trigger date. The employee receives compensation income at payout (no chance to obtain long-term capital gains treatment).

Phantom stock produces a financial statement impact as well. The phantom stock account is treated as a liability of the company and changes to the account are treated as financial statement expenses. Because of the extensive bookkeeping required, phantom stock is not as popular as restricted stock and stock options.

The overall arrangement is one type of deferred compensation and is treated as such for income tax and financial statement purposes.

STOCK APPRECIATION RIGHTS

SARs are very similar to phantom stock and have some features associated with stock options. A future compensation event to the employee is based on the change in value (appreciation) of the stock from the date of grant until the date of exercise. Although phantom stock is most often paid out at the company's date of choice (plan design), SARs are usually controlled by the employee. The employee can trigger the payment (sometimes in stock) by exercising the SAR.

The exercise of an SAR triggers compensation income. The company is entitled to a deduction for the amount of income received by the employee.

COMPANY BENEFITS AND POLICIES

Early on in the new venture, attention should be focused on establishing company benefits and policies that will meet the needs of the business as it grows. Company benefits should be evaluated based on competitive pressures (the need to attract and retain talented employees).

MEDICAL BENEFITS

Medical benefits are often a key factor in employee benefits. Traditional insurance programs [either health maintenance organization (HMO), preferred provider organization (PPO), or indemnity plans] can be supplemented with pretax employee contributions and pretax flexible spending accounts.

Many businesses require employees to contribute to medical benefit programs (share insurance premiums). The employer can lessen the impact on the employee by permitting the employee to pay for his or her share with pretax dollars. Many medical insurance providers, as well as some payroll providers, offer this feature.

An additional benefit is the creation of flexible spending accounts. Flexible spending accounts permit the employee to set aside pretax dollars for medical costs not covered by insurance. Flexible spending accounts are also permitted for dependent care expenses. There are a series of special rules associated with operating these plans, which must be kept in mind. In addition, any pretax features will require an annual information filing (Form 5500) regardless of the number of employees.

There are groups that specialize in the administration of these programs. Administration includes collection of funds from payroll and making payments when the proper documentation is received from the employee.

RETIREMENT BENEFITS

There are many different qualified retirement plans available to businesses, each providing benefits that may be more or less favorable to the entrepreneur in relation to the other employees. Some plans require more administration than others. In general, the qualified plans are formulated as either defined benefit plans or defined contribution plans.

Defined Benefit Plans

A defined benefit plan is the traditional pension, that is, the employee receives a monthly pension equal to a certain dollar amount. The amount received each month is based on specific variables such as length of service and earnings. These plans tend to benefit older employees and employees with many years of service. Because company contributions must be actuarially determined each year, they produce an administrative burden (and potential financial statement impact if not property funded). A defined benefit plan will *require* annual contributions by the company and therefore may put a strain on the cash flows during the initial years of operation. The administration and financial impacts have made these plans unpopular. In fact, many large companies have dismantled their defined benefit plans in recent years.

Defined Contribution Plans

A defined contribution plan does not guarantee any particular dollar amount at retirement. Instead, it is the annual contributions to an employee account that are determined each year. The contribution may depend on the age of the employee as well as the profits of the company. Defined contribution plans are easier to maintain and operate year to year, and they are more portable, that is, they can be carried from employer to employer. One form of defined contribution plan, the 401(k) plan, permits employees to save funds on a pretax basis. This is an especially popular benefit program.

The best retirement plan for the company will depend on multiple variables. In emerging-stage companies, ease of administration is a key feature and the defined contribution plan with a 401(k) feature is most popular.

EMPLOYEE STOCK PURCHASE PLAN

Once a company goes public, it may provide the employees with the opportunity to purchase shares of company stock on a discounted basis. Employee stock purchase plans (ESPPs) are designed so that an employee may to set aside funds on a payroll deduction to purchase company stock. The plan is typically designed to extend over a set time period and will provide for the purchase of company stock at specific intervals within this time period (either at the beginning of the period or the end of the period). When the stock is purchased, the purchase price could be discounted as much as 15 percent. These plans were wildly popular during the Internet boom days.

Historically, these plans did not have any financial statement impact. However, the changes to the stock option plan financial accounting will likely impact ESPPs as well. In the future, it is likely that the maximum discount will be reduced from the current 15 percent level.

PUBLICLY TRADED COMPLICATIONS

Once an emerging-stage company is ready to make an IPO, it needs to address a variety of issues. These include enhanced financial statement disclosures and restrictions, securities law compliance, and contractual issues with the underwriters.

SARBANES-OXLEY ACT

While operating as a privately held company, the entrepreneur's venture will not be subject to the rules and restrictions imposed by the Sarbanes-Oxley Act (signed into law in 2002). In addition to making changes in the conduct of audit and financial reporting for publicly held companies, the Sarbanes-Oxley legislation also imposes restrictions on the interaction between publicly held companies and their executive officers. These restrictions include the prohibition of personal loans between companies and their executive officers. The prohibition will encompass loans made to assist an executive officer with the purchase of a home or for the exercise of their company stock options.

Companies going public need to review interactions and arrangements with auditors and executives to make sure they are in compliance. Violations of Sarbanes-Oxley requirements trigger criminal charges as well as financial penalties.

LOCKUP AGREEMENTS

The lockup agreement is a private contract between the company going public and the underwriters of the IPO. The purpose is to prevent employees and their families from selling stock during the IPO period. Most often, employees and their immediate families are prohibited from selling (but not from buying) company stock for 180 days following the IPO. In theory, the lockup period is negotiable. In practice, it is rarely changed.

The lockup period can be very frustrating for employees and their families. It poses a significant danger for those who exercise stock options during this period (triggering income tax with no ability to sell stock to pay the taxes).

BLACKOUT PERIODS

The creation of blackout periods is a reaction to federal securities laws that prohibit trading on inside information. In order to prevent inadvertent trading, a company will create policies designed to prohibit certain suspect employees from trading during certain periods. These periods usually begin 2 to 6 weeks before the release of financial statement data and end several days after the public release. During the blackout period the designated employees are not permitted to sell stock.

Blackout periods are designed to prevent shareholder lawsuits and criminal prosecution for employees that might have access to material nonpublic information. Although there is some discretion over how to determine who is subject to blackout, it is an area in which a company and its legal advisors are generally very careful. Exercising stock options during blackout periods must be done with great care.

Affiliated Individuals

Certain individuals are treated as *affiliates* for federal securities laws. There are severe restrictions on the ability of an affiliate to sell stock. Only certain numbers of shares or dollar amounts are permitted each month and year. These rules are quite complex and require the assistance of a securities law attorney.

The Securities and Exchange Commission (SEC) has specific rules for determining who is an affiliate for purposes of these restrictions. The goal is to prevent significant owners from dumping their stock on an unsuspecting public. The result is that certain significant owners remain at risk even after a liquidity event. Affiliated individuals must be extremely careful about stock option exercises because their ability to sell stock is so constrained.

Prearranged Selling Programs

Prearranged selling programs are a recent SEC concept. Employees normally subject to certain blackout restrictions can create prearranged selling arrangements that should not result in liability for insider trading. The selling arrangements may be for certain share or dollar amounts on certain dates, or may involve formula triggers (certain trading ranges, etc). The triggering feature of the selling program must be determinable.

These selling programs are locked in to prearranged times, dates, and amounts. They can produce undesirable results if the stock price is not cooperative.

Susan registers a selling program where she will sell 1,000 shares on the 15th of every other month. The stock market seems to bottom out in the middle of each month. Susan is becoming disgusted with the prices she is getting for the stock and wants to end the program. Her SEC attorneys tell her that ending the program is not a good idea.

CONCLUSION

Entrepreneurs should surround themselves with outstanding employees, personal advisors, and business advisors. They should consider flexibility to be a key feature in any benefit plan. Entrepreneurs should be wary of those who claim to be expert in all areas or who think there is a single answer or approach.

Author Background

Bill Fleming is the Director of Personal Financial Services for PricewaterhouseCoopers LLP in the Hartford and Boston offices. Prior to joining PricewaterhouseCoopers in 1987, he was a principal of Ayco Corporation. His financial planning clients include prominent or retired executives at large Fortune 500 companies as well as start-up (pre-IPO) companies. In addition, Bill provides succession planning to the owners of smaller businesses as well as sophisticated plans for wealthy individuals. Bill is an attorney licensed in both Massachusetts and Pennsylvania. He is a member of numerous professional organizations relating to estate and financial planning and has Certified Financial Planner™ and Accredited Estate Planner designations. He has co-authored several PricewaterhouseCoopers publications dealing with life insurance and estate planning.

Daniel Carbonneau is a Senior Manager in the Personal Financial Services Practice group of PricewaterhouseCoopers LLP. Based out of the Boston office, he helps lead a group of twenty-five professionals in providing tax and financial planning services. Daniel has over seven years providing tax compliance and tax, financial, and wealth planning to corporate executive, entrepreneurs, and high net-worth individuals. He is a practice resource in the area of Wealth Transfer Services both locally and nationally throughout the firm.

Richard Kohan is the Partner in charge of PricewaterhouseCoopers Personal Financial Services Practice for the Northeast region. In addition, he is the firm's National Trust & Estate Service Line Leader. In these roles, Rich manages the implementation of the national PFS strategy in the Northeast region and advises clients on a variety of issues relating to their personal tax and wealth transfer needs. He is the client engagement manager on several corporate executive estate, financial, and tax consulting programs. Rich frequently speaks on leading edge financial planning topics such as executive wealth transfer techniques, investment strategies, employee benefits, stock options, and retirement planning. He often leads seminars on various aspects of financial planning for PricewaterhouseCoopers professionals, as well as top executives in a number of Fortune 1000 companies. Rich serves on the faculty and advisory committee for the Georgetown University Law Center Advanced Estate Planning Institute.

Chapter 2

Trust and Estate Basics

A. Silvana Giner and Kimberly E. Cohen

Estate and wealth transfer planning is a process that every entrepreneur should undertake, whether or not he or she is just beginning a career or is already established, and regardless of whether any significant wealth has yet been created. Of course, these two factors will influence the focus of each entrepreneur's planning process.

The goals of entrepreneurs' trust and estate planning vary and often include wealth transfer to future generations; directing the disposition of assets at death; preserving and managing the estate the entrepreneur has worked hard to create; minimization of estate, gift, generation-skipping transfer, and income taxes; protecting assets from the claims of the entrepreneur's creditors and the creditors of his or her family; and diversification of the entrepreneur's assets.

Minimizing transfer taxes (estate taxes and gift taxes) is frequently a significant goal for an entrepreneur because for estates in excess of $1.5 million or gifts in excess of $1 million, gift and estate tax rates currently (2004) start at 41 percent for gifts (45 percent for estates) and climb to 48 percent for estates or gifts in excess of $2 million. Because the rates are so high, there is a powerful incentive to minimize transfer tax costs.

In addition to estate and gift taxes, transfers to grandchildren or more remote descendants (or unrelated persons in the same generation as grandchildren) are subject to an additional flat tax assessed at the highest estate tax rate (currently 48 percent). This tax is known as the *generation-skipping transfer tax* (GST tax).

Under current tax law, each individual who is a U.S. resident or citizen is entitled to pass during lifetime $1 million of property free of any gift tax and a total of $1.5 million of property (less lifetime gifts) at death free of estate taxes. This amount is known as the *exemption equivalent* amount.

In addition, while you are living, you can also transfer $11,000 a year per person to an unlimited number of people (husbands and wives may gift $22,000 on a split gift basis). This kind of transfer (otherwise referred to as an *annual exclusion gift*) is totally disregarded for gift tax purposes. It is not a taxable gift. Further, you may pay tuition (not room and board) or medical expenses for anyone so long as those payments are made directly to the school or medical care provider. Such transfers are also ignored for gift tax purposes.

U.S. citizen spouses are treated as one economic unit and may transfer assets freely between themselves without any adverse income, gift, or estate tax consequences. For gift and estate tax purposes, this unrestricted transfer of assets is called the *unlimited marital deduction*. With proper estate planning, the unlimited marital deduction permits deferral of the payment of estate taxes until the death of the surviving spouse. Note that different and complex rules apply for transfers to non-U.S. citizen spouses.

The Economic Growth and Tax Relief Reconciliation Act of 2001, a $1.35 trillion federal tax-cut bill, was enacted in June of 2001. Under the provisions of the Act, the estate tax and the generation-skipping transfer tax are repealed. Barring further legislative changes, the effective date of the repeal (except for interim changes in exemptions and rates as set forth below) is not until 2010. Furthermore, the Act contains a "sunset" clause under which all of its provisions expire on January 1, 2011, unless otherwise extended, meaning that the estate and GST tax in effect in 2001 will be reinstated.

The gift tax, however, has not been repealed. It has been suggested that the retention of the gift tax is to prevent taxpayers in high income tax brackets from giving appreciated property to younger-generation family members, in lower income tax brackets, to sell and incur lower (or no) short-term capital gains tax. Because the gift tax will not be repealed, the $11,000 gift tax annual exclusion (which is indexed for inflation) and the special gift tax exclusions for payment of tuition and medical expenses are retained.

Under the 2001 Act, the maximum estate and gift tax rates will be reduced over the next several years leading up to repeal. The GST tax rate will equal

Table 2.1

Year of Gift or Death	Maximum Gift, Estate, and GST Tax Rate	Gift Tax Exemption Equivalent	Estate and GST Tax Exemption Equivalent
2004	48%	$1 million	$1.5 million
2005	47%	$1 million	$1.5 million
2006	46%	$1 million	$2 million
2007	45%	$1 million	$2 million
2008	45%	$1 million	$2 million
2009	45%	$1 million	$3.5 million
2010	No estate or GST tax; 35% gift tax rate	$1 million	Unlimited
2011+	55%	$1 million	$1 million

the maximum estate tax rate. In addition, the exemption equivalent for estate tax (but not gift tax) purposes will be increased as shown in Table 2.1.

In addition to the exemptions described, any assets given to qualifying charitable organizations are free of estate and gift taxes, and, if made during the donor's lifetime, may be deducted against adjusted gross income.

BASIC WEALTH TRANSFER TOOLS

THE WILL

Every adult should have a will. The will is important in that it is where you appoint an executor of your estate and name guardians of minor children. Without a will explicitly nominating a guardian or guardians for your children, the Probate Court will select the guardian. In addition, the will is also the vehicle pursuant to which you direct the disposition of your assets upon death. If you die without a will (i.e., intestate), the ownership of your property is governed by the law of the state in which you lived at the time of your death.

The laws of intestate succession are an attempt on the part of a state to dispose of your property as you would have if you had executed a will. In this context, "property" includes all property owned solely in your name, but does not include joint property that automatically passes to the surviving tenant or property that has a designated beneficiary, such as life insurance and qualified benefit plans, which passes by operation of law to the named beneficiary.

For example, if you die intestate as a resident of Massachusetts, not married and without children, all of your property will pass to your parents or parent, if only one of them is living. If neither of your parents is alive, your property will pass to your living siblings or the children of your deceased siblings. If you have no siblings, your property will pass to your next of kin (i.e. uncles, aunts, cousins), and finally, if you have no living next of kin, your property passes to the Commonwealth of Massachusetts. Many people might find that this disposition closely replicates what he or she may have chosen anyway.

A Massachusetts resident who dies intestate and who is married but has no children, however, may be surprised by the manner in which his or her property passes. Specifically, the first $200,000 of any property you own will pass to your surviving spouse. However, if you own property in excess of $200,000, only half of the excess will pass to your surviving spouse while the other half passes as though you were a single person. For example, if you own property totaling $400,000 and you die intestate, your surviving spouse will receive $300,000 of your property and your parents (assuming they are both living) will receive $100,000. Satisfied with the result?

Suppose you are married, have one or more children, and die intestate? Given this scenario, one-half of your property will pass to your surviving spouse, whereas the other half will pass directly to your children in equal shares. The unlimited marital deduction does not defer taxes on property passing to your children and, depending on the value of your estate, estate taxes could be payable at your death. If you die intestate survived by children but not by a spouse, all of your property will go directly to your living children in equal shares.

Once you have executed a will, you should update your will whenever a major life event occurs. Marriage, divorce, birth of a child, death of a family member, or a significant increase in the value of your assets are events the occurrence of which should prompt you to review your will and determine if changes should be made. As a rule of thumb, you should review your estate planning documents at least every five years. At that time, you can reassess the appropriateness of people named as executor, guardian, and trustee.

THE REVOCABLE TRUST

A revocable trust is a trust document established during lifetime that provides for the disposition of assets both during life and after death. The person who establishes the trust is often referred to as the *grantor*, *settlor*, or *trustor*. Most often, in sophisticated estate planning, the will provides that all of the decedent's probate assets pour over into the revocable trust and the trust serves the role of a will substitute. The trust can also be funded during lifetime (i.e., assets can be contributed to the trust while the grantor is still alive). If funded during a grantor's lifetime, the revocable trust provides immediate access for the trust beneficiaries to all assets held in the trust at all times, including whenever the grantor may be incapacitated or incompetent or upon the grantor's death.

Assets held in the revocable trust at death do not pass through the Probate Court and there is no public record of the assets held in the trust. As a result, privacy is maintained for the grantor and his or her family. Finally, a revocable trust generally contains a formula that defers any estate taxes until the death of the surviving spouse while minimizing aggregate estate taxes of the grantor and the surviving spouse.

THE BENEFITS OF LIFETIME GIFTS

In addition to setting up basic estate planning documents, including the will and the revocable trust, it is often sensible for an entrepreneur to consider making lifetime gifts. In addition to the $11,000 annual exclusion gifts and the payment of tuition and medical expenses, discussed previously, making lifetime gifts can often save significant amounts of transfer taxes. Even though gift and estate tax rates are currently the same, lifetime gifts, even if they result in paying a lifetime gift tax, may be a useful tool to save estate taxes later on. First, when an asset is gifted away, all subsequent appreciation in the asset escapes the estate and gift tax system. In addition, in response to reduced revenues received from the Federal system, many states have enacted their own estate tax systems, although few states have a state gift tax system. Therefore, lifetime gifts generally avoid taxation at the state level.

Basic Vehicles for Lifetime Gifts

After consulting with your estate planning attorney, if it is determined that lifetime gifts are appropriate, there are numerous vehicles that the entrepreneur should consider for making a lifetime gift. These vehicles are discussed in detail in the next section.

Your estate planning attorney will be able to explain the benefits of each of the different vehicles for lifetime gifting.

PRESALE AND PRE-IPO PLANNING

The most important thing entrepreneurs should keep in mind when considering estate and gift tax planning is that a little forethought goes a long way. Considering that for gifts in excess of $1 million and estates in excess of $1.5 million, transfer tax rates quickly reach 48 percent, estate and gift tax planning must be done before the value of the entrepreneur's assets appreciate substantially. When an entrepreneur starts a business, the value of which he or she expects will appreciate significantly over the lifetime of the business, he or she should consider gifting some equity in the business before this appreciation takes place. In addition, if an entrepreneur expects that the company will be acquired or that the stock of the company will ultimately be listed on a public exchange, the sooner such business interests are gifted, the better. There are numerous vehicles to make pre-IPO or presale lifetime gifts. These include:

- Outright gifts
- Custodial accounts and/or minority trusts for children under age 21
- Gifts to irrevocable trusts
- Gifts to grantor retained annuity trusts (GRAT)
- Sale to an intentionally defective grantor trust (IDGT)
- The use of family limited partnerships (FLPs) or limited liability companies (LLCs)

OUTRIGHT GIFTS

Although outright gifts are the easiest, cleanest, and least expensive technique for transferring assets to family members, there are often significant drawbacks to making such gifts, especially when the beneficiary is a minor or may have future creditor issues. Nevertheless, there are times when outright gifts are the most sensible option available to the entrepreneur.

GIFTS TO CUSTODIAL ACCOUNTS

Custodial accounts are also simple and inexpensive to create. A custodial account is essentially an account held for the benefit of a minor and managed by an adult or institution that is named as the custodian. The role of the custodian is similar to that of a trustee of a trust, but state law, rather than a trust instrument, sets forth the custodian's role. Gifts to custodial accounts qualify for the $11,000 gift tax annual exclusion. The custodian has the power to make payments to or for the benefit of the minor for whom the account has been established. The entrepreneur should not act as the custodian for gifts he or she makes. Otherwise, if the custodian were to die while assets remained in the custodial account, such assets would be included in the estate of the custodian, thereby negating the benefits of the planning. Income in the custodial account is taxed directly to the minor, but be aware that children under age 14 are treated as falling within the parent's marginal tax rate bracket.

If a minor dies before turning 21, the property must be paid to the minor's estate. If the minor survives to age 21, the property in the custodial account must be distributed outright to the minor upon his or her birthday. As a result, control over the assets is lost once the minor reaches 21. Such assets are thereafter subject to the claims of the creditors of the beneficiary of the custodial account and are included in the beneficiary's estate for estate tax purposes.

MINORITY TRUSTS

Much like custodial accounts, gifts to minority trusts also qualify for the gift tax annual exclusion. The trust must be structured so that the trustee has absolute discretion to distribute assets to or for the benefit of the minor. Neither the minor's parents nor the donor should serve as trustee of a minority trust.

As with the custodial account, if a minor dies before turning 21, the property in the minority trust must be paid to the minor's estate or as the minor directs. Unlike a custodial account, the minority trust may continue after the minor has reached the age of 21 so long as the minor received notice that he or she had at least a 30-day time period to demand that the trust property be distributed to him or her. If no such demand is made, then the property may continue in trust for a longer period of time as provided in the trust document.

GIFTS TO IRREVOCABLE TRUSTS

Frequently, early in the life of a business an entrepreneur may consider making gifts of such business interests, whether it be stock, partnership interests, or the like, to an irrevocable trust for the benefit of his or her family. The dispositive provisions of the trust can be drafted in any manner the entrepreneur deems satisfactory. We typically advise clients to make the trust instrument as flexible as possible. That is, rather than dictate specific distributions and termination, the trustees are given broad discretion to make distributions to, or terminate the trust in favor of, the beneficiary. The trust does not terminate at any specific age because of the uncertain future. There could be reasons relating to poor health, exposure to law suits (including divorce), money management abilities, and tax savings weighing in favor of continuing the trust into the next generation. To assist the trustees in making these decisions, it is wise to provide them with a letter setting forth your wishes regarding trust distributions and termination.

An important part of creating a trust is selecting a trustee to manage the assets based on the instructions contained in the trust instrument. Once again, the entrepreneur should not act as trustee. Given the very important role of the trustee, we often suggest that the entrepreneur retain the ability to remove the trustee and replace the trustee with another independent trustee, and that a similar power also be given after the entrepreneur's death to the surviving spouse or the trust's beneficiaries.

The advantage of making a gift to an irrevocable trust compared to some of the more sophisticated alternatives discussed below is that it is simple and it is proven. Once the assets are transferred into the irrevocable trust, the gift is complete for gift tax purposes and the terms of the trust document cannot be changed.

Restricted Stock

In some situations, the entrepreneur may have started a business with other individuals or funding may have been received from one or more outside sources. As a result, the entrepreneur may hold restricted stock in the new company. Although restricted stock can be transferred, the entrepreneur should first clear the transaction with the company's in-house counsel. In addition, the entrepreneur should make sure that any instrument to which the stock is transferred is in compliance with any restrictions in any applicable restrictive stock agreement.

Although restricted stock may be gifted, it is possible that the Internal Revenue Service (IRS) may try and argue that stock subject to forfeiture is not a completed gift. Many commentators in the estate and gift tax planning arena believe that the possibility of forfeiture should impact the value of the stock but not whether a completed gift has been made. The entrepreneur should be aware, however, that there are additional risks when planning is undertaken with restricted stock.

An entrepreneur in the early stage planning of a new company receives restricted stock. The entrepreneur has made no prior taxable gifts and his or her entire $1 million gift tax exemption equivalent amount is available. Assuming the entrepreneur has an interest in the new business worth $5 million, he or she decides to transfer in year 1 business interests worth $500,000 to an irrevocable trust for the benefit of the entrepreneur's children. In April of year 2, the entrepreneur must file a gift tax return disclosing the gift and applying $500,000 of his or her gift tax exemption amount to the gift. The entrepreneur also may allocate on that gift tax return a portion of his or her GST tax exemption to the gift if the entrepreneur expects the stock will appreciate significantly and that his or her children will not fully use the trust property during their lifetime. Allocating GST tax exemption allows such property to be later distributed to grandchildren and more remote descendants without incurring a second level of tax known as the GST tax. If, however, the entrepreneur expects that his or her children will need all of such property, GST tax exemption should not be allocated.

Assume now that in year 3, the business is sold and the entrepreneur's share of the proceeds, including the assets that have been transferred to the trust, is $10 million. As a result, the value of the interest in the trust is worth $1 million but the entrepreneur has transferred this amount while only using up $500,000 of his or her exemption amount. If the entrepreneur had waited until after the business had been sold to gift such property to the trust, he or she would have expended his or her entire $1 million gift tax exemption equivalent amount.

Valuation Issues

Whether an entrepreneur transfers restricted stock in a new company or other business interests of a closely held company, such property must be valued for gift tax purposes.

When an entrepreneur gifts a closely held business interest, an outside independent appraiser should be retained to value such an interest for gift tax purposes. Valuations conducted by directors of the company or the company's accountant increase the risk of an IRS audit. In addition, so long as the gift of stock is fully disclosed on a timely filed gift tax return, the gift tax return starts running the current three-year statute of limitations as to when the IRS can audit such a gift. However, the statute of limitations does not begin to run if the gift is not fully disclosed. Full disclosure requires a complete description of the gifted property and how the value of the property was obtained. By including an outside appraiser's report, you are more likely to meet the requirements of full disclosure.

COMPLEX WEALTH TRANSFER
AND ESTATE PLANNING ISSUES

As we begin to discuss some of the more sophisticated planning options available to an entrepreneur, let us first summarize the two critical planning goals on which the entrepreneur should focus. The first is to *freeze the value* of his or her assets. Certain vehicles, such as a grantor retained annuity trust (GRAT) or an installment sale to an intentionally defective grantor trust (discussed below), can be used to transfer growth at little or no gift tax cost. In addition, as previously discussed, making gifts allows the entrepreneur to remove appreciating assets from his or her estate. Finally, the transferred asset is frozen at its fair market value on the date of transfer for transfer tax purposes.

The second planning goal is to use techniques that allow the entrepreneur to *discount the asset's value* for transfer tax purposes. Gifting minority interests, restricted or nonvoting stock, or partnership/LLC interests that are not marketable and can qualify for valuation discounts, reduces estate and gift taxes.

Finally, in an ideal situation, the entrepreneur should try and integrate both freeze and discount strategies.

GRANTOR RETAINED ANNUITY TRUST

A GRAT involves the transfer of assets by the entrepreneur into an irrevocable trust. The initial value of the assets contributed to the trust, with interest, will be distributed back to the entrepreneur over a fixed term of years as an annuity. Upon the expiration of the GRAT term, all of the appreciation in the GRAT (i.e., the property remaining after all of the annuity payments have been made to the entrepreneur) passes to the trust beneficiaries free of any gift or estate taxes. In order for a GRAT to be successful, only property that is expected to appreciate at a rate greater than the interest rate mandated by the IRS when the GRAT is established should be contributed to the GRAT.

> An entrepreneur transfers $2 million of closely held stock to a GRAT with a three-year term, structured so that the annuity payments made over the three years will equal the $2 million transferred to the GRAT (plus the deemed interest).
>
> The IRS-mandated interest rate for the month in which the transfer is made is 3.6 percent. Because the assets are deemed to appreciate at this rate, in order for anything to pass to the remainder beneficiaries, the assets must outperform this rate. In order to zero out the remainder (so that there are no gift taxes associated with the transfer), the entrepreneur retains an annual annuity payment of $715,000.
>
> The stock appreciates by 15 percent per year for the three years of the GRAT term. After the final annuity payment is made to the entrepreneur, $558,000 will pass to the remainder beneficiaries at the end of the term, free of gift and estate taxes. If the GRAT fails to generate the 3.6 percent required rate

of return, there is no residual value to pass along to the GRAT beneficiaries. In this case, the GRAT is said to have "failed," but the only cost to the entrepreneur is the initial cost of setting up the GRAT. No part of the lifetime exemption is wasted.

An advantage of the GRAT is that the IRS and the tax code provide a road map for the entrepreneur and his or her advisor to follow. A disadvantage of the GRAT is that if the entrepreneur dies during the term when annuity payments must be made to him or her, all of the property in the GRAT (including appreciation) is likely to be reincluded in the entrepreneur's estate and nothing will pass from the GRAT to the named remainder beneficiaries. In addition, GST tax exemption cannot be allocated to the trust until the end of the entrepreneur's retained term. Therefore, a GRAT is not an effective vehicle for making gifts to grandchildren and more remote descendants.

INSTALLMENT NOTE SALE TO INTENTIONALLY DEFECTIVE GRANTOR TRUSTS

An intentionally defective grantor trust (IDGT) is a trust that is structured so that the assets in the trust are excluded from the grantor's estate for federal estate tax purposes, but the grantor, in our case the entrepreneur, is treated as the owner of the assets for income tax purposes. The result is that any trust income is reported on the grantor's individual tax return. Such an arrangement can be advantageous because, under current law, the grantor's payment of such income taxes is not a gift for gift tax purposes as he or she is required under the tax code to pay the income tax liability. In addition, sales transactions between the grantor and the trust are ignored for income tax purposes (because the grantor is deemed to be selling the assets to himself or herself).

The technique works as follows: The entrepreneur sets up an IDGT for the benefit of his or her descendants. Assume that in order to give the trust a strong economic basis to purchase assets, the entrepreneur makes an initial gift (seed money) to the trust of cash or other liquid assets equal to 20 percent of the value of property that he or she intends to sell to the trust. The entrepreneur then sells the business asset (stock, LLC membership interests, or other interests in a closely held business) that he or she expects will appreciate significantly over the next several years to the trust in exchange for the trust's promissory note. Because the grantor is deemed the income tax owner of the trust, no gain is recognized on the sale.

The promissory note back to the entrepreneur requires that interest only, at a rate established by IRS tax tables, be paid until a balloon payment is due at the end of term. Again, because the entrepreneur is treated as the income tax owner of the trust, payments of interest and return of principal are income tax-free to the entrepreneur.

Appreciation in the assets sold to the trust exceeding the interest rate of the promissory note passes to the trust beneficiaries transfer tax-free. The initial cash funding of the trust is a taxable gift, but the sale of the stock or other business interest to the trust is not a gift because it is for full fair market value.

For example, assume the entrepreneur gifts $400,000 of cash to an IDGT. Assume further that the entrepreneur sells $2 million of closely held stock to the IDGT for a nine-year promissory note (assume an interest rate of 3.06 percent as mandated by the IRS tables). The trust will have to make annual interest payments back to the entrepreneur of $61,200. Upon the expiration of the nine-year term, the $2 million must be repaid (although it can be prepaid at any time without penalty).

Any excess appreciation over the 3.06 percent interest rate remains in the trust for the benefit of the trust beneficiaries. If the average annual return on all the assets held in the IDGT is 10 percent over the nine-year term, the remainder passing to the trust beneficiaries would be approximately $2.8 million at a gift tax cost of only $400,000.

One advantage of an installment sale to an IDGT, as compared to a GRAT, is that the assets are excluded from the grantor's estate as soon as they are sold to the trust. If the entrepreneur were to die during the term of the note, the note would be included in the entrepreneur's estate, but any appreciation occurring after the note was created and before the death of the entrepreneur would escape transfer taxation. In addition, GST exemption must only be allocated to the initial cash gift to the trust. Assets sold to the trust for full fair market value are not subject to GST taxes. Therefore, if the goal of the entrepreneur is to move assets down to grandchildren and more remote descendants, the installment sale to an IDGT is preferable to the use of a GRAT. A disadvantage of this technique is that there is no road map provided by the IRS. In addition, the IRS has begun attacking some similar such sales. Finally, the entrepreneur must have additional liquid assets to fund the trust equal to 20 percent of the face amount of the promissory note.

FAMILY BUSINESS ENTITIES: FAMILY LIMITED PARTNERSHIPS AND LIMITED LIABILITY COMPANIES

Both the GRAT and the installment sale to a IDGT are excellent planning techniques for assets that have not yet obtained high values. However, what is the entrepreneur to do once he or she has had a successful business for some time, and the value of that business is substantial? In this case, the entrepreneur must focus on planning techniques that discount the value of the interests to be transferred.

Although FLPs and LLCs are similar, and have many of the same advantages, many practitioners prefer to use an LLC rather than an FLP because an LLC does not require a general partner. As a result, there is no individual or entity with general liability. Rather, all people with an interest in an LLC have limited liability. Therefore, for simplicity, we focus hereafter on the LLC as a planning vehicle.

An LLC is an effective means to have limited control and to centralize the management of family assets and to inhibit the transfer of interest in such property to outsiders. Furthermore, an LLC also provides certain creditor rights protections and may entitle the holder to minority and lack of marketability discounts when interests in the LLC are transferred, either during life or upon death. Often, in order to retain better control over the LLC interests after making transfers to descendants, transferability of LLC interests may be restricted, under the operating agreement, to family members.

An LLC has the tax advantages of a partnership and the limited liability advantages and potential unlimited life of a corporation. The owners of the LLC are called the *members*. The only rights conferred on a member are those granted under state law, generally limited to the right to an accounting by the managers. The members are analogous (but not identical) to shareholders of a corporation, except that members do not have the right to vote, nor do they have the right to force the liquidation of the LLC.

The initial members of the LLC are generally the entrepreneur and his or her spouse. In addition, other family members or related entities that contribute assets to the LLC also will be members. If the entrepreneur gifts interest in the LLC to other persons or entities, then such persons or entities become members as well.

The managers of the LLC are the persons who control the affairs of the LLC. They determine, among other things, when, whether, and in what amounts to make distributions of profits (or other LLC property) to members. Their role is analogous (but not identical) to the role of a board of directors in a corporation or a general partner in a partnership.

The managers also may (but need not) be members. Historically, the entrepreneur and his or her spouse have served as the managers of the LLC. However, in light of recent judicial developments, and in order to protect assets in the LLC that have been gifted to family members from being reincluded in the entrepreneur's or his or her spouse's estate for federal estate tax purposes, neither the entrepreneur nor his or her spouse should retain any power in the LLC relating to distributions of LLC assets or to the dissolution of the LLC. In addition, neither the entrepreneur nor his or her spouse should have any power to amend the LLC agreement.

The entrepreneur and his or her spouse may serve as managers of the LLC for investment purposes only. All other management powers should be held by a nonfamily member who also serves as the manager (often referred to as the *independent manager*). In order to retain control over the LLC, the entrepreneur may hold the power to remove the independent manager and replace him or her with a different independent manager.

Generally, members contribute assets to the LLC in exchange for LLC interests. Upon the death of a member, the estate tax value of his or her LLC interest may be discounted for lack of marketability and for ownership of a minority interest. By making lifetime gifts of discounted LLC interests, an entrepreneur can leverage his or her exemption equivalent amount and his or her GST tax exemption. Although there is no set rule with respect to whether, and to what extent, a discount may be allowed for lack of marketability and ownership of a minority interest, case law indicates that a combined discount of between 10 and 60 percent is appropriate. It often is reasonable to discount LLC interests gifted to nonmanaging members by 30 to 35 percent. An independent appraiser should determine the applicable discount.

Most LLCs are organized under Delaware law. The laws governing the rights of members of a Delaware LLC are highly advantageous in supporting discounted values for gift tax purposes. The LLC is a separate entity and will be taxed as a partnership for federal income tax purposes (unless the entrepreneur were to elect to treat the LLC as a corporation, a choice he or she would almost certainly never make).

There are significant advantages associated with using an LLC for estate planning. There are also some disadvantages. First, LLCs can be expensive to create and complex to maintain. Second, FLPs and LLCs are often challenged by the IRS. Therefore, in order for the entrepreneur to minimize his or her exposure to such an attack, it is important that the LLC have a business purpose and that the entrepreneur and those handling the LLC observe the formalities of a business.

In some cases, it can be advantageous to combine the use of LLC interests and an installment sale to an IDGT, or a gift to a GRAT. In such a case, the entrepreneur is not only freezing his or her asset, but also taking advantage of discounting, thereby best using his or her exemption equivalent amount.

SUMMARY

Every entrepreneur should engage in some level of estate planning, whether limited to setting up a basic will and living trust or involving more significant planning vehicles. Entrepreneurs should be sure to plan early in order to maximize savings. Your attorney can better help determine which of the aforementioned techniques are right for you.

Author Background

A. Silvana (Nan) Giner is a senior partner in Hale and Dorr's Private Client Department. She represents company founders and other entrepreneurs, and domestic and international families and serves as a professional trustee. Nan assists her clients on a broad range of personal planning matters, with an emphasis on sophisticated wealth transfer strategies. She lectures frequently on estate planning and fiduciary matters and is a member of the Massachusetts and Boston Bar Associations and the Boston Estate Planning Council. Nan is a trustee of the Social Law Library and the Brain Science Foundation. She also serves on the Advisory Board of the Commonwealth College of the University of Massachusetts-Amherst.

Kimberly Cohen is a junior partner in Hale and Dorr's Private Client Department. Her practice is concentrated in the field of estate planning, focusing on the development and implementation of sophisticated planning techniques to aid clients with accumulation, preservation, and transfer of wealth, including entrepreneurs, venture capitalists, private and public company officers and shareholders, and high net-worth individuals. She counsels clients whose companies encompass vastly different stages of development, including pre-and post-IPO planning for company founders. Kim has been significantly involved with planning for venture capitalists including structuring venture capital funds to facilitate gift and estate tax planning. She is a member of the Massachusetts and Boston Bar Associations.

Chapter 3

Life Insurance:
From the Basics to the Advanced

Herbert K. Daroff

Why should an individual buy life insurance? Ask yourself the following questions:

1. What is my current income? Who relies on my income? What will they do if that income is turned off? How much capital will be needed in today's investment markets to replace that income?
2. How much debt do I have in place for mortgages and loans?
3. Where will my children go to school? How much will that cost in today's dollars? Will they be able to afford those increasing expenses if I am not there to pay for them?
4. For private business owners, how much insurance do I carry on my most valuable pieces of equipment? How much do I carry on the life of my most valuable employees? How will the loss of a key piece of equipment or a key employee affect my life, and my business? The analogy is the same if your family loses you.
5. What kind of legacy do I want to leave to my heirs? Do I have enough now to provide sufficiently for them if I died today?

These questions and your answers illustrate the basic need for life insurance. How much of your wealth and ability to generate future income can you afford to self-insure? Once these questions have been answered, the next step is determining the type of coverage. The two types of life insurance from which you may choose are *permanent insurance*, with its subcategories of *whole life* and *universal life*, and *term insurance*.

PERMANENT INSURANCE

Whole life, which has a *guaranteed annual premium* and universal life, which has a *planned or scheduled annual premium that can change,* but include a tax-advantaged savings component. With these types of insurance, payments above the insurance premium accumulate tax-deferred and can be accessed during lifetime tax-free, provided the policy remains in force. These policies allow you to skip premiums in the event of financial hardship, or for any other reason, without losing your coverage. They are available either in a *fixed* account form (whereby the insurance carrier selects how your cash value is invested, typically weighted toward bonds and mortgages) or in a *variable* account form (where you retain control over how your cash value is invested, including stocks and bonds, both in the United States and internationally).

TERM INSURANCE

Term insurance provides coverage for a set period of time and pays benefits only in the event of death, if the coverage remains in force. Missing any premium results in losing the coverage.

There is considerable debate as to whether term insurance is better than permanent (cash value) life insurance, and, if permanent insurance is chosen, whether universal is better than whole life and whether fixed (traditional) is better than variable. The answers to these questions depend to a large extent on your age and the degree to which the beneficiaries will depend on the money they receive upon your death.

WHAT PRODUCT IS BEST?

The only good life insurance product is one that is in place when you die. As I have told clients for years, "If you could answer three simple questions for me, I could tell you precisely what you should do:

1. When do you plan to die?
2. What will investment returns be between now and then?; and
3. What will tax rates be on those invested returns?"

Then, I could develop the optimal blend of coverage for them.

In simple terms, if you die young, term insurance is the better choice. First, you will have paid fewer insurance premiums relative to the death benefit your beneficiary receives. Second, the cash value of a permanent policy, had you chosen this option, would not have had much time to take advantage of taxdeferred compounding. All else being equal, if investment returns are high and tax rates on investments are high, then permanent insurance makes more sense than term. The benefit of tax-deferred compounding inside the insurance vehicle increases as investment returns and taxes on those returns increase.

BUYING TERM AND INVESTING THE DIFFERENCE, BUT IN A TAX-ADVANTAGED MANNER

A common strategy is to buy term insurance and invest the difference. However, the invested difference is subject to the ordinary income tax rate on interest and short-term gains and to the capital gains tax rate on dividends and long-term gains, subject also to triggering the alternative minimum tax.

Think of cash value inside a life insurance policy as you would a clear plastic bag that keeps your food fresh. Inside the plastic bag, all of the tax consequences that would otherwise be lost, annually and/or upon rebalancing, are retained and continue to grow. When is a 10 percent return better than a 12 percent return? When the 12 percent return is taxed as ordinary income and/or capital gains and you net only 7 to 9 percent. Remember, it's not what you make. It's what you keep that counts.

When you cancel an insurance policy, or it lapses during your lifetime, then any growth of the cash value over the policy's cost basis is taxable as ordinary income. If the policy is in force when you die, all of the death benefit is received free of income taxes by your beneficiary (unless ownership of the policy was changed).

HOW YOUR MONEY GETS INVESTED

Table 3.1 is an example of how four major life insurance companies invested their money.

Table 3.1

	John Hancock	MetLife	Northwestern	Prudential
Equities:				
Stocks	4.5%	5.9%	6.6%	3.7%
Real estate	1.4%	3.9%	2.0%	0.5%
Fixed income:				
Bonds	68.5%	63.9%	53.7%	65.3%
Mortgages	18.3%	17.6%	18.4%	11.3%
Policy loans	3.2%	3.9%	11.0%	6.0%
Cash equivalent	1.6%	2.9%	2.4%	7.4%
Other:	2.6%	1.9%	5.8%	5.7%

Source: Vital Signs, year-end 2001.

This is how traditional whole life cash values are typically invested, and also how the premium stabilization reserves for term policies are invested. Compare the general account asset allocations in Table 3.1 to a series of sample asset allocation portfolios in Table 3.2.

Now, let's look at the performance (measured by five-year average returns) of these portfolios between 1970 and 2001 in Table 3.3 and 3.4. With a variable cash value policy (either whole life or universal), the asset allocation can be changed to look more like the traditional allocation if desired. Then, the portfolio could be dollar-cost-averaged back to the other models (if you could only have guessed correctly—timing the market requires a very clear

Table 3.2

	Income	Growth/Income	Growth	Aggressive
Equities:				
Large growth	6%	16%	18%	18%
Large value	12%	24%	30%	28%
International	5%	14%	18%	26%
Small cap	0%	6%	9%	18%
Fixed income:				
Bonds	42%	26%	15%	0%
High-yield	15%	9%	5%	5%
Cash equivalent	20%	5%	5%	5%

Source: Baystate Financial Services.

Table 3.3

	John Hancock	MetLife	Northwestern	Prudential
Average five-year returns	7.70%	7.41%	7.17%	6.77%

Returns shown are based on the asset allocations in Table 3.1.
Source: Vital Signs, year-end 2001.

crystal ball). All of this can be accomplished without incurring any income tax consequences, and in most cases without incurring any expenses for reallocation.

Variable products do not perform well if they are allocated in asset classes that do not perform well. Variable products whose subaccounts were shifted to look more like general account holdings fared better as the stock market declined in the late 1990s and early twenty-first century. The key to variable account products is that the policyholder can exercise asset allocation control over the cash value. You can dollar-cost-average in and out of the asset allocation models, and this can be done without incurring tax consequences or new acquisition charges.

EXPENSES

Care must be taken in selecting products based on subaccount choices and the expenses associated with your selection. Higher-expense products can erode a significant portion of the return. Index funds typically have lower expense ratios and offer greater diversification.

Variable account products (both whole life and universal life) do have greater expenses than their traditional counterparts, but they offer the ability to benefit from the stock market (and also suffer greater losses). Fund expenses have continued to decline in recent years. For example, an S&P 500 index fund may only carry 31 basis points inside a variable policy, which is competitive with its retail counterpart. Of course, every insurance policy carries with it insurance expenses. The younger and healthier you are when you take out the coverage, the lower will be the mortality charges.

Table 3.4

	Income	Growth/Income	Growth	Aggressive
Average five-year returns	9.9%	12.0%	12.7%	13.4%

Returns shown are based on the sample asset allocations in Table 3.2.
Data Source for the index returns: Ibbotson Associates.

ACCESSING CASH VALUE DURING LIFETIME

In addition to the tax-deferred accumulation of cash values, both traditional and variable life insurance also offer significant tax advantages when accessing the cash value during lifetime for any number of purposes such as funding education costs, supplementing retirement income, or providing funds in the event of an emergency. Life insurance distributions are made on a first-in first-out (FIFO) basis. The first dollars removed can be a withdrawal of the cost basis (the premium dollars contributed). Thereafter, dollars removed are treated as policy loans. In traditional products, the interest rate for borrowing is set by the policy contract usually at 6 percent or 8 percent. Variable products offer effective loan rates that are typically at 1 percent or less. The larger-premium products will frequently have effective loan rates around 25 basis points, or even "wash" loans with no borrowing cost. In essence, this is accomplished by borrowing from the insurance company (not your policy) at, say, 6 percent; then the insurance company pulls funds from your variable cash value subaccounts of an equal amount and places them in their fixed account. By contract, this fixed account earns between 100 basis points and 0 basis points less than the loan rate. So, in the case of the 25-basis point scenario, you borrow at 6 percent and earn 5.75 percent on the same amount of money now in the fixed account.

SELECTING THE RIGHT PREMIUM AMOUNT

The amount of the premium selected to fund the life insurance, especially in a variable product, is quite important. Using high projected investment returns and then funding a very low premium over a very long period of time can result in undercapitalizing the product. Lower returns or losses can result in the coverage lapsing, thus triggering income tax consequences on the growth over the policy's cost basis.

Variable products usually provide a *minimum premium,* a *target premium*, and a *7-pay* or *maximum premium* that allows the policy to retain its tax-advantaged status as life insurance and not become a modified endowment contract (MEC). To the extent possible, often it is better to fund closer to the MEC limit than to the minimum premium. You also should look to products that offer flexibility in selecting which subaccount is used to pay the mortality costs (the pure life insurance element).

Selecting a guaranteed premium results in a higher payment since the insurance company, in order to guarantee the payment, will apply a relatively low investment component in their calculations. A scheduled or planned premium is not guaranteed. Neither the amount nor the duration is fixed.

When choosing a scheduled or planned premium, the duration of premium payments is dependent on the performance of the cash value. If the performance exceeds expectations (as reflected on the initial policy projection), then fewer premiums may be needed to keep the coverage in-force for as long as you may want it. Future performance may still cause additional premiums to be needed. If the performance lags the expectations, then additional premiums will be needed. Projections should be updated periodically to see how you are doing.

Like thinly capitalizing a business, a life insurance policy funded with the lowest premium can result in higher premiums being due in the future, premiums being due for much longer than original projections, or the coverage lapsing. Funding larger amounts enables the cash value to grow (without current tax consequences) and may provide a cushion for weaker future performance.

SELECTING THE RIGHT PREMIUM PAYER

An employer can pay the premium on behalf of an employee, independent contractor, or director. If the business deducts the premium, then the employee picks up the premium as ordinary taxable income.

An employee can have a qualified retirement plan pay for life insurance premiums. Since the contributions to the plan are pretax, allocating a portion to premiums makes the premiums pretax. The qualified plan must provide for life insurance in order for an employee to make the selection.

Another pretax alternative is covered under the voluntary employee benefit association (VEBA) rules or under Code Section 419A of the Internal Revenue Code. These plans have been under a great deal of IRS and Tax Court scrutiny, under which the deductions have been denied entirely or for amounts in excess of a term insurance cost.

All other premiums either paid by individuals or paid by businesses use after-tax dollars. When a business uses after-tax dollars to pay for a life insurance policy, the program falls under *split-dollar* rules, which have also received a great deal of attention recently. However, unlike the 419A rules, there are specific split-dollar arrangements that have received approval. Final regulations were issued on September 17, 2003.

Split-dollar works best when the premium-paying business is in a lower tax bracket than the employee. Take, for example, a C corporation whose first

$50,000 of earnings before income taxes is in a 15 percent federal tax bracket. If the employee is in a 40 percent bracket, then the employee would need $16,667 pretax in order to net $10,000 to pay that as a premium for a $1 million policy, for example. The C corporation would only need $11,765 to net $10,000. Therefore, annual savings of $4,902 result. The employee is taxed on the pure death benefit that his or her beneficiary would receive if he or she died that year. This so-called *Table 2001 cost* would be only $1,530 for a 45-year-old. In a 40 percent bracket, that erodes the first year tax-adjusted savings by only $612. As the insured gets older, the Table 2001 cost increases. Another way to look at these split-dollar plans is to treat them as an interest-bearing loan of the premium. With low interest rates, these programs may be quite beneficial. As interest rates rise, so will the cost of these programs.

Another benefit of split-dollar (even when the income tax bracket difference is not present) is the use of the Table 2001 rate to measure the gift of an insurance policy in order to remove the death benefit proceeds from a taxable estate. In addition to life insurance that insures only one party, many married couples take advantage of one insurance policy that insures both spouses, payable upon the death of the surviving spouse. With an unlimited estate tax marital deduction, estate taxes may be postponed until both spouses have died. The adjusted Table 2001 rates for these survivorship policies are quite low. For example, for a couple, both of whom are age 45, the measure of the gift may be as low as $234 for $1 million instead of $1,530 for an individual policy, both of which are lower than the $10,000 premium.

WHO SHOULD OWN THE INSURANCE?

There are four major parties to a life insurance contract. We just covered the premium payer. The other three are the *insured,* the *policy owner,* and the *beneficiary.* No more than two people should hold these last three roles. For example, it is okay for the insured also to be the owner of the policy or the owner also to be the beneficiary of the policy. Of course, the insured of a life insurance policy can never be its beneficiary.

When the insured is also the owner, all incidents of ownership are retained (e.g., ability to name the beneficiary, select the dividend options or variable subaccounts, withdraw cash value or borrow against it). As a result, however, the death benefit is included in the taxable estate.

If the insured is not the owner, then the owner also must be the beneficiary (e.g., an irrevocable life insurance trust). Irrevocable trusts frequently are used to hold life insurance death benefits outside of the insured's taxable estate. However, as the name implies, these trusts cannot be changed, but they do keep the death benefit proceeds out of the insured's taxable estate.

In most cases, when there are three different people or entities holding these three roles, adverse income tax consequences arise at some point. For example, if the business is the owner of a policy on the life of an employee, with the employee's spouse as the beneficiary, absent a split-dollar program, the proceeds at the employee's death may be taxed as ordinary income to the spouse. Another example would be an irrevocable life insurance trust that owns the policy on the life of the trust's grantor, but the grantor's spouse is the beneficiary. This results in pulling the proceeds into the spouse's taxable estate.

When someone other than the policy owner pays premiums, tax considerations must be evaluated. If a business pays for a policy owned by one of its employees, the payment is likely to be part of the employee's taxable income (and will be deductible by the business if it does not result in unreasonable compensation). However, as described above, the business may pay the premium under a split-dollar plan in order to create some other benefits for both parties. Private split-dollar plans are becoming more prevalent as estate planning techniques. They can facilitate having large insurance policies excluded from people's taxable estates while keeping the premiums within gift limitations.

WHO SHOULD BE INSURED?

Today, most insurance has one party insured (individual coverage). However, since the creation of the estate tax marital deduction, policies are also available with two insured parties (typically husband and wife) with the death benefit payable after both have died (which is when the estate tax would be due). Generally speaking, if it costs $1.00 to insure the husband (usually older than the wife, and the cost of insuring men is higher than the cost of insuring women), it costs about $0.75 to insure the wife. It costs about $0.50 to insure the second-to-die. Survivorship coverage can be used for more than estate taxes. Since the cost of insurance is lower, the cash value can provide other benefits during lifetime for children and grandchildren (such as providing for education costs).

CONCLUSION

Regardless of your conclusions regarding whether to purchase life insurance or the amount or type of coverage, please remember this: Once the insurance contract is put in force, the insurance company cannot cancel it, even if your health deteriorates. They cannot require you to take new physical exams or provide periodic reports from your doctors.

Compare this to property and casualty insurance. Take homeowners' coverage, for example. If your chimney has sparks coming through the bricks, your coverage can be rated (i.e., higher cost for the coverage). If you point the bricks and make other repairs, your cost can go down. If you don't and the problem worsens, your cost can be increased or the coverage can be canceled.

With life insurance, if your coverage is rated and your health improves, you can go back to the insurance company and reduce your premium. However, if your health gets worse, you can retain your coverage and your premium.

If you carefully consider how much coverage you need, if any, and you diversify your coverage selections and put them in the right trust, LLC, or FLP structures, you will be well positioned to be sure your death does not burden others or, better yet, leaves a lasting financial legacy.

Author Background

Herb Daroff is an attorney by education and a financial planner by profession. He heads up Estate and Business Planning for Baystate Financial Services in Boston, where he provides custom case design and is also available on a consultation basis. Herb is listed as one of the 250 Best Financial Advisers in America by *Worth* magazine (August 2002); as one of the Top Planners in the Northeast in *Mutual Funds* (October 2001); and as one of the 150 Best Financial Advisers for Doctors in *Medical Economics* (December 2002). He is Past President of the Greater Boston Chapter of the International Association for Financial Planning (IAFP, now the Financial Planning Association, FPA). He currently serves as an officer of the Society of Financial Service Professionals (SFSP) in Boston.

Chapter 4

Negotiating the Deal

F. George Davitt and Barry Nalebuff

Congratulations. Someone wants to buy your company. Now what? This chapter offers a short guide to some of the questions you need to answer before embarking down this road. It addresses the primary negotiating and legal issues that you likely will face during the process of selling your company.

SELL YOUR COMPANY RIGHT

The first point is that as much as you might like to, it doesn't make sense to dip your toe in the water. If you decide to sell your company, then go ahead and sell it the right way. A smart buyer will do everything in his or her power to convince you that you will be better off just negotiating with him or her.

Our reasons for taking this rather extreme position are several. The most important is that sticking a toe in the water is an illusion. Once you head down this road, circumstances start taking on a life of their own. Indeed, this was the logic behind the Camp David peace process. If you can get two parties to negotiate together in good faith, there is a pretty good chance they will do a deal, even if one side doesn't think it is possible going into the process.

AN OPEN SELLING PROCESS

As a buyer, the last thing you want is to have to outbid other potential acquir-ers. In the same spirit as "Speak now or forever hold your peace," if a com-pany is coming up for sale, many firms will take a look knowing that this is their only chance to buy it. Your company might have been on their distant radar, but now they are forced to pay attention.

Academic evidence suggests that when buyers face competition for a target company, they generally end up overpaying, and, as the seller, that's what you want. The negotiations will end with the synergy and cost savings going to you in the form of increased purchase price rather than to the buyer's share-holders. So that is why buyers prefer to negotiate. Indeed, that is the reason many companies insist on getting a right of first refusal before even begin-ning the negotiation process.

An open selling process can bring out bidders for all sorts of reasons. Sometimes the aim is to prevent your company from falling into a rival's hands. If you want to sell to Coke, there is nothing like getting Pepsi's inter-est and vice versa. Indeed, the beverage company SoBe was almost sold to Coke. Pepsi felt excluded from the deal. When Coke balked, Pepsi was excited to be back in the game. SoBe is now part of Pepsi. It is a good bet that Pepsi's eagerness was fueled by their opportunity to beat Coke.

A CLOSED SELLING PROCESS

Now, having said that you should prefer an auction to a one-on-one negotia-tion, let us give the other side of the argument. We have a client who sold one of his books to a publisher that made a preemptive bid. The publisher under-stood that it was about to face an auction in which it had an uncertain chance of winning. From the client's side, there was also a chance that the auction would fail. If few bidders showed up, then the publisher would end up bid-ding less than its preemptive offer. Also, the publisher's excitement for the book would be greatly diminished. That matters when it comes time for mar-keting budgets. And, in the case of selling a business, it matters to you if your purchase price includes a postclosing payment dependent on the perform-ance of the business, that is, an *earn-out*. Thus, it is possible to get some, or even all, of the benefit of an auction without running one by allowing poten-tial bidders to make a preemptive bid. However, this requires that the bidder believe that it will have to compete in an auction if its preemptive bid fails.

A second reason not to have a full-fledged auction is that your company may have proprietary processes and other sensitive information. Thus, the value of your company will go down if more people really understand how you make money.

One of the key lessons that you know from business is to put yourself in the shoes of the other party. Being a bidder is a big distraction. Some firms might not enter the competition unless they think they have a respectable chance of winning.

PAYING BIDDERS TO PLAY

One strategy you might not have considered is to pay bidders to play. That payment might be in the form of cash, typically through a breakup fee. It might be in the form of a supply contract. That way, the potential buyer knows that its efforts won't go fully unrewarded at the end of the day.

A great example of this occurred during the hostile takeover attempt by Craig McCaw for LIN Communications. The example may be a bit extreme, but it shows what is possible.

LIN's CEO, Donald Pels, was no fan of McCaw and put a poison pill into place to prevent the takeover. As a result, McCaw was thwarted. The problem is that the share price also fell as a result of LIN no longer being a takeover target.

Pels went to Bell South and invited them to make a friendly bid for his company. But the smart folks at Bell South realized that McCaw would most likely outbid them. Sure they would be delighted to buy LIN at the current price, or even at McCaw's first bid. But that wasn't going to be McCaw's best bid. Why go through all the distraction only to have McCaw end up with the company?

LIN gave Bell South 54 million reasons. If their initial bid was topped, they would get a $54 million breakup fee. Under those terms, they agreed to bid. And sure enough, their bid was topped. After they bid approximately $110 a share, McCaw countered with $115. LIN wanted Bell South to bid again, and for another $10 million they were willing to play along. McCaw outbid them again, and this time also paid Bell South $22.5 million to stop bidding. (Keep in mind that LIN was a public company and that different rules apply when bidding for public companies. Consult your attorney for advice on developing bidding incentives in the context of a sale of a private company.)

Bell South did great in that it turned a losing hand into approximately $80 million of profit. Although it is true that Donald Pels ended up paying a lot for this extra competition, McCaw's final bid added an extra billion dollars to LIN's valuation, at which point Pels decided that McCaw wasn't such a bad guy after all.

The takeaway point is that we often assume that bidders will provide their competition for free. That's the American way. Some firms may enter the ring just to have a chance of winning. But you can't presume that you will get enough competition for free. Thus, you should think who else you might like to enter the game and how you can reward that bidder. Eighty million was a bargain price to get McCaw to raise his bid by a billion.

RIGHT OF FIRST REFUSAL

The buyer asks for a last-look provision. Under a last-look (also known as a *right of first refusal* or *right of last offer*), the buyer gets a chance to see all the other bids and if he or she is willing to match the highest bid, can then buy the company at that price.

If so, the buyer knows what he or she is doing. Do everything you can not to give a last-look provision. The reason is that few other bidders will be willing to look at your company if they know that someone else can always outbid them. This will not only depress the value of your company to other bidders, it will also depress how much the bidder with the last-look will pay because this bidder can anticipate how others will react.

RIGHT OF FIRST OFFER

The best solution here is to offer a right of first offer. This sounds similar to a right of first refusal but is quite different. A right of first offer solves some of the same issues as a last-look provision without giving away the store. Under a first offer, the buyer states a price and you can either accept or reject. If you accept, the deal is done. If you reject, you are free to sell the company to any other bidder provided that you can get a higher price. If you can't get a higher price, you don't have to sell. But if you still want to, the first buyer isn't required to keep his initial price on the table. You have to offer the buyer with the right of first offer a chance to buy your company at the best price you've obtained. With a right of first offer in place, other bidders can still buy your company without having to let someone match them—provided they bid high enough. Thus, they are not at such a disadvantage that they won't play.

AN OFFER YOU CAN'T REFUSE

The buyer says: "Sell to me or I will enter your market and compete with you." This can be done as a threat or even in a friendly way: "We think this is a great market. We plan to enter. We'd prefer to enter by buying you, but this is a market we want to be in."

Either way, you are in a tough position. There's good and bad news here. If the buyer is the right buyer for your company, then the threat is more serious. But if the buyer isn't the best one, then you should be less worried. There is often a right time to sell a company. Doing so before a major competitor comes into the market is one of those right times.

PROFESSIONAL HELP

By the way, if some of this confusing to you, this is as good a signal as any that you need professional advice. Although you may have sold a company in the past, chances are that you don't have that much experience in this process. In contrast, your buyer has probably done this before. Good investment banks and (mergers and acquisitions) M&A lawyers have seen all of these contract provisions before, as well.

A second reason to get professional help is that you care too much. As Herb Cohen, author of *Negotiate This,* emphasizes, you should care, really care, but not that much. It is hard to discuss in dispassionate terms something that you've created. In many cases, you will end up having to work with (or for) the buyer when the deal is done. If you are the one doing the negotiation, it is almost impossible to prevent bad feelings, unless you end up being too much of a softy.

EARN-OUTS

Many times buyers will want to include an *earn-out* provision. You have provided them with some estimates for future sales. Part of the payment for the company will be contingent on making those sales forecasts.

How you feel about this provision will depend quite a bit on whether you are planning to stay with the company. If the factors (advertising, sales force) are not in your control, then you are taking a much bigger risk in accepting an earn-out.

However, the earn-out provision can be a great tool for resolving valuation debates. You say that the company is worth $100 million because its sales are projected to grow from $10 million this year to $20 million next year. The buyer says the company is only worth $50 million because they have doubts about the size of the market. In that case, you can say: "Well, then you should have no problem paying us $100 million if we actually hit those targets."

Be careful here. Almost by the very fact that you are running this business, you are an optimist about the future. You may have more facts, but it is hard to be objective. That said, rather than simply accept $50 million, there is no reason not to push for the upside. Indeed, if the buyer was bluffing on this point, this is a good way to find out.

EARN-INS

You can also turn an earn-out around. Consider an earn-in. Many companies will claim that they are a great strategic buyer. They will claim that they can bring your company to the next level. They can give you access to distribution, production, international markets, and more.

The problem is that they may not deliver. This will be especially painful if you find yourself holding their stock as compensation.

A solution here is to give the buyer control of the company subject to hitting certain performance measures. Today the buyer pays for a call option, the right to buy the company at a fixed price. The buyer quite rightly does not want to have to pay a much higher price for the company, having been the one to add this value. But the buyer's ability to exercise the call is contingent on meeting performance goals.

With these negotiating tactics in mind, let's turn to a discussion of the legal aspects of the transaction you are about to enter. The next part of this chapter addresses issues related to the trade-offs between going public versus being acquired, the process of negotiating and putting together a contract, and the key provisions that should be included (or excluded) from the contract. Finally, it touches on the differing implications of being acquired for cash versus stock.

COMMONLY MISTAKEN ASSUMPTIONS

Let's conduct a little practical test. True or False:

1. If I sell my company for stock instead of cash, I can avoid paying capital gains tax.
2. If I sell my company for stock, I can immediately sell the stock I receive.
3. If, instead of selling my company, I undertake an initial public offering (IPO) of my company's stock, I can keep control of my company and sell stock whenever I personally need cash.

If you answered true to any of the above questions, you're wrong. There are many cases in which each statement is incorrect. If you answered false, you're probably wrong, too. There are cases in which the statement is correct. It may come as a surprise to you that the correct answer to each question is a resounding maybe.

How can this be? Is there no certainty on something as fundamental as obtaining liquidity for one's company? The laws—both tax laws and securities laws—that govern the questions posed are complex and have been developed over time. As a result, there is a veritable patchwork quilt of laws and regulations that apply. In some cases, a sale of your company for stock instead of cash is taxable and in other cases not. In some cases, you can immediately resell stock you receive as consideration for the sale of your company and in other cases not.

The important lesson to take away from these questions is that you cannot assume anything, even the most intuitive conclusions, when considering the sale of your company. Each aspect of a potential transaction must be considered from a business standpoint, and then analyzed carefully under applicable corporate, securities, and tax laws.

SALE OR IPO?

America loves an IPO. During the 1998–2000 bubble, during which the NASDAQ Index soared above 5,000 and every week seemed to create a new Internet billionaire, everyone wanted an IPO. The cake being served by the equity markets was so rich that conventional businesses turned their attention away from their core businesses and instead focused on developing an Internet strategy. Wall Street thought, and most of us bought into it, that the Internet would fundamentally and quickly change the way business was conducted. One investment bank ran an ad campaign under the slogan "Are you still calling it the new economy?"

We all now know that the cake was too rich, that the Internet is best viewed as another channel of distribution—adding to and not displacing conventional channels—and that business is, once again, all about making profits.

THE IPO ROUTE

Assume, however, that you've got that remarkable company that can go public. Should you do it? It depends on your objectives. The best reasons for undertaking an IPO are:

- To raise a significant amount of equity capital in order to fund rapid growth
- To have a noncash "currency" that can be used for acquisitions, which is common in rollup and consolidation strategies
- To take advantage of higher valuation multiples that may exist in the public markets for companies in your particular industry
- To facilitate the sale of stock at different times by different family members or owners of the company
- To help create a stock incentive program for employees

Another reason commonly given is that going public will give the company a sales boost because it's easier to compete as a large, public company. But this reason is specious. Once a company is public, the world can see its financial results and thus determine with great certainty precisely how large or small the company is and precisely how strong or precarious is its financial position. Large companies do not point to this reason for going public.

THE SIZE OF YOUR COMPANY MATTERS

A good reason to undertake an IPO is that if the company is large enough, the owner can obtain some liquidity by selling a minority position and still maintain control. The reason the company has to be large is that in order to have a successful offering, the IPO must offer both a relatively large number of shares to ensure a liquid market and a price per share high enough to attract institutional investors.

For example, a company with an equity value of $1 billion can sell 20 percent to the public and have a market float of $200 million. If 10 million shares were offered, the stock would have a price of $20 per share. This would seem to be a sufficiently large market float to offer liquidity and a high enough per share price to attract an institutional following. A 100,000-share lot would cost $2 million and yet constitute only 1 percent of the market float. However, if the company had an equity value of $100 million, a sale of 20 percent would yield a market float of $20 million. If 10 million shares were offered, the stock would have a per share price of $2, which no underwriter would propose. If two million shares were offered, the stock would have a price of $10 per share. While $10 per share seems high enough in the abstract, a $2 million investment would require the purchase of 200,000 shares and constitute a full 10 percent of the market float. Unloading a 10 percent position in any stock is not simple. Although there are plenty of underwriters who would recommend an IPO of 20 percent of a company with a valuation of $100 million, the owners may be surprised by the lack of institutional interest in the stock after the completion of the offering.

The important point here is that $20 million isn't enough to have a liquid market, whether it is one share at $20 million or 20 million shares at $1. Just as you can't make more pizza by cutting it into smaller slices, you can't make a stock more liquid by creating more shares with a lower price. Liquidity is determined by investors' ability to sell some dollar amount of stock in a day. If there is only $20 million of stock that can be traded, it is next to impossible to for an institution or large investor to trade more than $1 million without having a significant impact on the price.

CHANGE OF CORPORATE STRUCTURE

What if your company is organized as an LLC or S corporation? Can it maintain that status and still go public? No. A public corporation cannot be an S corporation for federal income tax purposes in the United States. Although there are no strict limits on the number of members of an LLC, except for real estate investment trusts (REITs), the public markets do not want to invest in pass-through entities. You should assume that your LLC or S corporation will have to become a C corporation for federal income tax purposes at the time of its IPO. This means that the company will be taxed at the corporate level going forward.

REPORTING REQUIREMENTS

After an IPO, your company will be subject to the full panoply of the periodic reporting regime of the federal securities laws. With the recent amendments to the securities laws and the regulations promulgated by the Securities and Exchange Commission (SEC) as a result of Congress' enactment of the Sarbanes-Oxley Act of 2002, it has been estimated that the cost of compliance to be public is between $0.9 and $3.5 million. While this seems extremely high, even if your company's costs were 50 percent of those amounts, it's a staggeringly expensive administrative burden. Cutting costs in the compliance area is not an option, especially in light of the new criminal penalties enacted by Congress.

GETTING LIQUIDITY THROUGH AN IPO

IPOs fall into two categories: primary offerings and secondary offerings. A primary offering is an offering of shares newly issued by the company. The net proceeds of the offering are payable to the company. A secondary offering is an offering of shares held by a shareholder. The net proceeds of the offering are payable to the shareholder. (The terms are not uniformly used. Occasionally, you'll hear underwriters talk of a secondary offering when they mean the sale of shares by a company in an offering after an IPO. The better term for this is a *follow-on* offering.) An IPO can be either a primary offering or a secondary offering, or it can be both. If both, the company would issue some shares to be sold to the public, and the company's existing shareholders would sell some shares to the public.

Can you can sell some of your shares in an IPO so that, at least in part, the IPO of your company is a secondary offering? The answer is maybe. If your company is large enough, the answer is likely to be that you may indeed sell some shares in the IPO. Your stake in the company is probably so valuable that the underwriters can explain to the institutional investor community that you are selling to obtain some modest liquidity and that your stake in the company is still large enough to keep you highly motivated. On the other hand, if your company is more modest in size, the answer is likely to be no. The underwriters will explain to you that the institutional investor community will want all net proceeds of the offering to be used in the business.

LIQUIDITY CONSTRAINTS

After an IPO, contrary to popular belief, you cannot sell stock anytime you like. First, as part of the IPO, the underwriters will require you to sign a lockup agreement, pursuant to which you agree not to sell any of your shares for at least 180 days following the offering. Second, unless you have rights to require the company to register your shares under the Securities Act of 1933 in order to permit you to resell them to the public (commonly called *registration rights*), the federal securities laws limit the amount of stock that you as a controlling person can sell. In general, in any three-month period, you can sell up to the *greater* of 1.0 percent of the number of outstanding shares or the number of shares equal to the average weekly trading volume (over the most recent four weeks). See the discussion of Rule 144 below. Third, you cannot sell shares at any time when you are in possession of material non-public information, which usually means that you can sell only when the "window is open" under your company's insider trading policy.

Many founders of companies that have gone public take advantage of the SEC's Rule10b-5.1. This rule enables a company insider to sell at regular intervals a set number of shares previously announced to the market without being subject to blackout periods.

IPO UNDERPRICING

What about price? Can you get more for your company in an IPO? Academic research suggests that IPOs are typically underpriced; the 6,249 IPOs between 1980 and 2001 rose by an average of 18.8 percent on their first day of trading.[1] What that means is that you are effectively selling your stock at a discount and this can be thought of as one of the costs of going public. Of course, if you are only selling 10 percent of the company and there is an 18.8 percent discount, then the true cost is still under 2 percent.

You might even think these discounts are good for your company. If there were no discounts, then people would not have any incentive to invest resources to learn about your company (why do research in order to buy shares in a company that is fully priced?). To the extent that fund managers have done well with your stock, they may be more willing to invest in further offerings down the road. There is nothing that makes for less happy investors (and bankers) than starting off with a decline in price so that everyone invited to the party will have lost money.

SELLING RATHER THAN GOING PUBLIC

INTERMEDIARIES

So, after all this, you might have ruled out an IPO. Let's now discuss the sale process from commencement to completion. Do you need an intermediary to help you sell your company? These intermediaries (investment banks, business brokers, M&A advisory firms) charge a fee or commission if the business is successfully sold. From a legal standpoint, you can sell a company without an intermediary. However, the majority of companies owned by entrepreneurs get sold with the help of an intermediary. Why? The reasons include:

- The intermediary's knowledge of the value of the business and hence the sale price that the owner can expect to receive
- The intermediary's knowledge of the likely buyers and contacts within an industry
- The intermediary's experience in closing sale transactions
- The intermediary's time both to prepare a description of the business (often called an *offering memorandum,* or *book*) and to manage the sale process

An intermediary will ask you to sign an engagement letter formally setting out the terms of the intermediary's deal. Do not sign the engagement letter without having it reviewed by counsel. In addition, be careful not to make oral statements to the intermediary that you will retain the intermediary. The case law in this area is riddled with claims by intermediaries who did not have written contracts but who nonetheless sued the seller of a business claiming that the seller owes the intermediary a fee based on an alleged oral contract. In many jurisdictions, these contracts are enforceable.

The fees of intermediaries vary, depending on the size of the deal and the nature of the intermediary. The "bulge bracket" investment banks (including Citigroup, CSFB, Deutsche Bank Alex Brown, Goldman Sachs, JPMorgan, Lehman Brothers, Morgan Stanley, and UBS) usually have high minimum fees that make them logical intermediaries only for deals with transaction values over $100 million, although these institutions often compete for deals with lower transaction values. The middle and small business markets are served by a large number of intermediaries, including boutiques who specialize in selling businesses, often within a particular industry. Many intermediaries ask for an up-front retainer or monthly fee, although some are willing to be paid only if a sale transaction successfully closes, with what is called a *success fee*. Any retainer or monthly fees should be creditable against the success fee. The intermediary's expenses are typically reimbursed, sometimes subject to a negotiated limit.

Engagement letters usually provide for a *tail* period. If you do not successfully sell your company within the period of engagement—usually one year—the engagement letter will specify that the intermediary will be paid if a sale is completed within a period of time after termination of the engagement. This tail period is usually an additional year, although for larger transactions the bulge bracket firms have begun to insist upon two years. You should focus on this provision of the engagement letter because you might have to pay two success fees if you engage a new intermediary and subsequently close a sale. You should try to limit your obligation to pay the first intermediary only for sale transactions closed with parties with whom the intermediary has had meaningful discussions, often limited to those who sign a confidentiality agreement.

CONFIDENTIALITY AGREEMENTS

Your lawyer or intermediary will work with you on the form of a confidentiality agreement that all prospective buyers are asked to sign. It is customary to obtain a signed confidentiality agreement before giving information about your business to any prospective buyer. You may find yourself frustrated with the amount of time spent negotiating what should be a straightforward agreement (or frustrated at having to pay a lawyer to negotiate a number of these agreements). However, it's money well spent. Among other things, these agreements typically impose obligations on prospective buyers to:

- Keep your information confidential
- Not to discuss the fact that you are for sale with any third party
- Not to solicit or hire your employees
- Not to contact your employees, customers, or suppliers except as permitted by you or your intermediary during the sale process
- Acknowledge that you can sell to anyone you like, or choose not to sell
- Acknowledge that you are not obligated to sell until a definitive sale agreement is signed

OFFERING MEMORANDUMS

You and your intermediary will likely prepare an offering memorandum or book on your business. The book typically introduces the company, its industry, and value proposition. Both historical financial statements and projections are typically included. Often, the summary financials will contain adjustments showing expense savings that a prospective buyer will enjoy, such as the elimination of your compensation and benefits or the closing of an administrative office. You should have your counsel review the offering memorandum.

LETTERS OF INTENT

A letter of intent in the context of the sale of a business is an expression of mutual intent of the parties to proceed with due diligence and negotiation of a definitive acquisition agreement. The letter of intent usually describes the basic economic deal: how much the buyer will pay, whether the consideration is cash or stock, the structure of the deal (e.g. an acquisition of stock or assets or a merger), and whether the buyer is assuming that the business will have certain attributes, such as minimum working capital or the services of named employees. These provisions are usually expressed to be nonbinding. This means that, at this juncture in the process, the parties do not intend to be legally bound. Ordinarily, the buyer needs to complete its due diligence investigation of the business, as well as to negotiate the terms of a definitive acquisition agreement, before the buyer is ready to be legally bound to buy the business.

It is extremely important to have counsel review any letter of intent before it is signed. The case law is littered with cases brought by would-be buyers or more numerous would-be sellers claiming that the letter of intent created a legally binding obligation. In some states, unless a letter of intent contains language expressly contemplating a subsequent definitive acquisition agreement, it will be held to be binding.

A letter of intent also usually contains binding provisions that relate to the procedure to be followed as the parties move forward to negotiate and sign a deal. A buyer will typically ask for a period of exclusivity, often called a *no-shop*. During the no-shop period, the seller agrees to deal exclusively with the buyer and not to discuss the sale or provide materials on the business to any other potential buyer. A typical no-shop period can be anywhere from 14 to 60 days, depending on the bargaining leverage of the parties. If the seller's business has attracted significant buyer interest, a skilled intermediary will negotiate a short no-shop period.

In the sale of some businesses, the buyer and seller proceed directly to the negotiation of a definitive acquisition agreement, and a letter of intent is not required.

DUE DILIGENCE

Due diligence is the process performed by the buyer to investigate the business proposed to be sold. In the context of the sale of a large business—for example, one with a purchase price over $100 million—the intermediary will run a process that will require potential buyers to complete or nearly complete their due diligence prior to submitting final bids. In the sale of a more modest business, a potential buyer will have done some due diligence prior to signing a letter of intent but will not have completed its due diligence investigation.

Normal due diligence will include an investigation of:

- Financial records, including the company's bookkeeping system, accounting ledgers, financial statements, audit work papers (if the company has audited financial statements), and related accounting and financial data
- Legal records, including the company's certificate of incorporation and bylaws, minutes of meetings of the board of directors and shareholders,

and material contracts (such as leases, intellectual property licenses, and significant customer and supplier contracts)

- Environmental matters, if applicable to the nature of the company's business, including possibly an initial investigation by an independent environmental consultant of the company's compliance with applicable environmental laws and regulations and an investigation of the company's facilities
- Tax records, including the company's tax returns and tax work papers
- Employee matters, including employment contracts with key employees, vacation and benefits records, compliance with workplace laws and regulations, and records relating to pension or defined contribution plans
- Capitalization matters, including any debt or capitalized leases and stock and option records
- Intellectual property records, including patents, trademarks, copyrights, and documentation relating to the proper assignment of intellectual property rights from employees to the company
- Other matters, including customer and supplier relationships and industry-specific items

A well-prepared seller will have worked with its intermediary and counsel to prepare due diligence materials in advance of any due diligence investigation. This has two big advantages: First, it facilitates a potential buyer's completion of due diligence and, second, it enables the buyer's advisors (lawyers, accountants, industry consultants) to conclude that the business is well run.

DEFINITIVE ACQUISITION AGREEMENT

The definitive acquisition agreement is the legally binding agreement signed by the seller and the buyer setting forth the rights and obligations of each of them in the purchase and sale of the business. It is usually a long, complicated agreement negotiated between buyer and its counsel, on the one hand, and seller and its counsel, on the other. The form of the deal is important. Sales of businesses are usually given legal effect through one of three ways: asset sales, stock sales, and mergers.

Asset Sale

An asset sale is the sale of the company's assets and assumption by the buyer of certain of the company's liabilities. A definitive acquisition agreement in the form of an asset sale, called an *asset purchase agreement*, lists the assets to be sold to the buyer and the liabilities to be assumed by the buyer. Buyers typically like to structure acquisitions as asset purchases because they can specify the types of liabilities that they are willing to assume (such as trade payables) and not assume (such as, in some cases, debt obligations). Buyers also like asset acquisitions because, for U.S. federal tax purposes, they can step up the tax basis of the acquired assets to fair market value and therefore enjoy a bigger depreciation and amortization deduction.

Sellers are usually amenable to asset acquisitions if the business is organized as an S corporation for tax purposes or LLC because the deal can generally be structured to result in one level of tax, namely, at the shareholder level. However, if the seller's company is organized as a C corporation for tax purposes, an asset sale will result in two levels of tax: one at the company level on the gain from the sale of the assets and, when the proceeds of the sale are paid out by way of a dividend to the stockholders, a second level of tax at the stockholder level. Table 4.1 is illustrative.

Stock Sale

A stock sale is the sale by the company's stockholders (and not by the company) of the company's outstanding shares of capital stock. As a result, the buyer becomes the owner of the company. Unless the company has transferred out certain assets or liabilities prior to the closing of the transaction, the company retains all of its assets and liabilities.

Table 4.1

	C Corporation	S Corporation or LLC
Asset sale proceeds	$10,000,000	$10,000,000
Tax basis of assets	4,000,000	4,000,000
Gain on sale	6,000,000	6,000,000
40 percent corporate tax*	2,400,000	—
Net gain at corporate level	3,600,000	6,000,000
Distribution of net proceeds	3,600,000	6,000,000
20 percent individual tax[†]	720,000	1,200,000
Net after-tax proceeds	$2,880,000	$4,800,000

*Assumed combined federal and state corporate tax rate.

[†]Assumed combined federal and state individual tax rate applicable to dividends or capital gains. Actual tax rates may differ, including whether the owners of an S corporation or LLC recognize capital gains or ordinary income on the sale.

A definitive acquisition agreement in the form of a stock sale, called a *stock purchase agreement*, must be signed by each stockholder. A stock sale is feasible if there are a limited number of stockholders, all of whom support the transaction and are willing to be subject to the obligations of the stock purchase agreement. However, it is not feasible if there are a large number of stockholders—even 10 or 20 stockholders can make it unworkable. A stock sale is also not feasible if a single stockholder rejects the terms or refuses to be subject to the obligations of the stock purchase agreement. Although it is legally possible for a buyer to acquire less than all of the outstanding capital stock of a company, buyers ordinarily want to acquire 100 percent of a company and generally do not want to go into business with a former fellow stockholder of the seller. A stock sale usually results in the same net after-tax proceeds whether the business is organized as a C corporation, S corporation, or LLC (in which all outstanding interests are sold). This is because the company is not a party to the transaction and thus does not recognize any gain or loss; the company merely experiences a change in controlling stockholder, from seller to buyer. A buyer generally will not be willing to pay the same purchase price in a stock acquisition as in an asset acquisition. This is because the buyer will not be able to step up the tax basis of the assets as the buyer would be able to do with an asset acquisition.

Merger

A merger is a creature of corporation law and permits one corporation to combine with or merge into another. The company into which another company is merged is called the *surviving corporation*. As part of the transaction, stock held by stockholders of the company whose separate existence ceases is changed into something else, usually, in the case of the sale of a business, the right to receive cash or securities of the buyer. As with a stock sale, the buyer becomes the owner of the company and, unless the company has transferred out certain assets or liabilities prior to the closing, the company retains all of its assets and liabilities.

The primary advantage of a merger is that it permits a business to be sold without the consent of each stockholder. When public companies are sold, the form of the transaction is invariably a merger agreement for the simple reason that it would be impractical for buyer to enter into an acquisition agreement with each stockholder. A definitive acquisition agreement in the form of a merger, called a *merger agreement* or an *agreement and plan of merger*, is only required to be signed by the company, not by each stockholder. It is common that controlling stockholders also sign a merger agreement, but it is not necessary as a matter of law.

Before the company can close a merger transaction, the merger must be submitted to stockholders for approval. In some states, such as Delaware, unless the stockholders have agreed to a higher threshold, a merger can be approved by the holders of 50.1 percent or more of the outstanding capital stock. In other states, the approval requirement is higher, such as two-thirds or 75 percent of outstanding capital stock. Once approved by the required majority, the merger can close and is effective for all stockholders, even for stockholders who vote against the merger, unless a particular stockholder exercises dissent rights. Dissent rights permit a stockholder to ask a court to determine the fair value of his or her shares. Dissent rights are rarely exercised in the case of a sale of a company if the consideration to be received in the merger has been negotiated in good faith at arm's length. This is because it would be difficult for the stockholder to prove that the fair value is greater than the price obtained in an arm's length negotiated sale.

Because mergers can be approved by less than 100 percent of the stockholders of a company, they enable a controlling stockholder to cause a business to be sold even if the minority stockholders do not favor a sale. For this reason alone, in cases in which there are more than a few stockholders, buyers and sellers usually prefer that the form of the transaction be a merger.

REPRESENTATIONS AND WARRANTIES

In the definitive acquisition agreement, irrespective of the form, the seller will make statements about the company and the condition of the business. These are called *representations and warranties,* which if not true at the time of closing, may entitle the buyer not to close or to make a legal claim against the seller. Typical representations and warranties include:

- The company is duly incorporated and in good standing
- The company has corporate power and authority to conduct its business
- The company has taken any necessary corporate action (such as a stockholder approval) to authorize the transaction
- The consummation of the transactions contemplated by the acquisition agreement will not contravene the certificate of incorporation or bylaws of the company or any of the company's contracts (such as leases, credit agreements with lenders, etc.)

- A statement as to the capitalization of the company, including debt and equity securities, such as stock, warrants, and options
- A list of the company's material contracts
- A list of the company's employees and their compensation arrangements as well as a list of company benefits and benefit plans
- A list of the real property assets owned or leased by the company and a statement as to the condition of the company's facilities
- A list of the personal property assets of the company and a statement of their condition
- A description of any transactions or ongoing arrangements between the company and its affiliates, including its stockholders, directors, and officers
- A list of the company's intellectual property assets and statements as to the ownership, registration, and protection of them
- A statement as to the accuracy of the company's financial statements and, in some cases, the projections or forecasts prepared by management
- A statement as to the company's insurance arrangements
- A statement that the company does not have undisclosed liabilities

Representations and warranties represent a snapshot of the business as of a moment in time. Typically they are required to be made on the date of signing and, if different, on the date of closing of any acquisition transaction.

COVENANTS

A covenant is an agreement to do or not to do something. It is a promise to take or refrain from taking action. Any acquisition agreement, irrespective of form, will usually contain covenants binding upon either or both of the parties. Some covenants operate only between signing and closing, such as the typical promise by the seller to conduct the business in the ordinary course and not to enter into any material transactions between signing and closing without the consent of the buyer. Other covenants operate after the closing, such as the typical promise by the seller not to compete with the business just sold to the buyer.

CLOSING CONDITIONS

If the definitive acquisition agreement is signed with the intent of closing it at a later date, the agreement will contain closing conditions. Closing conditions are matters that the parties have agreed must be satisfied or waived in order for the closing to proceed. Some will be applicable to both parties and some will apply only to the buyer or seller. For example, if the transaction has a purchase price of over $50 million, it will likely be subject to antitrust review under the Hart-Scott-Rodino Antitrust Improvements Act of 1976. The buyer and seller will be required to file a prescribed form with the Federal Trade Commission (FTC) and the Department of Justice, who then have 30 days to review it. As a result, a typical closing condition will provide that neither the buyer nor the seller is obligated to close unless the waiting period under the Hart-Scott statute has expired. Other closing conditions, but ones that apply only to the buyer's obligation to close, include:

- The seller's representations and warranties are true on the closing date.
- The seller has taken all action required under the covenants set forth in the agreement to have been taken by the closing date.
- Certain named employees have entered into agreements with the buyer to continue to work for the business after the closing.
- In the case of a merger agreement, holders of not more than, for example, 5 percent of the outstanding shares have exercised their dissenters' rights to demand an appraisal of the value of their shares.

Because the seller's representations and warranties must be true at the time of closing, at least in "all material respects"—which is a commonly negotiated middle ground—sellers must be extremely careful about rushing to sign a definitive acquisition agreement. Typically, a deal is announced after the definitive acquisition agreement is signed and before closing. However, once announced, employees, customers, and suppliers expect that the deal will close. If the representations and warranties are not true on the signing date, the buyer is entitled not to close, and, if the deal does not close, the seller could end up holding a company that in the market is viewed as "damaged goods." In this circumstance, too, a buyer typically will attempt to renegotiate the purchase price or the terms of the deal in exchange for the buyer's waiver of the closing condition.

INDEMNIFICATION

Businesses are not generally sold on an "as is, where is" basis. A buyer customarily will be entitled to be indemnified by the seller for problems that are discovered by the buyer after the closing. Of course, not all problems are indemnifiable, only those problems that amount to a breach of the seller's representations or warranties or a breach of the seller's covenants or agreements. For example, if the seller neglected to include in its representation about material contracts a statement disclosing a material contract pursuant to which the business agreed to supply a significant amount of product at what had become a below-market price, the buyer would likely have a claim against the seller for the burden of fulfilling the obligations under the undisclosed contract. Or, if the seller failed to disclose that the company had received a letter threatening a lawsuit and the lawsuit was subsequently brought, the buyer would have a claim against the seller for the burden of defending the lawsuit and ultimately settling it or paying a damages award.

Why indemnification? Why not just a common law claim for breach of contract? The reason is simple: An indemnification claim usually includes coverage for all costs and expenses, including legal fees.

Is the seller responsible for every penny's worth of problems that the buyer suffers after the closing? In general, no. Most indemnification provisions contain limitations that apply so that the seller is not responsible unless problems aggregate to a particular dollar amount. The buyer and seller usually negotiate whether this amount is a mere threshold beyond which the buyer can recover from the first dollar or is a true deductible or "basket" beyond which the buyer can recover only the excess. In addition, sellers usually try to negotiate a limitation or cap on the aggregate amount of their liability under the indemnification provisions. A logical cap is 100 percent of the purchase price, but many sellers are successful in negotiating a cap that is lower, sometimes significantly lower.

SALE FOR CASH OR STOCK

Often the most misunderstood issue in the mergers and acquisitions world is the importance of the form of consideration; that is, whether the business is being sold for cash or stock or (sometimes) both.

Cash is simple. The sale will be a taxable transaction for U.S. federal and state income tax purposes, and the amount of net after-tax proceeds kept by the seller will depend on the form of the transaction and whether the business is organized as a C corporation or as an S corporation or LLC. (See the discussion above under Definitive Acquisition Agreement—Asset Sale.)

Stock is more complicated. The sale may be a tax-free transaction for U.S. federal and state income tax purposes, but it may not be. The rules are extremely complex, and you must consult a tax advisor for advice in the context of any sale of a business, especially the sale of one for stock. In general, you should not expect the stock portion of any transaction to be tax-free unless more than 50 percent of the aggregate consideration is stock. There is some support for a lower percentage, but most tax advisors generally will insist upon at least 50 percent. This may seem straightforward, but it is not. What happens if the value of the deal consideration is 55 percent stock and 45 percent cash measured at the time of the signing of the deal, yet by the time of closing, the buyer's stock has fallen in value so that the value of the stock has become 40 percent of the deal consideration? It is a good idea to consult a tax advisor early in the sale process.

Can you immediately resell any stock that you receive? As noted early in this chapter, it depends. Let's assume, for purposes of this discussion, that the buyer is a public company. This means that the buyer files periodic disclosure reports (such as 10Ks and 10Qs) with the SEC. Let's also assume that the buyer's shares are traded on an exchange (such as the New York Stock Exchange) or in an interdealer quotation system (such as the NASDAQ National Market). The securities laws in the United States require that any company selling shares of stock must file with the SEC a registration statement for those shares and sell the shares pursuant to a prospectus—or must be entitled to an exemption from the registration requirements. There are considerable regulations and case law dealing with these requirements. You might think that the buyer is not selling shares of stock, but that the buyer is making an acquisition of another business using shares of its stock as its currency. However, the securities laws treat any sale of stock as the same— whether for cash or for consideration consisting of property (i.e., the seller's business). As a result, the federal securities laws apply to the buyer in the case of an acquisition as equally as they apply in the case of a sale of stock for cash. Consequently, whether the buyer is issuing 100 shares or a million shares of its stock, it must register the shares or find an applicable exemption.

In most acquisitions of private companies, the buyer issues shares of its stock pursuant to an exemption. The exemption most often used is the *private placement* exemption, which permits the buyer to issue shares to a limited number of persons, ideally persons who are accredited investors. There is some disagreement among lawyers as to the number of persons to whom a buyer can issue shares in an acquisition and still claim to rely on the private placement exemption. However, in practice, the problem tends not to be the number of accredited investors; the problem tends to be the existence and number of sellers who are not accredited investors.

An individual is an *accredited investor* under federal securities laws if his or her net worth individually or jointly with his or her spouse exceeds $1 million or if that person's net income in each of the two most recent years exceeded $200,000 or $300,000 with that person's spouse. There are other rules applicable to entities. Consequently, if every seller is an accredited investor, the buyer will generally rely on the private placement exemption in issuing shares of stock in the acquisition. Buyers will usually require sellers to represent and warrant that they are accredited investors.

If some sellers are unaccredited, the private placement exemption may still be available, but there are procedural requirements that must be followed in the transaction, as well as a 35-person limit on the number of unaccredited sellers. This tends to be an issue in practice because almost all private companies have stockholders who include Aunt Millie, the proverbial widow whom the securities law were designed to protect.

Let's assume that you and a partner are the only shareholders and that you both are accredited investors. The buyer is therefore comfortable that it can rely on the private placement exemption in issuing shares of stock to you and your partner as acquisition consideration. When can you and your partner sell the shares the buyer issues to you?

The shares issued to you pursuant to the private placement exemption will be restricted shares under federal securities laws. Unless the buyer agrees to register the shares for resale, you and your partner cannot sell them on the market for at least one year. The share certificates will likely bear a legend indicating that the shares have not been registered, and no transfer agent or brokerage firm will accept them as good delivery in any market sale. It is possible that you and your partner may be able to sell them in a private transaction, in which the person who buys the shares from you agrees that the shares remain restricted, but the market for such outright sales is limited—other than in connection with hedging transactions, which are discussed in Chapter 7.

If you and your partner hold for a year and then want to sell on the market, can you? Let's assume that you became a director and officer of the buyer and that your partner left the business and became a full-time amateur golfer. Let's also assume that you received 5 percent of the outstanding common stock of buyer and that your partner received 1.5 percent. After one year, you and your partner are each entitled to sell, during any three month period, the *greater* of (1) 1 percent of the outstanding common stock of the buyer or (2) the average weekly trading volume for the buyer's common stock for the four calendar weeks preceding the sale. Therefore, if your partner has not agreed to any other restrictions on his ability to sell, your partner would be able to sell his entire position within six months (i.e., two three-month periods) and possibly less time if the trading volume for the buyer's common stock is high. On the other hand, because your position is larger, it will take longer for you to sell your entire position, potentially as long as 15 months (five three-month periods).

What if you and your partner hold for two years? Because you elected to become a director and officer of the buyer, federal securities law treats you as having become an affiliate of the buyer. After holding restricted stock for two years, your partner could sell his entire position without regard to the volume limitations described above. On the other hand, because you are an affiliate of the buyer, you are still subject to the volume limitations.

Sales of restricted stock in compliance with the SEC's safe harbor described above are called *Rule 144 sales*. Most major brokerage houses have special departments to handle Rule 144 sales. In addition, there are paperwork requirements, including SEC filings and legal opinions. If you will receive restricted stock in any sale of a business, you should contact your broker and tell him or her that you ultimately expect to sell under Rule 144. Your broker should be familiar with the procedures required to be followed or will have a department dedicated to handling Rule 144 sales.

If you and your partner insist upon receiving freely tradable shares, is there any way that a buyer can satisfy your objective? Yes. The buyer can agree to file a resale registration statement in which you and your partner would be identified as the sellers. While the registration statement will describe the buyer's common stock, it will state that none of the proceeds from the sale of the shares covered by the registration statement will be paid to the buyer and that all proceeds will go to you and your partner. The SEC will have to declare the resale registration statement effective before you and your partner can sell. You and your partner will then sell the shares of buyer stock pursuant to a prospectus, which you (through your broker) will be obligated to deliver to any buyer. If you and your partner are successful in convincing the buyer that it must agree to register the shares issued to you in the acquisition, none of the limitations under Rule 144 will apply and you could sell your entire 5 percent interest and your partner could sell his or her entire 1.5 percent interest as quickly as the market trading volume for the buyer's common stock would permit. Again, you have to work through a major brokerage house in a transaction like this because of the prospectus delivery requirement that accompanies each sale.

What if, instead of 5 percent, you received 25 percent of the buyer's common stock in the transaction? You know you will end up holding the stock for some time, but you do not want to be limited to selling under Rule 144.

If the weekly trading volume is not meaningful, you can be limited to 1 percent every three months and thus take more than six years to sell down the entire position. If the buyer agrees to file a resale registration statement covering all of the shares, and to update and maintain the effectiveness of the registration statement until your position is fully sold, then you can sell the shares freely until your entire position is sold down. However, if the buyer refuses to register all of your shares and wants you to have to hold at least some of the shares for a period of time, you could attempt to negotiate registration rights pursuant to which you have the right to require the buyer to register a certain number of shares periodically.

Registration rights fall into two types: *demand* rights and *piggyback* rights. Demand rights give you the right to require the buyer, upon your demand, to register a certain number of shares. The buyer will likely limit the number of demands that it is willing to give to you. Piggyback rights give you the right to ask the buyer to register your shares whenever the buyer itself is registering shares either on behalf of itself or on behalf of others. Registration rights are a way of protecting you against the illiquidity of a large single stock position.

CONCLUSION

The architect Ludwig Mies van der Rohe (1886–1969) is known for his view, "God is in the details." The attention to detail is what turns ordinary work into a work of genius. The flip side is the maxim of pop musician Blixa Bargeld who says, "The devil is in the details."

From either perspective, when it comes to selling your company, the details matter more than you might ever expect. This starts with the negotiation phase all the way through the contract terms of the sale and postsale tax issues.

If you are selling your company, the first detail to attend to is to get professional advice. This may mean retaining an intermediary—an M&A professional at an investment bank—and it will mean retaining an M&A lawyer. An intermediary should know your industry as well as having M&A expertise. Your lawyer may have to be different than your regular counsel. Ideally, your lawyer will have industry expertise, too, but it's more important that your lawyer be an experienced M&A lawyer than an industry insider.

M&A professionals are well versed in the process of selling a private company. Follow their advice. Although you'll pay what may seem like high fees, you're undertaking what may arguably be the most important business transaction of your life. The odds are that it will go more smoothly and that you'll successfully complete a transaction if you build upon the experience of your professional advisors. The topics covered in this chapter should give you a head start in knowing what to look out for and what to ask for.

Notes

1. This data comes from Ritter, Jay, and Ivo Welch. "A Review of IPO Activity, Pricing and Allocations," *Journal of Finance*, August 2002. During the dot-com bubble, those discounts became much larger; some stocks doubled on their first trading day. One response to the IPO discount is to reduce the size of the offering, wait until a market price is established, and then sell more shares in a secondary offering. Another innovation is the IPO auction approach, created by the boutique investment bank W.R. Hambrecht & Co.

Author Background

F. George Davitt is a partner at the Boston law firm of Testa, Hurwitz & Thibeault, LLP. An experienced mergers and acquisitions lawyer, Mr. Davitt's has handled acquisition transactions in many industries including information technology, media and consumer products. Mr. Davitt was educated at the University of Toronto and Oxford University and is a member of the New York bar (1984) and the Massachusetts bar (1995).

Barry Nalebuff is the Milton Steinbach Professor of Management at Yale University School of Management. An expert on game theory, he has written extensively on its application to business strategy. He is the coauthor of *Thinking Strategically: The Competitive Edge in Business, Politics, and Everyday Life* and *Co-opetition*. His most recent book, *Why Not?* provides a framework for problem solving and ingenuity. Professor Nalebuff is on the boards of Trader Classified Media and Bear Stearns Financial Products, and is the chairman and cofounder of Honest Tea. A Rhodes Scholar and Junior Fellow at the Harvard Society of Fellows, Nalebuff earned his doctorate at Oxford University.

II

After Selling Your Business

Chapter 5

How Your Life Changes: Psychology of a Windfall

Marty Carter and Charles W. Collier

You have sold your business and received substantial money: your reward for many years of vision, creation, risk, and uncertainty while working 75 hours or more a week. You are successful! So why do you have lots of stress, worry, and questions? It is because the sale encompasses more than a successful transaction and the creation of a windfall. It becomes a major transition in your life and the life of your family. With careful thought and planning, entrepreneurs can make the transition productive, fulfilling, and enjoyable. Many people having sold or in the process of selling their business ask similar questions about what happens next:

- What do I do now?
- What will be my identity in the community?
- What impact could this have on my family?
- Will this money spoil my children and grandchildren?
- Now that I am wealthy, everyone seems to want a piece of my money or me!

- What should I do with this money?
- What are the family's attitudes toward this money?
- What do I tell my children about my wealth and when?

IMPACT OF THE SALE ON THE ENTREPRENEUR

MAINTAIN A HEALTHY BALANCE
BETWEEN THE BUSINESS AND FAMILY

Your relationships with your spouse, family, friends, and the community depend on how you balance your time, energy, and commitment to the family and to the business.

Successful entrepreneurs share similar characteristics: They are driven, highly motivated, astute visionaries, who are adept at making deals. They communicate effectively, translate vision into implementation, are shrewd managers, and possess acute business and financial skills. In addition, they must be able to maintain a healthy balance between family and business.

Imagine the family and the family business consisting of interlocking circles, as shown in Figure 5.1.

If the business circle is considerably larger than the family circle, the emphasis may generate a favorable bottom line. However, if most of the entrepreneur's energy is directed toward the business, this comes at the expense of

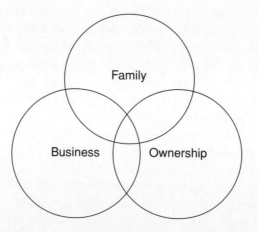

Figure 5.1   Interlocking Circles of Family and Business

the family. You may reap a substantial financial reward with the sale of the business, but find you have missed opportunities with your family.

One entrepreneur sold his business and turned attention to his children, eager to now be a part of their lives. He expressed frustration when his daughter declined his request to take her shopping for back-to-school clothes. "Dad, I'm 15, I can buy my own clothes." In families where the opposite is true, the business exists primarily to provide income and employment for family members, and eventually the business will atrophy when it can no longer meet those financial needs as the family increases in size. More attention has been given to maintaining lifestyles than addressing future needs of the business. Both business and family will need more attention at some times than others, and often both entities are demanding.

☛ Tip: Entrepreneurs who understand and maintain appropriate balances are more likely to be less stressed and anxious after the sale of their business.

MEASURING SUCCESS

Ask yourself: "What does success mean to me?" In some families, success is measured by money. In others, by work accomplishments; in yet others, by philanthropy. Success measured primarily by money only discounts gifts of talents, accomplishments, and being a "good person."

What will be your identity in the community after the sale of the business? In your family, you'll still be Mom or Dad, but will your identity in the outside world change?

☛ Tip: Ask yourself: "What would I like my identity to be?" and "What do I have to do to achieve that new identity?"

SECURITY

Now that you have money, do you feel secure? Do you fear you will lose it? Are you relieved that you do not have to worry about money? Do you worry about the impact wealth will have on your family?

☛ Tip: Engage a financial planner (preferably a firm that is fee-only) to assist you in setting income and capital appreciation goals and determining the funds necessary to meet those goals. Consider what joys can come from making a difference for others with your resources.

IMPACT ON HOME LIFE

After selling the business, the entrepreneur may suddenly have little to do if no transition planning has occurred. Suddenly, he or she has plenty of time with no commitments and may turn to the spouse, perhaps forgetting that marriage vows were "for better or worse" but not for lunch! Entrepreneurs who are married can disrupt the routine of the spouse at home. The at-home spouse has a regular schedule of activities and events and is now expected to drop everything and make lunch for the retiree?

Planning for the transition from CEO to the next chapter in your life requires thought. Take an inventory of your life outside business:

- Do you have a life outside your business?
- Do you have true friends?
- What amount of time do you spend with your friends, with your spouse and family?
- What is important to you? Many entrepreneurs say "family, friends, health, happiness, and security." Recently they have added "security" due to uncertainty and fear.
- What is meaningful to you?
- What brings joy to you?
- What is rewarding?

☛ Tip: Spouses should discuss their goals, such as time together, time with family and friends, travel, intellectual and spiritual pursuits, and the desire to make a difference to society. Revisit those goals. Schedule a yearly spousal retreat to review and update your joint goals.

IMPACT OF WEALTH ON THE ENTIRE FAMILY

ENTITLEMENT

In many families, particularly when money was created several generations ago, there is a tendency for the descendants to assume that the resources will never run out. Parents who have not acquired sound money practices do not instill such attitudes and behaviors in their children and often produce a next generation that always has its hand out. This is the meaning of entitlement. Picture this exchange: "Mom, you are spending my inheritance." "It's not yours, yet." Families with a great deal of wealth may think about money, usually in terms of spending and perhaps charitable giving, but seldom talk about money, or ask, "What is the purpose of money? How does money impact our relationships?"

Another by-product of entitlement is community adulation. When you meet someone with a name well known in your community, what goes through your mind? Hmm, lots of money, power, and influence. Do you think of them as being different? Wealthy people are often placed on pedestals and treated with deference if people see them as possible donors or clients. If overdone, this community adulation is absorbed and welcomed by some and causes others to retreat. Seeing the family name over the door of the new art center at best creates a selfless spirit of giving back to the community and, at worst, a sense of entitlement.

If significant wealth is produced when a family has both older and younger children, there may be a discrepancy in the ways children react to having money. Older children may not have had the benefit of the largess as family financial resources were poured back into the business, leaving little for "extras." These children may be resentful if younger children are showered with money and no boundaries or expectations on spending.

☛ Tip: Provide education to teach financial skills.

☛ Tip: Teach humility by stressing giving back to the community.

☛ Tip: Discuss with children why there is suddenly more money. Create a mechanism for fairness for older children. Set expectations and guidelines for spending, saving, and sharing.

VALUES

Families who have not set boundaries and expectations rear a next generation that may not feel worthy. If the message is, "There is plenty more where that came from," there is little or no incentive to do well in school and prepare for a job. As Willis notes in her book on the dark side of wealth, "A common reason inheritors develop late emotionally is that no one walks willingly into the kinds of experiences that tend to mature us, and many inheritors are quite successful in avoiding maturing experiences altogether." (Thayer Cheatham Willis, *Navigating the Dark Side of Wealth: A Life Guide for Inheritors.* Portland, OR: New Concord Press, 2003.)

A trust fund beneficiary was recently asked about the purpose of his trust, the first of several trusts created for him. His answer was startling: "It allows me to BUY anything I want to." Notice he did not say, "It allows me to DO anything I want to." His parents and grandparents inherited millions and none of them worked for pay, although several were heavily involved in community activities. The parents were concerned that they had not given very good messages about money to their children, and we were engaged to coach the nine children in the next generation to be wise about money.

As for the trust beneficiary, he has discussed his goals (hard for a 21-year-old to identify) and what was needed to accomplish them. Then some sticky questions: What were the values taught by his family that he would want to keep and pass on to his children? What were the things he would want to change? In a recent conversation, he said, "I've been thinking. . . . Now I don't want to sound disloyal to my parents, but I may want to do it differently. I mean how many houses, cars, and boats do I need?" Maybe there is hope for him! He is defining who he is and his relationship to money. That means setting goals, creating ways to be aware of the needs of others and to be involved in the community. This is a young person who has been kicked out of three schools and has done some soul searching about how being wealthy has not always been such a good thing for him. He needs to experience living his life differently.

☛ Tip: Hold family meetings to discuss what is important and meaningful. Engage your children in a discussion around this question: What are the strengths and *real* assets of this family, and how can we invest in them?

SELF-ESTEEM

Self-esteem, or lack of it, is a condition often exacerbated by wealth. Wealthy people are uncertain if they are liked by others for who they are or for how much money they have. They often feel isolated because others treat them deferentially. Or the opposite situation can occur: Young wealthy adults have complained that when they are hanging out with their friends, they are expected to pick up the tab. A 10-year-old commented that when a classmate returned his borrowed tennis racket and he discovered it was damaged, he said, "Hey, you need to fix my racket or get me a new one." The reply: "Buy a new one yourself. You're rich."

Another stumbling block to a healthy sense of self occurs in families in which success is measured by money. If this happens, then there is little attention given to other accomplishments that make a successful person—

intellectual capabilities, capacity to help others, and commitment to family and friends.

☛ Tip: Acknowledge and promote different forms of capital each individual has to offer: human (who you are), social (commitment to community), intellectual (lifelong learning), and financial (becoming a great steward of the family money).

DENIAL

Keeping up with the neighbors often drives families to make destructive financial decisions. It is not uncommon for families to take out a second mortgage to finance their daughter's debut. The cost of a wedding pales in comparison to a Mardi Gras presentation, but appearances mean a lot to some folks and can color their sound financial decisions.

Unfortunately, it's easy for families of wealth to live beyond their means. One wealthy woman was told that she will be insolvent within a few years if she does not drastically cut her spending. This will not be new information. Her advisors and managers have created every way possible to say, "You will run out of cash." The problem is that she doesn't want to hear it. She engages in excessive displays of wealth and makes philanthropic commitments that she financially cannot support. She could sell assets but the cycle would only continue. The history is that somehow she escapes each crisis because someone comes to her rescue and bails her out. The next family meeting will focus on what to do. Bailing her out is not working and she is not willing to cut spending.

☛ Tip: Engage a financial planner and investment manager to ensure that interests of the heart are fiscally prudent and wise.

GUILT

Some clients are ashamed of their inherited wealth, thinking, "I did not make it, I did nothing to create it." They do not want outsiders to know how much they have. Embarrassment can lead to behavior that either hides or denies the existence of the money in their family.

Consider the woman who owns a line of high-end children's clothing and yet dresses her children from Kmart. Another example: Once when walking to the speaker's rostrum, a colleague said, "In the audience, I see very old money: old Pendleton wool skirts, shabby cashmere sweaters and pearls." Women in the audience had intentionally dressed as an understatement and yet the understatement caught my friend's attention.

☛ Tip: Decide what image do you want to convey and what values support it.

RELATIONSHIPS

Relationships are often affected if each spouse comes from a different socio-economic background. The person growing up with less money can react on one end of the spectrum with continued frugality, or at the other end he or she develops an attitude of, "I've made it. Bring on the loot." Parents of new-lyweds are often concerned that the spouse of the inheritor will take advantage of the access to lots of money. As mentioned earlier, families often have limited experience talking constructively about money.

Consider the case in which it was Tuesday before a Saturday wedding, and the prenuptial agreement between two very wealthy individuals was bogged down by wrangling attorneys arguing over the agreement. The couple had not talked with each other or with their attorneys about what was needed and what was doable! The groom's attorney was anxious because he had recently negotiated the divorce from the first marriage in which he thought the groom gave away too much of his fortune. The bride was anxious because she had been through a nasty divorce with an aggressive attorney. The bride and groom sat down with a trusted counselor and talked about what was needed and what was doable for about 45 minutes. Then the attorneys put it in legalese and the couple beat the deadline.

☛ Tip: Use trusts, if at all possible, in lieu of prenuptial agreements.

Relationships are also affected by power and control issues with regard to money. A grandmother was worried by the poor academic performance of her grandson and, without checking with the parents, hired a tutor for him. You can guess that a blowup occurred. "Why did you do that without talking with us?" "Look, I'm paying for his tuition and I've a right to do what I think is correct." Don't forget: Grandchildren are OPC—other people's children!

Different members of the same family may have different amounts of wealth. Those who have it can feel put upon by family members asking for help, whereas others may want to be generous. Sometimes folks could use the financial help but have a great deal of self-respect and pride that makes it difficult to accept money, even for a most worthy cause. Wealthy families are often concerned when money marries no money and are reassured by the use of prenuptial agreements or other protective instruments. They want to protect the family wealth.

☛ Tip: Learn to talk about money: what money means to you, what it is supposed to do, and how to share it with no strings attached.

Financial Literacy

There is a tendency to think that wealthy families are sophisticated, but this is not always true when it comes to financial literacy and strategy. One wealthy person had never paid a single bill in his life! "He's totally helpless," his financial advisor laments. This advisor asked another one of her clients what he did before he retired. The client replied, "Before I retired I was a baby!"

However, other wealthy people keep close tabs on their investments, but are not always mindful of teaching their children sound financial strategies. College-bound kids should be encouraged to do their own due diligence on expenses, make a list, and talk with their parents to see what is needed, what is doable, and who will pay how much. If they have to figure out how to live on what they have, they'll be more careful, unless the parents capitulate to "Dad, my checking account is overdrawn."

☛ Tip: Talk to your teenage children about their financial skills and strategies. Discuss expectations and accountability with the money you give them and the money they earn.

Money Beliefs

Part of working with individuals and families is to provide financial and investment education, teach fiscal responsibility, develop passions for a philanthropic spirit, and increase understanding of the psychology of money. To do this, it is necessary for people to understand their *money beliefs*.

Attitudes and behaviors with money define what you will do with it. Following a sudden windfall of money, people react differently. Those who are frugal, fearful, and anxious about spending will demonstrate similar behaviors after receiving wealth. Others may see the windfall as a chance to make up for lost opportunities, for example, travel or purchase a second home, provide monies for children and grandchildren, and perhaps share their largess philanthropically.

It is important to explore what messages about money are learned in growing-up years. Were you taught to be frugal, give to others, be careful? Did you learn the clichés: "Money doesn't grow on trees," "A fool and his money are soon parted," and "A penny saved is a penny earned"? In many families, the message is "Shhh, this family doesn't talk about money."

Money beliefs come from messages from parents while their children are growing up—what they said and what they did with money. Kids listen to some of what their parents say and pay even more attention to what their parents do with their money. If the messages were "Not to worry, there is plenty more," if parents do not set good examples by working (career or volunteer), then children will have little motivation to be productive, plan, delay gratification, and feel pride of accomplishment.

☛ Tip: Talk about money: What is it for? What does it mean to be responsible with money? Insist that children should have age-appropriate summer jobs. Use resources to teach children philanthropy: Take them on age-appropriate site visits and match their charitable gifts.

ESTATE PLANNING

All of a sudden you have more money than you dreamed of and how are you going to think about your estate plan? You should focus first on the "why" of the inheritance for your children before you work on the "how." That is, what are the principles and values that will drive your estate planning decisions? Determine those first and then the products of estate planning [trusts, family limited partnerships (FLPs), and limited liability companies (LLCs), for example] will naturally follow. Think about values and the impact of the inheritance first, estate planning vehicles second.

☛ Tip: Ask yourself these questions:

- What is an appropriate financial inheritance for my children?
- Will the amount I have in mind for them enhance their life course?
- When do we tell them?
- How much do we tell them?

- What will be the effect of this inheritance on them—and their own marriages?
- What will my children think if they don't have to work?
- Can we give them a say in their financial inheritance?

FACILITATING THE ENTREPRENEUR'S TRANSITION

Given the complex issues surrounding new and existing wealth, families have to come up with strategies to help facilitate the transition from entrepreneur to investor. Among these strategies is the facilitated family meeting. Structured as a series of family gatherings, the meetings generally focus on conversation surrounding money education, age-appropriate philanthropy, and questions facing the entrepreneur following the sale of the business, such as:

- What do I do now?
- How will life change?
- What impact will this money have on our family?

The broad money conversations explore such questions as:

- What does money mean to us?
- What do we want to do with it?
- What do we need to know to be good stewards of this wealth?
- How can we learn to be responsible with money?
- What are the good things that money brings to the family?
- What are the drawbacks of being wealthy?
- Do people like us for who we are or for our money?

All generations of family members from 8 years old and older are invited to a half- or full-day money conversation meeting. A genogram (family tree) is drawn on large sheets of paper and taped to the walls. The family is asked to introduce the facilitator to the cast of characters listed on the family tree. As the family recalls and shares stories about these people (who they were, where they lived and when, occupations hobbies, interests, living conditions in the context of the world at that time), family members begin to understand the influences and messages that pass down through the generations and how they impact who people are and what they do.

For example, one family told stories about a great-grandfather who was a circus rider going from town to town on horseback to conduct religious services.

The great-grandfather on the other side of the family was kidnapped, blind-folded, and led to a cave to provide medical attention to a man eager not to be recognized. The physician was warned by his captors to say nothing to any-one or he would be killed. The doctor told no one, but his great-grandson found a note in the family bible written by his great-grandfather. As the fam-ily story goes, the wounded man was Jesse James. Even though the family members had heard and retold these stories, they had not realized the con-nection with their own lives: Since time of the stories, three generations of men had entered the field of medicine or the ministry.

As the stories are shared, the facilitator begins to highlight the values that govern the family. In this example of the family of physicians and ministers, the shared values become apparent: healing, nurturing, caring, spirituality, and commitment to others. As the values are highlighted, individuals and families can encourage those values and support them. When people are con-sistent in their reporting of what is important to them, they are more likely to act in a manner that expresses those values.

At this point in the money conversation meeting, the opportunity arises for a discussion of where to go from here. Some families decide to allocate resources for money-related education for adults (many adults with inherited wealth don't balance a checkbook because someone else has always done it). Families often request help coaching the next generation in learning financial skills to spend, save, and share. Older children may be interested in under-standing investments. In introducing young adults to the concept of finan-cial planning, the facilitator suggests identifying short- and long-term goals and calculating what resources are necessary to accomplish them. In a follow-up meeting, the facilitator asks two cousins to put together a "ballpark" cash-flow analysis (they preferred this term to "budget," which implied they were not fiscally prudent) of funds needed for the coming collegiate year. They learned to collect data on rent, food, utilities, insurance of various types, transporta-tion, entertainment, travel, and "mad money." When they totaled the expenses, they were aghast and immediately took a "red pencil" to slash costs. These college students could readily afford all the expenses, but they were beginning to develop a conscience of what they really need versus what they might want and to make choices about how they want to spend their money.

When young adults marry and raise a family, big-ticket items, such as a house, cars, and tuition payments, can create anxiety. When working with a financial planner, the couple should spend time to do a money dynamics meeting to explore their behaviors and attitudes about money, the levels of compatibility in making money decisions, messages they got about money in their growing-up years, and what messages they want to pass on to their children. For instance, does the family value fiscal responsibility or is there a message implying: "There is plenty more where that came from"?

CONCLUSION

In summary, often families do not know how to talk about important and private matters, including money. The entrepreneurs are people who formulate an idea and turn it around in their head without talking about it to someone else. When they later talk about their decision, it sounds like an announcement, with little invitation for discussion. This creates a problem because families need to engage in a dialogue, a conversation not just an announcement. Facilitated family meetings help address these questions and anxieties about money.

Without planning, there will be no transition between life as the CEO and what will be the next chapter. A financial windfall can create many emotions: excitement, anxiety, uncertainty, joy, and fear. Families need to consider the impact of the new wealth, reconsider their life course, and define what they truly value. The goal for the senior as well as the next generation is to be fiscally wise and prudent with the money while encouraging all family members to lead their own lives as productive and contributing members of society. Asking the questions outlined in the chapter can help the entrepreneur be more thoughtful in creating a successful transition. With careful planning and family conversations, the entrepreneur and the family can chart a productive and fulfilling life course following a major transaction.

Additional Reading and Resources

Collier, Charles W. *Wealth in Families*. Cambridge, MA: Harvard University, 2001.

Gallo, Eileen and Jon. *Silver Spoon Kids*. New York: Contemporary Books, 2002.

Hausner, Lee. *Children of Paradise: Successful Parenting for Prosperous Families*. Los Angeles: Jeremy P. Tarcher, Inc., 1990.

Lansberg, Ivan. *Succeeding Generations: Realizing the Dream of Families in Business*. Boston, MA: Harvard Business School Press, 1999.

Parks, Sharon. *Big Questions: Worthy Dreams*. San Francisco: Jossey-Bass, 2000.

Price, Susan. *The Giving Family: Raising Our Children to Help Others*. Washington, DC: Council on Foundations, Inc., 2001.

Author Background

Marty Carter is the family communication advisor at Charles D. Haines, LLC, in Birmingham, Alabama. She is an experienced professional with 26 years of practice in family communication consultation. Her work with family-owned businesses and foundations has won her national recognition. As a partner with Charles D. Haines, LLC and the Family Business Alliance, Mrs. Carter speaks to issues facing families of wealth: the psychology of money, emotional and developmental impact of wealth transfer, money and kids, and life planning. She was recently awarded the Certificate in Family Business Advising with Fellow Status by the Family Firm Institute (FFI), an international professional organization dedicated to assisting and advising family businesses. She has presented or published nationally in the following sample of venues: the Council on Foundations and Family Foundation Conferences, FFI, the Center for Family Enterprise, Nation's Business, Family Business, Family Business and Professional Educators Association.

Charles W. Collier is the senior philanthropic advisor at Harvard University, and has also held positions at Princeton, Brown, Andover, and Dartmouth. He has worked with hundreds of individuals and families to shape their philanthropy, help them make tax-wise gift decisions, and advise them on family issues surrounding financial wealth. He is a senior fellow at The Philanthropic Initiative, and serves on the boards of the National Center for Family Philanthropy and The Catalogue of Philanthropy. Mr. Collier is a graduate of Phillips Academy, Andover, and holds a BA from Dartmouth College and an MTS from Harvard Divinity School. His book, *Wealth in Families*, was recently published by Harvard University.

Chapter 6

Overview of the Wealth Management Industry

David M. Spungen

During the 1990s, the booming economy and stock market resulted in a explosion of personal wealth. This extraordinary growth attracted the attention of virtually every end of the financial services industry, including banks, brokerage firms, and money managers. Although some companies always had viewed the private client business as their bread and butter, many of these firms previously had treated it as an afterthought, preferring to focus their attention on institutional business, primarily pension funds. However, as the growth in that sector slowed, more and more financial services companies began to position themselves as wealth managers, providing complementary services to their money management capabilities that would be attractive to wealthy individuals.

As a result, the high-net-worth client has a significantly broader array of providers from which to choose than was the case 10 years ago, with access to products and services previously available only to large institutional investors. These include sophisticated asset allocation analysis, specialist separate account managers, hedge funds, private equity, and venture capital. However, to the individual who just sold Worldwide Widget, Inc., for $50 million, the myriad of choices can be dizzying, and distinguishing one firm from the next can seem nearly impossible.

There is, however, a framework through which virtually any wealth manager can be viewed that can help to identify strengths and weaknesses and potential suitability for a particular client's needs. Matching a firm to one of three service models may require reading the fine print and asking questions that might not seem obvious, but it can save a client from unwanted surprises and potential disappointments. Those three service models are as follows:

1. Investment offices (Multifamily offices, investment consultants, financial planners)
2. One-stop shops (banks, brokerage firms, trust companies)
3. Hybrid (one-stop shops to varying degrees)

INVESTMENT OFFICE

The first model, the *investment office*, probably constitutes the smallest segment of the wealth management industry, and is populated by a significant number of smaller boutique firms, unaffiliated with large institutions. However, the popularity of this segment seems to be growing as an increasing number of investors seek alternatives to the bigger firms.

The defining characteristic of the investment office is independence from product and freedom from conflicts of interest; that is, investment office revenues derive primarily from advisory fees charged to the client, and not from fees or commissions paid from funds, managed accounts, or other products that the client is advised to use. As such, clients are unlikely to be steered towards higher-cost, higher-margin products that may not be the most appropriate alternatives.

Functionally, such firms can be seen to be similar to single-family investment offices, which have been established by mega-wealthy families like the (Bill) Gates and the (Michael) Dells to oversee the investment of their significant assets. Such families can afford to hire seasoned investment professionals whose loyalties are solely to their employers, and not to any product or provider. Those professionals are responsible for setting investment strategy, performing arms-length due diligence on independent managers for each asset class into which they invest, and measuring and monitoring performance. They also coordinate and optimize their client's investment, tax, estate, philanthropic, and liquidity objectives, working with internal as well as external professionals [i.e., CPAs (certified public accountants) and attorneys, among others].

Such operations bring to the founding families benefits of scale, freedom of conflicts of interest, and utilization of talented, experienced professionals. However, such family investment offices can be expensive to operate, and typically make economic sense only at asset levels of $500 million and greater.

Wealth managers who fit the investment office model work much the same way, and potentially bring similar benefits to clients who, unlike Bill Gates, share the resources of the firm with other clients. By essentially aggregating client assets to create scale, this kind of wealth management firm can underwrite and spread research and due diligence costs, bypass high minimum account sizes, and negotiate fees. They can bring sophistication, experience, and knowledge to the development and oversight of a client's portfolio free from conflicts of interest. They utilize an open-architecture approach, and seek multiple "best of breed" investment managers through which to implement their asset allocation strategies.

The advantages of the family office approach seem clear. As such, why would a high-net-worth individual not choose this type of firm? There are several reasons. First, most firms of this type are small (at least compared to banks, brokerage firms, and insurance companies) and owner-operated, and tend to be regionally focused. They are rarely household names, and typically depend heavily on a relatively small number of professionals, often the founders of the firm. It may be difficult for individuals with newly liquid wealth to take what may seem to be the leap of faith required to turn responsibility for that wealth over to this kind of firm, when bigger, more familiar alternatives may be available. Although this may be a triumph of perception over reality, it is nonetheless represents a significant barrier for many individuals.

Second, when compared to more product-oriented firms, the investment office model wealth managers generally experience lower profit margins. As such, they tend to be somewhat resource-constrained. They may not be as able to provide as broad an array of auxiliary services, such as banking and brokerage, "concierge" services (the proverbial walking the dog), and estate planning, as compared to larger firms. Their ability to develop or obtain cutting edge technology solutions for back-office and client reporting functions may be limited. Furthermore, their key professionals may be spread thinly across client service, new business development, and internal management.

The third potential disadvantage is that if a firm in this category is weak at selecting managers, it may take some time to become apparent. Managers, once hired, are usually expected to demonstrate value-added performance over a three- to five-year cycle. If performance is subpar, the manager may be terminated and replaced, based upon reasons other than the wealth manager's poor selection. It may take as long as 10 years for a pattern of consistently poor selection to become apparent.

The types of firms which fall into the investment office category vary, and include multifamily offices, consultants, and financial planners. Most, but not all multifamily offices (MFOs) started as single-family offices, that chose to offer their services to outside families. These firms bring the obvious benefit of having deep experience in dealing with the complex issues a typical wealthy family faces. However, they tend to have higher relationship minimums ($25 million and up) and, depending upon the proportion of founding family assets to outside family assets, new clients may have to compete for the firm's resources.

Many consulting firms that were founded to serve the needs of ERISA (Employee Retirement Income Security Act) plans have shifted their focus somewhat to wealthy individuals. They typically bring an academic approach to asset allocation and portfolio construction, and have extensive experience in researching money management firms. They tend to have lower, retainer-based fees, and similar to multifamily offices, often are unavailable below the $25 million to $50 million asset level. However, because much of their experience has been focused on tax-exempt entities, they may not be as tax conscious or well versed in estate planning and philanthropic issues. Consultants also suffer from the perception that they make safe recommendations, that is, recommendations for which they would be unlikely to be fired, even if the results were poor. As a result, returns tend not to deviate materially from the broad benchmarks.

Finally, financial planners provide a detailed focus on tax, cash flow, and retirement and education planning. Many developed their wealth management activities out of a CPA practice and so tend to have more of an accounting-oriented focus. Those that continue to prepare tax returns for their clients provide a high degree of coordination between their investment activities and their tax planning. They tend to provide a highly customized approach with a high degree of client service. They also tend to have lower minimums, and may charge hourly or retainer-based fees. Due in part to their planning-intensive focus, financial planners tend to provide more generic investment management solutions, often utilizing retail mutual funds or prescreened funds and/or separate accounts off of a turnkey asset management platform (TAMP). Therefore, investment expenses are typically high, their ability to negotiate fees limited, and exposure to cutting-edge investment products, such as alternative investments, is modest at best. Furthermore, many so-called *fee-based* planners actually derive a significant portion of their revenues from commissions from insurance products and 12b-1 fees from mutual funds, both of which constitute conflicts of interest.

ONE-STOP SHOP

The second wealth management model, the *one-stop shop*, is probably the most common and represents a significant portion of the assets under management in the industry. Dominated by banks and brokerage firms, the one-stop shop firms fulfill most of their clients' investment needs with internally managed products. As the name suggests, a key advantage to the one-stop shop is the convenience and simplicity of having all of your assets under one roof. Firms tend to be large and resource-rich, and can generally afford to provide a broad array of complementary services. These may include banking, brokerage, fiduciary services, estate planning, and philanthropic advice. They also may provide the ability to structure and execute complex derivative transactions to hedge concentrated stock positions or enhance the tax-effectiveness of a particular investment. Although some firms have suffered with bulky legacy systems, they have the ability to invest in technology to support back-office and client reporting functions. There is obviously variation from firm to firm; however, many have outstanding core investment products, with deep teams of experienced professionals and strong track records. There typically is not a particular reliance on one or a few people, so the "getting hit by a truck" risk is limited.

A comparison to the investment office model, however, reveals some of the potential pitfalls of the one-stop shop. The lack of "open architecture" means that the selection of investment alternatives is limited to those under the firm's roof. Clients are not afforded the benefits of other outstanding investment managers and products, unless they identify and choose them on their own, diminishing some of the simplicity benefit. In particular, a client may be exposed to the firm's investment philosophy, as compared to an open-architecture platform utilizing multiple managers. Moreover, if a firm's core investment product deteriorates, the client cannot simply fire the manager; he or she must uproot the entire wealth management infrastructure and move it to another firm.

The large asset base of many one-stop shops limits their ability to allocate to specialty or niche asset classes with limited capacity. For example, most small-cap equity managers must limit their size to a few billion dollars at most to avoid taking on excessive illiquidity. For a wealth manager with $50 billion to $100 billion, meaningful small-cap allocations within the firm are simply not possible. Additionally, such firms, by virtue of limiting their offerings to in-house products, may lack the flexibility to quickly respond to opportunities in markets that may arise if they do not already have that product "on the shelf." Similarly, it may be difficult to reduce allocations to asset classes where they have substantial infrastructure in place.

Another possible shortcoming of the one-stop shop is that, being large, mostly public firms, ownership is widely dispersed, and professional turnover tends to be relatively high. Experienced client relationship managers are in high demand, and often will change firms for a better offer. This can be quite disruptive to the client, who must decide whether to follow the person with whom he has developed a relationship, or stay put, but work with a new person with whom they may or may not be compatible and have no history.

On the investment side of the house, professionals, having built a track record and a reputation at a large firm, often leave to start their own shop, or to join a more entrepreneurial venture in which they may have a significant ownership stake. Although investment products at one-stop shops do not typically rely on a star manager, the talent pool can be diminished, leading to mediocre results. Such firms have often been involved in merger and acquisition activities, which can also be disruptive to the client, but which may bring new or better products or services inside the firm.

Finally, the most glaring weakness of the one-stop shop is the many conflicts of interest, particularly where the firm is involved in multiple lines of higher-margin businesses. The most clearly documented example has been in firms that derived significant fees from underwriting initial public offerings (IPOs), which were then highly recommended to their clients, despite dubious prospects. Although there are other less dramatic examples, internally generated, high-margin products may drive the investment decision, as opposed to an arms-length, thoughtful, due diligence process on the client's behalf.

The one-stop shop category includes banks, trust companies, multiproduct asset management firms, and brokerage firms. In the post-Glass-Steagall era, the lines between these can be quite blurred, and combinations of these types of firms can coexist under the same holding company. However, banks, trust companies, and asset managers tend to have more of a fiduciary culture, whereas brokerage firms have more of a product-oriented, sales mentality. Banks and trust companies tend to have narrower product lines and may have limited exposure to alternative investment products. Brokerage firms generally have a broader array of offerings and are quicker to develop new products in response to opportunities or client demand. Although this can be a positive, it also gives rise to greater conflicts of interest. Brokerage firms are often more transaction-oriented, particularly where the client relationship manager is selecting individual securities, and receive a significant portion of their compensation in the form of sales commissions.

HYBRID

The final wealth management service model is the *hybrid.* This is typically the result of a one-stop shop firm that has opened up its investment architecture to include unaffiliated investment managers and products. The advent of the so-called *wrap* or *separately managed* account has transformed many brokers into financial consultants, and converted commission-based revenues to fee-based income. This has brought many of the advantages of the investment office model, and in many cases the hybrid may be difficult to distinguish from the investment office on the surface. However, the opening up of the investment platform at these firms has not eliminated conflicts of interest. Higher-margin, proprietary products remain a staple on the menu at the hybrids, and client relationship managers often are given strong incentives to favor those products.

Additionally, the sales culture of the brokerage firms often has led to a reputation of "selling performance," that is, to recommend managers who have just completed a period of unusually strong returns, which is often a precursor to a period of underperformance. Many clients of hybrid firms discovered during the 2000–2002 bear market that the multiple managers they had selected to diversify their equity portfolios were essentially large-cap growth managers who had excelled in the several years prior, and whose poor performances were highly correlated when that style subsequently fell out of favor.

Furthermore, while some brokerage separate account programs provide access to a broad array of outstanding investment managers, many other attractive firms may not be available. They choose not to participate, because taking part in a separately managed account program entails a significant commitment of resources on the part of an investment management firm. Handling smaller account sizes, often as low as $100,000, requires a meaningful investment in back-office personnel and technology. Furthermore, marketing and client service requirements increase because they need to court and support a firm's client relationship managers. Hybrid firms that offer separate account programs have also applied increasing pressure on investment managers to lower their fees (without always passing this along to the end client). As a result, many managers, particularly those with limited capacity, have decided that participation in such programs is unattractive.

Larger hybrid firms also tend to choose managers with significant capacity so that they can be widely utilized across the firm. Again, this has often led to a less than optimal asset allocation and manager selection because the preponderance of assets in separate account programs are with large-cap managers and, in fact, with a relatively small subset of the manager universe.

These descriptions of the three wealth management models are generalized. Wide variations may exist from firm to firm. As opposed to determining which model is superior, this analysis is meant to outline a framework for determining how a particular firm operates, and whether it is well suited for a client's specific needs. It is critically important to understand a firm's financial motivations, as well as those of the relationship manager with whom you would be working, so that if conflicts of interest do exist, you can be aware of them and attempt to take them into account when reviewing recommendations. It is also important to understand what type of client fits in the firm's "sweet spot," and whether you fit that profile.

HOW TO EVALUATE
WEALTH MANAGEMENT FIRMS

The following questions are among those that should be asked of a potential wealth manager:

1. What are the sources of the firm's revenues? How much comes from advisory fees versus product fees? How much comes from wealth management versus other lines of business?
2. How are client relationship managers compensated? Are they paid a salary and bonus or commissions? How are they compensated on proprietary products versus outside ones?
3. How long has the client relationship manager who will be working with you been with the firm? What has the turnover of people in that role been? What departures have there been of key investment professionals?
4. What is the average size of the firm's high-net-worth relationship? What is the largest? The smallest?
5. How has the number of clients and the assets under management changed from year to year?

6. How has a typical client's portfolio performed? (Note: For firms utilizing outside managers, do not accept the historic returns of managers currently being recommended as indicative of historic performance.)
7. If the firm utilizes outside managers, which firms have been utilized over the past several years that are no longer being recommended? When were they terminated and why? What was their performance while included in client portfolios?

In addition to asking questions directly, valuable information can be gathered indirectly. Request the firm's SEC Form ADV Parts I and II, which they are required to provide to new clients, which contains valuable information on the firm's ownership, key professionals, fees, and potential conflicts of interest. Check the SEC's website to see if the firm has had any violations or if the individual you would be working with has. Ask for references, and check them.

It also is important, before selecting a wealth manager, to perform an honest assessment of your own needs and desires:

1. How active do I want to be in managing my portfolio? Do I want to pick my own securities? Do I want to pick my own managers?
2. How much control am I comfortable delegating?
3. Do I want to be given guidance and advice, or be sold ideas?
4. How much do I value brand names, versus smaller boutiques? What has worked for me in other professional relationships (CPAs, banks, attorneys)?
5. Would I rather be a very important client at a less well-known firm, or a less important client at a firm with name recognition and cachet?
6. Are my financial affairs relatively organized? Will I benefit more from assistance in creating order out of chaos, or from better execution of my already well-defined strategy?

Generally speaking, more active investors who want to retain a significant level of day-to-day control over their portfolio are better suited to the one-stop shops and hybrids, whereas clients who want to articulate their objectives and leave the day-to-day work to investment professionals work better with the investment office model.

Remember, when going through this process, that performance, while an important consideration, should not be given too much weight in the decision process. As the fine print says, past performance does not guarantee future results, and recent outstanding returns may not be repeatable. It is important to confirm that the wealth manager is competent and can add value. But value can be added in a variety of ways, and firms with good returns and poor service can have unhappy clients.

Wealth management can and should be a long-term and ongoing process. Selecting an advisor who can successfully guide you through that process is of critical importance. Take your time, ask the hard questions, meet with many firms in each of the categories, and ultimately choose a firm with whom you believe you can develop a long, trusting relationship.

Author Background

David Spungen is Managing Partner and Founder of Hillview Capital Advisors. He brings a wealth of experience on all aspects of capital markets investing to his clients. David heads up the firm's asset allocation optimization, portfolio construction, manager selection/monitoring, and investment product generation efforts. Prior to founding Hillview Capital Advisors, David was one of the founders of the Capital Management division within CMS Companies in 1989. David also served as a partner of CMS from 1995–1999. Prior to joining CMS in 1989, he was an associate with Ryan, Beck & Company. He has served as a Director of M Funds, Inc., M Financial Investment Advisors and the Hirtle Callaghan Trust.

Chapter 7

Managing Concentrated and Restricted Stock Positions

David N. Elan

RESTRICTED STOCK AND EQUITY RISK MANAGEMENT

Issues related to restricted stock, or risk management of a concentrated position in a single stock, are high-class problems. If you are considering restricted stock issues, it likely means you are contemplating a liquidity event such as an acquisition or an initial public offering (IPO), or that you have already completed such a transaction.

Should you be fortunate enough to own a large holding in a single stock, resulting from periodic purchases or grants of company stock, an inheritance, or wise investments, the management of such a position will share many of the risk reduction and tax-related goals common to owners of restricted stock. Protection from declines in the share price and postponement of capital gains tax liability are common goals of owners of large single-stock positions, whether or not the stock is considered restricted.

DEFINITIONS AND EXAMPLES

The term *restricted stock* has more than one meaning. Throughout this chapter, restricted stock will mean stock that must be sold in accordance with procedures established under the Securities Act of 1933 and Securities and Exchange Commission (SEC) Rule 144. This definition contrasts with stock granted by an employer to an employee with restrictions related to vesting, but also often called restricted stock by the issuer.

A good working definition of restricted stock is this: If you acquired shares of stock in a manner other than by purchasing those shares on a public stock exchange or inheriting shares from someone who purchased them on a public stock exchange, you likely own restricted stock. In addition, if you are a senior executive, shares of your company's stock, regardless of how you acquired them, are likely to be defined as control stock, and are subject to the same kinds of trading constraints as if they were restricted stock.

Here are a few examples:

Smith is a member of the founder's team of ABC Technology, Inc., and owns shares of founder's stock. ABC Technology will sell shares of its stock in an IPO later this year. Concurrent with the IPO, Smith's founder's shares will be converted to shares in the newly public company. Since Smith's founder's shares were not acquired through a transaction on a public stock exchange, Smith's shares of publicly traded stock arising from the conversion of private to public stock will be restricted stock.

Brown is a senior executive of XYZ Enterprises, Inc., a private company being acquired in a stock-for-stock transaction by a competitor with publicly traded stock. Brown owns shares of XYZ as a result of yearly grants of stock to key employees. After the acquisition, Brown's shares will be exchanged for shares of the acquirer's publicly traded stock. Since Brown's shares of XYZ were acquired through private grant, the shares of the acquirer's publicly traded stock received in exchange for XYZ shares will be restricted stock.

Jones is a general partner at Foundation Ventures, a venture capital firm. Foundation made an investment in GenCo, a private company now being acquired in a stock-for-stock transaction by Multi, Inc., a company with shares listed on the New York Stock Exchange. Jones will receive a distribution of Multi, Inc., stock when the transaction is complete. Since Foundation's shares in GenCo were acquired through a private investment, the shares of Multi received by Jones will be restricted stock.

Johnson is Chief Executive Officer of Multi, Inc., and through his stock-broker periodically purchases shares of Multi that trade on the New York Stock Exchange. Although Johnson purchases his Multi shares on a public stock exchange, because of his position as CEO at Multi, his shares will be treated as if they are restricted stock. In addition, Johnson will be subject to provisions of Section 16 of the Securities Exchange Act of 1934 that will constrain the kinds of transactions Johnson may engage in with Multi stock.

PUBLIC POLICY AND RULE 144 OF THE SECURITIES ACT OF 1933

Before we discuss the mechanical steps required to comply with laws regulating the sale of restricted stock, a short discussion of the public policy behind the provisions of Rule 144 may be helpful in understanding the provisions of the rule. The terms *distribution of securities* and *trading in securities,* as these terms underlie the intent of Congress behind the regulations imposed by the Securities Act of 1933 (the Act), are central to the discussion.

We are all familiar with a public offering of stock, involving investment bankers and one or more broker-dealers. Within the atmosphere of sales hype surrounding a public offering, Congress deemed it important that prospective investors have adequate disclosure of the risks involved in purchasing the publicly offered stock. The Act addresses this concern by requiring that securities being offered for sale in a public offering go through a procedure known as *registration*, at some point between issuance of the stock by the corporation and purchase by the investor. The registration procedure requires the public disclosure of information about the corporation issuing the stock, including the risks involved in ownership of the stock. Usually, this involves the preparation and distribution of a prospectus, and the approval of the level of detail and disclosure within the prospectus by the Securities and Exchange Commission (SEC).

With distribution of securities at one end of a transactional spectrum, the other end of the spectrum is trading in securities. The distinction between the terms is not precise, and rests partially on the absence of promotional activities surrounding a particular securities transaction. Individual investors, unaffiliated with a particular company and engaged in the day-to-day sales of that company's stock, clearly are trading in securities. The Act does not seek to impose the burden of registration on the activities of individual investors transacting in public markets in trading uncoordinated with sales of other individual investors, and without the promotional activity common to a public offering.

The term *distribution* describes a sale of stock subject to regulation by the SEC, and although the term is not specifically defined in the Securities Act of 1933, there is a body of case law and administrative interpretations that contribute to an understanding of the concept. A public offering is a distribution. But any person, or group of persons, may, through their individual or collective sales of stock, also be considered as having effected a distribution. The key concept to this discussion is that a distribution of securities requires registration, and registration takes time and costs money. Sellers of restricted stock would prefer to sell their stock without the time and expense of the registration process.

In 1972, the SEC adopted Rule 144 to provide sellers of restricted stock with a road map of how to sell stock in a manner that will not be considered a distribution, and accordingly, will not become subject to registration. Rule 144's Preliminary Note provides the points that the SEC deems important in determining whether the sale of stock constitutes a distribution:

1. Since a major policy of the 1933 Act is to protect investors by ensuring their decisions are informed, adequate current public information concerning the issuer must be available before securities can be resold without compliance with the registration provision of the 1933 Act.
2. In order to ensure that the person wishing to sell restricted securities is not participating in a distribution, a holding period is required to guarantee that the person has assumed the economic risks of investment.
3. To minimize the impact on the trading markets of a mass resale of an issuer's securities, volume requirements are imposed.[1]

Rule 144 provides an exemption from the time and expense of registration. The conditions under which restricted securities can be sold to the public without registration comprise the road map:

1. *Holding period*: A minimum of one year must elapse after the acquisition of and full payment for the shares.
2. *Public information:* Current financial information on the company must be available to the public. Companies that are required to file periodic reports with the SEC, and that have made the required filings, usually satisfy this requirement.
3. *Disclosure:* For sales of more than 500 shares, or shares valued at more than $10,000, the seller must file a Form 144, "Notice of Proposed Sale of Securities," with the SEC and the exchange on which the shares trade. The filing is effective for 90 days. The Form 144 must be post-

marked no later than the day on which the first shares are sold and becomes public information, available on the SEC website and through commercial distributors of financial information such as Yahoo Finance and Bloomberg.

4. *Manner of sale:* The selling shareholder may not solicit or arrange for solicitation of the sale. That is, the sale cannot be advertised. In addition, the seller may not make any payment in connection to the sale of the securities other than a reasonable and customary brokerage commission to the broker who executes the order.

5. *Volume limitation:* If the securities have been held for between one and two years, the volume that can be sold in any 90-day period may not exceed the greater of (1) 1 percent of the company's outstanding common shares or (2) the average weekly trading volume of the company's stock during the preceding four weeks.[2]

Adherence with the sale conditions specified by Rule 144 allows both the intent of Congress articulated in the Preliminary Note to Rule 144 to be met, together with the efficient and cost-effective sale of restricted stock by shareholders.

REGISTRATION RIGHTS

In addition to the safe harbor provided by Rule 144 to allow the sale of restricted stock without requiring registration of the shares, it may be possible to negotiate registration rights from an acquiring company. The right to have one's shares registered, without incurring the expense of registration, provides an additional route by which the shares can be sold. A large company engaged in regular acquisitions will often register a block of shares with the intention of using these shares as acquisition currency. The recipient of such preregistered shares will have the benefit of registration without the need to negotiate for the rights.

Registration rights, when shares are not preregistered, come in two general forms: *piggyback* and *demand.* Piggyback rights allow the holder of unregistered shares to have those shares included in a registration of other shares when and if the company engages in a registration process. Demand rights allow the holder of unregistered shares to compel a registration of its shares.

HEDGING AND TAXATION

The one-year holding period imposed by Rule 144 has, and properly so, caused the most concern to holders of restricted stock. Watching the daily price swings of a concentrated equity position that represents the fruits of years of investment risk may be emotionally unsettling. It certainly violates the precept of diversification at the core of prudent investment policy. Apart from the principles of risk management, a holder of restricted stock may wish to realize the monetary reward locked up in the stock prior to the expiration of the mandatory one-year holding period.

Alongside the goals of managing the financial risk and gaining liquidity is often the goal of minimizing the tax consequences of whatever strategy is implemented. Prior to the enactment of the Taxpayer Reform Act of 1997 (TRA 1997), concentrated stock positions, whether restricted or not, were commonly hedged by selling short a number of shares identical to the shares to be hedged. Known as a *short against the box,* this strategy provided liquidity, locked in the price of the stock being hedged, and deferred tax consequences until the actual sale of the shares being hedged or the closing of the short position. TRA 1997 targeted the short against the box strategy, and effectively removed it as a viable choice for hedging, by defining it as a *constructive sale* and making the hedged gain an immediately taxable transaction. You are treated as having made a constructive sale of an appreciated financial position if you:

1. Enter into a short sale of the same or substantially identical property
2. Enter into an offsetting notional principal contract relating to the same or substantially identical property
3. Enter into a futures or forward contract to deliver the same or substantially identical property (including a forward contract that provides for cash settlement)
4. Acquire the same or substantially identical property (if the appreciated financial position is a short sale, an offsetting notional principal contract, or a futures or forward contract)[3]

With the short against the box removed from the menu of risk reduction techniques, the financial engineers, lawyers, and attorneys on Wall Street turned to other strategies. In December 1999, the SEC issued a no-action letter at the request of a major brokerage firm that has provided the legal comfort behind the use of the variable prepaid forward (VPF) contract (more on this later) as a hedging technique, particularly for corporate insiders and affiliates.

With a bit of taxation history behind us, we turn first to the choices available to holders of restricted stock subject to a one-year holding period. Note that prior to engaging in hedging strategies, if you are an employee of the company whose stock you wish to hedge, you should check with your company to be sure it allows hedging by its employees. Many companies have strict policies prohibiting the purchase or sale of derivatives (or equivalent strategies) in the company stock.

DERIVATIVE STRATEGIES

PURCHASE OF PUT OPTIONS

Owning a put option gives the holder the right, but not the obligation, to sell his stock at a prearranged price, known as the *strike price*, for a specified period of time. A put option will effectively place a floor price beneath a restricted stock position until the one-year holding period is satisfied, without placing a cap on the appreciation of the share price.

However, like insurance, this protection comes at a cost. And like insurance, the cost is known as a *premium*. For example, as I am writing this, the premium for a put option on Microsoft stock that provides 90 percent protection for one year will cost approximately 7.3 percent of the share price. That means Microsoft stock must decline by more than 17.3 percent before the shareholder will feel the economic benefit of having purchased the puts.

In addition, if the stock being protected through the purchase of a put has not reached a long-term holding period for tax purposes, the purchase of the put will extinguish the stock's holding period. The higher tax rate imposed upon the sale of short-term assets must be considered when evaluating the strategy.

Unlike put options bought and sold on public exchanges, over-the-counter (OTC) puts can be customized to meet a particular client need, and can be settled either in cash or physically. Under cash settlement, the buyer of the put will receive a cash payment equivalent to the dollar amount by which the share price of the stock being hedged is less than the strike price of the put, multiplied by the number of shares being hedged. Cash settlement is not considered a sale of the shares being hedged. Rather, a taxable event has occurred relative to the gain realized through the purchase and subsequent sale of the put. A subsequent sale of the shares will create a second taxable event.

Under physical settlement, the shares are delivered to the counterparty in exchange for cash equal to the strike price multiplied by the number of shares. A physical settlement is, in fact, a sale of the shares to the counterparty and is considered to be a sale at the strike price for tax purposes.

An advantage of hedging stock with put options is that the combination of the stock and the put creates a stable, creditworthy portfolio that can be used as collateral for a margin loan without risk of a margin call. This theme will reoccur during our discussion of collars, which have a put option as part of their structure. Most large investment banks will lend up to 90 percent of the protected value of the stock when the purpose of the loan (known as a *non-purpose* loan) is to do almost anything except buy publicly traded equity securities. If the loan proceeds will be used to purchase publicly traded equity securities (known as a *purpose* loan), the bank is restricted, under Federal Reserve Board Regulation T, from lending more than 50 percent of the protected value.

The implications of Regulation T may appear to be in conflict with good public policy, but nevertheless, they are what they are. A holder of restricted stock who hedges with put options and uses the combined stock/put position as collateral for a 90 percent loan can use the proceeds of the loan to gamble, buy a yacht, or finance an extraordinary shopping spree. But if this same stockholder uses the loan proceeds to invest in equity securities, the loan proceeds can be no more than 50 percent of the protected value of the stock.

SALE OF CALL OPTIONS

A call option is the flip side of a put option. Rather than the right to sell, conveyed by the purchase of a put, the sale of a call creates the obligation to sell stock at a prearranged price for a specified period of time if the person to whom you sold the option requests you to do so. Because it is a sale, rather than a purchase, the premium is received by you, the shareholder, rather than paid. Receiving the premium creates a dollar-for-dollar buffer that serves as a thin insulation from a decline in the share price. But the obligation to sell creates a ceiling on the stock's appreciation beyond which the shareholder will not benefit.

The sale of a call option on Microsoft with a strike price 10 percent over the price at which Microsoft trades on a given day might generate a premium of, for example, 9 percent of the share price. Accordingly, a holder of Microsoft stock who sells these calls would be economically indifferent to a 9 percent drop in share price during the life of the option. But this same shareholder will be fully exposed to decreases in the share price below that level, and will not enjoy any future appreciation in the share price greater than 10 percent.

From a tax holding period perspective, the sale of OTC calls will, as in the case of the purchase of puts, extinguish the holding period of short-term assets. Although OTC options may be either cash settled or physically settled, should a stock appreciate substantially beyond the strike price of a call option, it may be financially painful to cash settle, making the mandatory delivery of a short-term asset the only practical settlement choice. This may not be the best settlement choice for tax purposes.

COLLARS

For shareholders who desire the insurance protection conveyed by the purchase of a put option, but without the out-of-pocket premium, a *collar* may be the answer. A *collar* combines the purchase of a put with the sale of a call. The premium received through the call sale is used to partially or fully offset the premium used to purchase the put. When the put and call prices are adjusted so the premiums are exactly equal, the collar is commonly known as a *zero cost* or *zero premium* collar.

A shareholder who hedges stock with a collar will be fully protected should the share price fall below the strike price of the put, and will be limited in the possible appreciation of the share price by the strike price of the call. Using a collar has the advantage that the strike prices of the put and call can be adjusted to reflect the shareholder's degree of risk and outlook toward the stock's future movements.

However, to avoid being considered a constructive sale, the shareholder must remain subject to some downside risk. The Internal Revenue Service (IRS) has never definitively specified just how much risk is enough to ensure that the collar not be construed as a constructive sale, but most practitioners are comfortable when the put strike protects 90 percent of the downside. Said another way, when the put strike is 10 percent below the current share price, the IRS has historically been unlikely to consider the collar as a constructive sale. However, you should consult appropriate counsel when using collars, as the rules and boundaries defining constructive sale are subject to change.

While a stock is subject to a collar, the shareholder retains ownership, voting rights, and will receive any dividends.

As with stock protected by puts, stock subject to a collar will make excellent collateral for a margin loan, with little or no risk of a margin call. Similar to put and call transactions, collared stock that has not yet reached a long-term holding period will have the holding period extinguished and the potential realization of a short-term, rather than long-term, gain must be evaluated before initiating the strategy.

The taxation of collars is complex. Shareholders should consult with an experienced tax counsel before entering into a collar to thoroughly understand the tax consequences and the optimal manner to unwind the collar at maturity. The complexity in taxation results from a combination of three factors: (1) the IRS tax straddle rules, (2) whether a collar is cash settled or physically settled, and (3) whether the shares underlying the collar have a short-term or long-term holding period.

A *tax straddle* is "any offsetting position on personal property" and includes stock when "at least one of the offsetting positions is an option to buy or sell the stock or substantially identical stock or securities."[4] The taxation of a straddle can be summarized by the following rule of thumb: Whatever is the worst outcome for the taxpayer is probably what happens. In summary:

- If the shares underlying the collar have already reached a long-term holding period before the collar is initiated, then, when closed out, any loss in either the put or the call position is taxed as a long-term capital loss. Likewise, when closed out, any gain in either the put or the call position is taxed as a short-term capital gain.
- If the shares underlying the collar have a short-term holding period before the collar is initiated, the holding period of the shares is extinguished, and the holding period "clock" will not start again until both the put and call positions are closed. Any gain or loss from either the put or the call position is taxed as a short-term capital gain or loss.
- Any loss realized on closing out either the put or the call position is deferred until the entire collar is closed out and the gain or loss is recognized.
- If the collared stock is used as collateral for a loan, any interest paid on the loan, if otherwise deductible, is capitalized. Furthermore, there is a limitation on the amount of capitalized interest equivalent to the amount of interest paid in excess of dividends received on the stock underlying the collar.

NONDERIVATIVE STRATEGIES

VARIABLE PREPAID FORWARDS

As discussed earlier, with the passage of the Tax Reform Act of 1997, Wall Street engineered the variable prepaid forward (VPF) as a hedging technique that would not run afoul of the constructive sale rules. When dissected into its component parts, the VPF looks a lot like collared stock used as collateral for a margin loan. But there are legal and structural differences that give the VPF several advantages over a collar with a margin loan for shareholders who wish to harvest a large portion of the cash value represented by the stock, particularly if the shareholder is a corporate insider or affiliate.

A VPF is not a loan. Instead, it is a contract between a shareholder and a counterparty under which the shareholder agrees to sell a contingent number of shares of stock to the counterparty at some prearranged future date in exchange for a cash payment from the counterparty at the inception of the contract. The number of shares that will be delivered to the counterparty in the future is determined by a formula tied to the future price of the stock, and it is this uncertainty that keeps the VPF from being considered a constructive sale. Part of the formula is a cap on the number of shares that could ever be delivered to the counterparty, even in the event the stock price went to zero at the maturity of the contract. This provision provides the same kind of downside protection to a shareholder as does the put option within an equity collar. In fact, the counterparty will hedge its own position in a manner economically similar to a collar, but in the counterparty's name, rather than the shareholder, and then essentially pass the economics of the hedge to the shareholder through the VPF contract.

Because the contract is not a loan, it is not subject to the restrictions of Regulation T, and a large percentage of the value of the stock can be paid to the shareholder regardless of how the funds will be used. There are no ongoing interest payments or additional loan paperwork that must be negotiated and executed, and the cost of funds implicit in the cash advance is fixed, rather the variable interest rate that is seen in a margin loan.

There may be regulatory advantages to using a VPF over a collar as well if the shareholder is an insider or affiliate of the corporation issuing the shares. Insiders and affiliates are subject to the provisions of Section 16 of the Securities Exchange Act of 1934. Among these provisions are trading limitations and the obligation to disgorge back to the issuer profits obtained through buying and selling company equity securities, or derivatives of company equity securities, if the profit is derived through trades occurring within any six-month period. Known as *short-swing profits,* profits derived through any combination of purchase and sale, or sale and purchase, or the earning of an option premium that expires worthless within a six-month period, or cash settlement of certain derivative hedges may trigger the obligation to disgorge.

Equity collars, with their explicit put and call positions, place an insider or affiliate at greater risk of having engaged in a transaction subject to short-swing profit disgorgement. In contrast, the VPF transaction has the advantage of an SEC no-action letter, discussed earlier, that provides a legal comfort zone for insiders and affiliates wishing to hedge stock. Essentially, for SEC purposes, the date of sale is the date the VPF contract is executed, but for tax purposes, the date of sale is the maturity date.

EXCHANGE FUNDS

An exchange fund can be best thought of as a private mutual fund. But instead of buying shares in the fund with cash, a participant in an exchange fund contributes a block of stock in exchange for a partnership interest representing a pro rata interest in all of the different stocks contributed to the fund. The contribution and exchange are not taxable events. To receive the maximum tax benefit, the investor must remain in the fund for at least seven years, after which the investor may withdraw from the fund, receiving a basket of the fund's component stocks, albeit with the same tax basis as the shares originally contributed. Swapping exposure to a single stock for tax-efficient exposure to a diversified portfolio is the rational behind exchange funds, and superficially that is exactly what happens. But the exchange fund technique has several disadvantages that must be carefully weighed:

- An investor considering an exchange fund should view the transaction as a total return swap; that is, an investor will swap the return on a concentrated stock position for the return on a diversified portfolio. Apart from the worthy goal of diversification, an investor's enlightened self-interest should suggest that if the expected return on the diversified portfolio (which should be similar to an index return) is likely to outperform the expected return on the single-stock position, then joining the exchange fund will be a good trade. What this means is that investors will not contribute stocks likely to outperform an index to an exchange fund, and that the exchange fund will be left with only with stocks thought by their owners to be likely laggards. The firms sponsoring exchange funds try to address this concern by providing a list of all the stocks proposed as participants in the fund, along with the number of shares and percentage of the overall fund, prior to the fund's closing date. Each investor will then have a short window during which to evaluate the overall fund and make a final decision about whether to participate.
- Exchange funds are generally structured to resemble a broad-based equity index and to provide a return similar to that of the index benchmark. However, the fees levied by the sponsor will be materially higher than fees charged by index funds and will create a drag on the exchange fund's return.
- Because the exchange fund sponsor is seeking a broad-based index return, the stocks most attractive for inclusion in an exchange fund are generally the high-capitalization stocks that comprise the major indexes. However, the shares an investor may be most interested in contributing

to an exchange fund may be the small-capitalization, thinly traded, and highly volatile stocks that will likely be ineligible for inclusion.

- The IRS requires that 20 percent of an exchange fund's assets be illiquid. Often, a sponsor will purchase special securities called *partnership preference units* issued by real estate investment trusts for this purpose. Without cash to make these purchases, the exchange fund will use a margin loan to provide liquidity, and the interest payments on the loan will create a drag on the fund's return.
- The deferral of capital gains taxes is an attractive feature of exchange funds. Presently, however, with the low capital gains rate enacted in 2003, but scheduled to increase again in 2009 (before a seven-year holding period would be achieved), the deferral is less attractive.

PRIVATE SALE

The most straightforward way to eliminate the risk of a restricted stock position is simply to sell the stock and pay the tax. A public sale will not be possible until a one-year holding period is satisfied, but a private buyer, usually an investment bank, may be a potential buyer. The purchase will be at a discount to the stock's market price, but the buyer takes on the price risk until the one-year holding period is satisfied, and the seller will have the cash.

A private sale can be weighted against a VPF by considering the percentage of purchase discount and the likely rate of appreciation of the stock during the term of the VPF, versus the cost of funds and other fees impounded within the VPF, together with the value of the tax deferral.

RULE 10B(5)1 SALES PLANS

In October 2000, the SEC made a change to the insider trading rules by adopting Rule 10b(5)1 to the Securities Exchange Act of 1934. The new rule provides an affirmative defense against charges that a corporate insider, subject to Section 16, sold or bought stock on the basis of material nonpublic information in breach of a duty of trust or confidence.

To use the affirmative defense, *before becoming aware of material nonpublic information,* a corporate insider must have done one of following:

1. Entered into a binding contract to purchase or sell the security
2. Instructed another person to purchase or sell the security for the instructing person's account
3. Adopted a written plan for trading securities

Any contract, instructions, or plan to trade securities must:

1. Specify the amount of securities to be purchased or sold and the price at which and the date on which the securities are to be purchased or sold.
2. Include a written formula or algorithm, or computer program, for determining the amount of securities to be purchased or sold and the price at which and the date on which the securities will be purchased or sold.
3. Not permit the person to exercise any subsequent influence over how, when, or whether to effect purchases or sales.
4. Provide that any other person who, pursuant to the contract, instruction, or plan, may exercise such influence must not be aware of any material nonpublic information when doing so.
5. Provide that the purchase or sale that occurs is pursuant to the contract, instruction, or plan. A purchase or sale is not pursuant to a contract, instruction, or plan if, among other things, the person who entered into the contract, instruction, or plan altered or deviated from the contract, instruction, or plan to purchase or sell securities (whether by changing the amount, price, or timing of the purchase or sale) or entered into or altered a corresponding or hedging transaction or position with respect to those securities.[5]

The practical use of Rule 10b(5)1 involves the selling shareholder, counsel to the selling shareholder, counsel to the company, a broker-dealer, counsel to the broker-dealer, and often an individual stockbroker serving the selling shareholder.

The selling shareholder and counsel to the company must be comfortable that the selling shareholder is not aware of material nonpublic information when adopting a written plan to sell company securities. To address this, it is common practice to impose a cooling-off period between the adoption of a Rule 10b(5)1 plan and the first transaction under the plan. In addition, because Rule 10b(5)1 does not override or replace the provisions of Rule 144 or Section 16, the selling shareholder, aided by counsel and corporate counsel, must comply with the notice, volume, holding period, and manner of sale requirements of Rule 144, and the short-swing profit rules of Section 16(b).

The broker-dealer and counsel to the broker-dealer must be comfortable that a written selling plan provides clear instructions relative to when shares are to be sold, how many shares are to be sold, and at what price shares are to be sold. The more complex and restrictive the instructions, the less likely the affirmative defense provided by Rule 10b(5)1 will stand close scrutiny. Many broker-dealers provide a specialized team, physically separate from the selling shareholder's stockbroker, to enter the actual order to sell or buy shares. This additional level of separation from the selling shareholder strengthens the argument that the selling shareholder was not able to exert any subsequent influence on transactions made under a written plan.

The company's investor relations department will often issue a press release disclosing the shareholder's adoption of a Rule 10b(5)1 selling or buying plan in advance of any transactions under the plan. This kind of telegraphing of intentions is exactly what the SEC intended. Public shareholders who are aware, well in advance, of automatic sales or purchases by corporate insiders are likely to draw more accurate inferences from those transactions. In contrast, public shareholders who learn of insider sales from the filing of Form 144s after the sale has taken place have had no opportunity to weigh the motivation or consequences of an insider's sale of company stock.

NEGOTIATING WITH BROKER-DEALERS AND FINDING THE BEST COUNTERPARTY

When looking for a broker-dealer to structure a derivative hedge and serve as counterparty, it makes sense to take the advice in the Motown hit by Smokey Robinson and the Miracles: "You better shop around." Each broker-dealer will have its own strengths, weaknesses, and appetite for your transaction. Pay particular attention to the word "counter" in counterparty; more often than not, the interests of the broker-dealer in pricing a transaction run counter to your interests.

It is a common misconception that a broker-dealer counterparty takes on all of the risk when, for example, your stock, hedged with an equity collar, suffers a steep price decline, requiring a substantial payment from the counterparty. In fact, the counterparty has hedged its position by selling short a large percentage of the same stock it has collared for you. If the price declines, the counterparty's short position will increase in value, offsetting its loss on the put. The actual process by which a broker-dealer hedges its derivative exposure is outside the scope of this chapter. The important point is this: The pricing of a derivative hedge has more to do with the profit margin a counterparty is hoping to earn than with the degree of perceived risk that a particular stock will rise or fall in price between the inception and maturity of the hedge. As the counterparty calculates its desired profit margin, it will estimate your stock's likely future volatility and trading volume, it will calculate how much stock can be borrowed and sold short, and it will estimate future interest rates, but it will not take much of a view on the company's fundamentals.

The pricing decision will have more to do with how familiar the firm's traders are with the stock, which is a largely a function of the number of shares of a particular stock a given broker-dealer transacts throughout the year. As a result of many factors, including investment banking relationships, research coverage, and institutional clients, the trading volume of specific stocks tends to cluster among a few broker-dealers. Should that be the case with your stock, those broker-dealers who trade the most volume are more likely to price a derivative hedge most competitively.

Another important consideration is the size of your transaction, and the potential of a future business relationship. It is no secret that assets tend to be "sticky." When your hedge matures, the broker-dealer who acted as the counterparty will be first in line to propose products and services relative to the management of your new liquidity. There is nothing inherently wrong with this. From your perspective, it is important to understand that the potential for a broker-dealer to earn future fees and commissions will likely influence pricing of today's hedge.

Finally, be aware of the profit centers within the potential counterparty: The more mouths to feed, the less competitive is the pricing. If your transaction is large enough, bypass the local stockbroker or financial advisor, and call the equity derivatives desk at the broker-dealer's main office directly.

In summary, pricing a derivative hedge is similar to buying a car. The large dealership with the most volume in the model you are seeking will probably, but not always, give you the best price. If you indicate that you will use the dealer's service department or buy another car in the future, that may have an effect on price. And if you can bypass the salesman and deal directly with the manager, you are likely to strike a better deal.

PHILANTHROPIC STRATEGIES

A discussion of choices facing a holder of a concentrated stock position would not be complete without touching on the philanthropic strategies that can allow you to do well while doing good. The addition of a philanthropic component to a hedging and selling program can add important income and estate tax benefits, while simultaneously fulfilling a charitable intent.

A simple donation of appreciated, low-cost-basis stock will:

- Remove the capital gain issue from the stock being donated. The beneficiary of a donation will take the capital gain within its own tax-exempt
  structure.
- Create a charitable deduction based upon the market value of the stock
  on the date of the donation.
- Remove the value of the stock from the donor's estate, thereby reducing
  the donor's estate tax liability.

When charitable intent is combined with a need for continued income, a
charitable remainder trust (CRT) allows a donor to swap a concentrated
position of low-cost-basis stock for a customized portfolio, tap the portfolio
for income during the donor's lifetime, defer capital gains tax, and ultimately
leave the remaining trust assets to a selected charity. Some people use CRTs
purely as a vehicle to diversify concentrated stock positions while deferring
capital gains tax, but the rules surrounding CRTs are complex, and professional advice should be sought.

When charitable intent is combined with a desire to leave assets to heirs, a
charitable lead trust (CLT) allows a donor to swap a concentrated position of
low-cost-basis stock for a customized portfolio and permit a selected charity
to receive a stream of income generated by the portfolio for a predetermined
term, after which the remaining assets will pass to heirs.

PROFESSIONAL ADVICE

Restricted stock and concentrated stock present a series of complex problems
as issues related to taxation, legal, and regulatory issues, financial analysis,
and market forces are considered. It is critical to consult with competent legal
and tax counsel, and to seek independent advice when structuring, pricing,
hedging, and engaging in other risk management transactions.

Notes

1. Quoted in Hicks, J. William. *Resales of Restricted Securities,* 1998 Edition. West
   Group; St. Paul, MN 1998, p. 4-1.
2. The volume of NASDAQ stocks is counted both when a share is sold and then
   again when it is bought, unlike volume on the New York Stock Exchange and
   the American Stock Exchange, which is counted only once when a given share
   of stock is sold. Essentially, this disparity in the method of computing sales
   volume allows twice as much volume of restricted stock to be sold for stocks

listed on the NASDAQ, while still remaining under the average trading volume restriction of Rule 144, than stocks listed on the New York or American exchanges.

3. IRS Publication 505, 2002, p. 37.

4. IRS Publication 505, 2002, p. 55.

5. *The Security Lawyer's Deskbook.* University of Cincinnati College of Law website. http://www.law.uc.edu/CCL/index.html.

Additional Reading and Resources

Knapp, Travis L., and Nathan L. Reneau. *Understanding Employee Stock Options, Rule 144 and Concentrated Stock Position Strategies.* iUniverse, Lincoln, NE, January 2000.

Thomas, Kaye A. *Consider Your Options: Get the Most from Your Equity Compensation.* Fairmark Press, Inc., Lisle, IL, April 2002.

Welch, Scott D. "Diversifying Concentrated Holdings: Having Your Cake and Hedging It, Too." *Bloomberg Wealth Manager* (April 2001). Mr. Welsh is a Managing Director of Lydian Wealth Management and has published several articles on issues surrounding concentrate stock positions. His articles are posted at http://www.cmsfs.com.

http://www.mystockoptions.com. My Stock Options.com is a good online source for information on employee stock options, restricted stock, and related compensation issues.

http://www.irs.gov/pub/irs-pdf/p550.pdf. IRS Publication 550 discusses the taxation of options, including application of the straddle rule.

Author Background

David Elan is a Principal at Windward Investment Management. He joined Windward from Ernst & Young, where he was a Senior Manager responsible for investments within the Personal Financial Counseling practice in New England. Prior to Ernst & Young, David was a Vice President in the Investment Management Division of Goldman, Sachs & Co. where he managed client portfolios of equities, fixed income, convertible securities and derivatives. He has extensive experience advising clients on hedging and risk management strategies. David is a Chartered Financial Analyst charter holder, a Certified Financial Planner™ practitioner, and a member of the Boston Security Analysts Society.

Chapter 8

Asset Allocation

Stephen J. Cucchiaro

As an entrepreneur, you most likely earned your wealth by being intensely focused on a single mission. You kept your focus through good periods and bad until you achieved your success. Now that you have personal wealth to manage, it's time to shift gears. Unlike your entrepreneurial experience, you have no operating control over the performance of a publicly traded company or security you may be investing in.

Of course, you want to manage your personal wealth for a high return on your capital. At the same time, after working hard to achieve your personal wealth, you also care about the return of your capital, or your ability to preserve the wealth you created. Therefore, as a passive investor, your ultimate goal is to earn a high, real (after inflation) investment return with as little risk of losing your investment as possible.

Fortunately, when investing in publicly traded securities, there is a way to target attractive investment returns while greatly reducing your risk of loss. This approach is commonly known in the investment community as *asset allocation*. The essence of asset allocation is to spread your personal wealth across several investments that do not move in lockstep with one another. The idea is that although one of your investments may be performing poorly over a certain time frame, another one of your investments with different characteristics may be performing well, offsetting your losses elsewhere. By investing your personal wealth into a collection or portfolio of investments with unique characteristics, your target return would remain high, but the investment performance you would experience over time would be much smoother than if you placed all of your wealth into a single volatile investment. In 1991, a widely cited study published in the *Financial Analysts Journal,* Brinson, Singer, and Beebower concluded that asset allocation was responsible for explaining 91.5 percent of an investor's variability of returns over the long run.[1] Since this study was published, an increasing number of investment professionals have realized that focusing on the asset allocation of a client's portfolio has a much greater impact on client investment performance over the long run than picking individual investment managers or securities.

Conventional wisdom teaches that publicly traded stocks offer investors the best chance to make healthy investment returns over the long run. By investing in one stock, you run the risk of losing all your capital if the company you invest in becomes insolvent. By diversifying your equity investments over several stocks with different characteristics, you can significantly reduce your chances of losing all of your capital. One way equity investors diversify is by choosing a variety of stocks from different industries or sectors of the economy. While one sector is slumping, another sector may be thriving, providing balance to your stock portfolio. Other diversification strategies include spreading your equity investments across large, medium, and small companies, across international and domestic companies, and across growth and value companies. Although all of these diversification strategies seem promising, it has been demonstrated time and again over decades of experience that professional investors who select individual stocks fail to beat the stock market averages around 75 percent of the time. Therefore, you increase your chances of earning high returns while at the same time reducing your risk of loss by simply owning a small piece of every public company traded on the stock market. Although this sounds impractical, index funds are portfolios that own the publicly traded stocks that belong to a particular index. By owning shares of an index fund, your capital can match the performance of the stock market while insulating yourself from the demise of any one particular company.

It would certainly be convenient if you could simply place all of your capital in a broadly-based equity index fund and be done with your investment decision making. Although investing in an equity index fund offers you a higher probability of success than attempting to beat the market by selecting individual stocks, placing all of your capital in the equity markets is a ticket to a roller coaster ride. If you placed all of your capital into the U.S. total stock market index (as measured by the Wilshire 5000 Index) on January 1, 1973, 30 years later you would have achieved a compound annual return of 10.5 percent. However, you would have experienced several severe plunges along the way. From January 1973 through September 1974, you would have lost 46.3 percent of your investment. During the crash of 1987, you would have lost 29.8 percent over a three-month period. And during the recent bear market, from September 2000 through September 2002, your investment would have dropped 44.1 percent.

A much better investment experience would be to achieve compound annual returns of around 10 percent over time, but without the severe drawdowns on your investment capital. The power of asset allocation provides the opportunity to realize attractive investment returns with much less risk. The approach is based on taking the concept of indexing beyond equities to a collection of asset classes including equities, bonds, hard assets (such as commodities and gold), real estate, and foreign currencies. Each of these asset classes responds differently to changes in the global economy. As a result, there is little correlation in the behavior of these asset classes with one another over time. Over the long term, each of these asset classes generates an attractive investment return. By diversifying your capital broadly across each of these asset classes, you have greatly increased your chances of simultaneously earning an attractive return and smoothing your investment performance, thereby avoiding the roller coaster effect.

Over the years, rules of thumb about how to allocate portfolio assets have evolved into widely practiced asset allocation guidelines. Conventional wisdom dictates that investors should divide their portfolio between equity investments and fixed-income (bonds and cash equivalents) investments. Equities are treated as high-return, high-risk assets, whereas fixed-income securities are considered low-return, low-risk investments. By adjusting the proportions appropriately, an investor can determine the asset allocation that matches his or her risk profile. The average investor is typically assigned an asset allocation mix of 60 percent equities and 40 percent fixed income. An investor with a higher risk tolerance would target an equity percentage higher than 60 percent of the total portfolio; conversely, an investor with a lower tolerance to risk would set an equity percentage below 60 percent.

This approach to asset allocation is widely accepted, yet at certain times following these guidelines could be dangerous and hazardous to your personal wealth. For example, during periods of rapidly rising interest rates, bonds can become more risky than equities. As prevailing interest rates rise, the market value of a bond's principal correspondingly declines. A bond issues a stream of fixed interest payments (or coupons) to its holders. As interest rates rise, because the coupons are fixed, a bond investor needs to pay less to own a fixed coupon stream and earn the new, higher prevailing interest rate. As a result, bonds can generate substantial losses during periods of rising interest rates. Since September of 1981, market interest rates have generally fallen. As a result, bondholders have had very little experience with a sustained, rising interest rate environment over the last two decades. However, the 1970s contained years of rapidly rising interest rates, resulting in substantial losses for bondholders. For example, a holder of top-rated municipal bonds of medium-term duration purchased in October of 1979 would have experienced a 23 percent plunge in total return in 18 months! In the early 1970s, as we experienced the economic condition known as stagflation (recession and inflation simultaneously), holding a portfolio allocated to equities and fixed income was generally a disaster as stocks declined from the recession and bonds declined from inflation and its associated rising interest rate environment. Because we could experience these or other harmful economic conditions in the future, it is wise to expand your asset allocation strategy to include assets that would actually benefit from turbulent times, thereby offsetting potential losses in your more traditional equity and fixed-income investments.

Figure 8.1 displays the investment performance of a broad collection of asset classes over two time periods. The top bar graph illustrates performance during the year 2002. The bottom bar graph shows the compound annual performance over the last 30 years ending December 2002. Many investors will remember the year 2002 as a year of great pain. The U.S. stock market, as measured by the popular S&P 500 Index of large U.S. publicly traded companies, lost over 22 percent of its value. The EAFE Index of large international (non-U.S.) publicly traded companies lost nearly 20 percent of its value. The NASDAQ 100 Index of large publicly traded technology companies lost over 37 percent during the year. Most investors who were overly exposed to equities, regardless of type, suffered severe losses in 2002. At the same time, there were several asset classes that performed extremely well during the year, benefiting from the same economic and geopolitical conditions that caused equity values to decline. As shown in the top bar graph of Figure 8.1, the Goldman Sachs Commodity Index (GSCI), which is composed of numerous commodities weighted in the proportion that each commodity is produced in the real economy, climbed over 30 percent in 2002. Gold prices

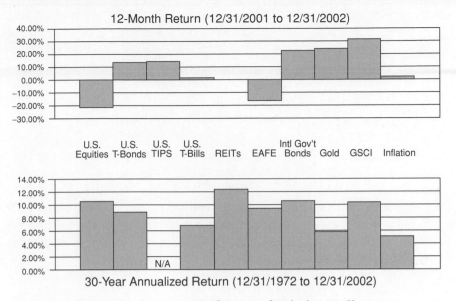

Figure 8.1 Short-term and Long-term Performance of Multiple Asset Classes
SOURCE: Courtesy of Windward Investment Management; Data Source: Ibbotson Associates.

rose over 20 percent, international government bonds gained over 15 percent, and Treasury Inflation Protected Securities (TIPS) increased over 15 percent. By expanding the universe of candidate asset classes beyond conventional stocks and bonds, it was quite possible to earn a positive investment return in 2002, despite the significant losses experienced by the world's major stock markets.

Although it's easy to reduce portfolio risk by diversifying across an expanded universe of asset classes, conventional wisdom suggests that investors would sacrifice their long-term investment returns as a result. Many believe that only stocks offer the opportunity to earn annual returns of 10 percent or more over the long term, and that all other asset classes drag down expected return as they reduce short-term risk. Conventional advice to long-term investors is to invest primarily in stocks, hold for the long term, and be willing to suffer the inevitable roller coaster ride along the way. As the bottom bar graph in Figure 8.1 indicates, there is a better way. Looking at performance of a variety of asset classes over the last 30 years, we can observe that U.S. and international stocks did earn about 10 percent a year on average. However, publicly traded real estate investment trusts (REITs), international government bonds, and commodities (GSCI) all performed as well or better

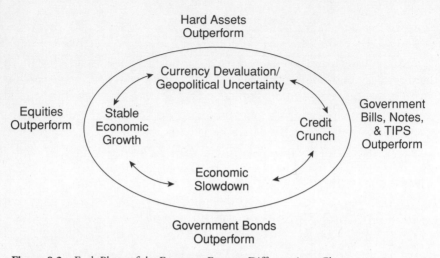

Figure 8.2   Each Phase of the Economy Favors a Different Asset Class
SOURCE: Courtesy of Windward Investment Management.

than stocks over the 30-year time period. In fact, over this time period all asset classes generated positive returns in excess of inflation. As a consequence, by diversifying your portfolio across an expanded universe of asset classes, it is possible to earn high, real investment returns, and at the same time, greatly reduce your risk of suffering investment losses.

Figure 8.2 further illustrates the importance of broadly diversifying your investment portfolio. As the economy enters various phases of the economic cycle, certain asset classes become favored investments. In an inflationary cycle, stable economic growth gives way to an overheated, inflationary economy, whereby currency purchasing power declines. As the central bank tightens monetary policy in an effort to control growth and inflation, a credit crunch ensues. The economy contracts, inflation and interest rates decline, and then stable economic growth resumes. In a deflationary cycle, stable economic growth gives way to falling prices and economic contraction. As credit demand slows, the central bank loosens monetary policy in an effort to reflate the economy. Currency valuation declines, inflationary expectations increase and the economy eventually reflates into stable, economic growth.

Unfortunately, these cycles do not occur over regular, easily predictable time periods. Changes in government policy, investor behavior, and the geopolitical environment can disrupt the economic cycle, causing large, unexpected shifts. As an investor, it is critical to recognize that because the economy can enter any of the four major phases identified in Figure 8.2 a portion of your portfolio should participate in each of the asset classes that benefit from each phase. In this way, part of your portfolio is always working in your favor, off-setting losses elsewhere in your portfolio. For example, suppose your portfolio allocation was 100 percent stocks. You could expect your performance to thrive under conditions of stable economic performance. Yet even if your portfolio was diversified among different types of stocks, your portfolio could suffer substantially during an economic slowdown, a credit crunch, a currency devaluation, runaway inflation, or geopolitical uncertainty.

As we discussed, conventional asset allocation practice suggests diversifying a portfolio 60 percent to stocks and 40 percent to bonds. The idea is that when stocks falter, bonds could potentially gain, smoothing returns. However, looking at Figure 8.2, you can see that stocks and bonds only protect you in two of the four major phases of the economic cycle. As a result, conventional asset allocation practice leaves investors vulnerable to half of the economic cycle. To protect your portfolio under all economic conditions, it is imperative to diversify beyond conventional stocks and bonds.

Figure 8.3 presents an expanded universe of candidate asset classes designed to support a more comprehensive, effective asset allocation strategy for growing and protecting your investment portfolio. Included are equities, bonds, TIPS, hard assets, real estate, and currencies across the United States, Europe, Asia, and emerging markets. To implement an investment strategy using these asset classes, a set of investable index instruments can be identified

	Equity	Fixed Income	Hard Assets	Real Estate	Currency
U.S.	S & P 500 Russell 2000 NASDAQ 100	10-Year Gov't 10-Year TIPS High Yield		NAREIT Equity Index	U.S. Dollar 3-month T-Bill
Europe	DAX FT-SE 100	10-Year German Gov't			Euro 3-month T-Bill
Asia	Nikkei 225 Hang Seng	10-Year Japan Gov't			Yen 3-month T-Bill
Global	S&P/IFC Emerging Markets	JP Morgan Emerging Markets	Goldman Sachs Commodity Index Gold		

Figure 8.3 Expanded Asset Class Universe
SOURCE: Courtesy of Windward Investment Management.

that correspond to each market index listed in Figure 8.3. Creating a portfolio strategy using index instruments rather than by trading individual securities can improve investment returns while lowering investment expenses. Numerous studies have shown that index instruments typically outperform the vast majority of professional investors that trade individual securities in an attempt to beat a market index. At the same time, trading costs are typically far lower for index instruments than for individual securities. Because index instruments hold large numbers of individual securities within them, it is much safer to own an index instrument than an individual equity or debt security that may become unexpectedly insolvent at some point in time. Relative to mutual funds, annual operating expenses incurred by mutual funds are typically 150 to 160 basis points (1.5 to 1.6 percent), far more than for index instruments, which typically incur annual operating expenses of 10 to 30 basis points. Because the composition of an index fund is relatively stable over time, taxable distributions are held to a minimum, unlike a typical mutual fund which by law must distribute most of its taxable gains generated by its high-turnover trading back to its investors.

Because employing an expanded investment universe of index instruments significantly increases the chances of earning a higher risk-adjusted investment return, one might ask why such an asset allocation strategy is not more commonly employed. The answer may lie in the evolution of the investment brokerage industry. Major brokerage firms are multifunctional in nature. Their fee income comes from a variety of sources, including investment banking, corporate finance, research, retail brokerage, and asset management. Investment banking, corporate finance, and research are referred to as the *sell side* of their business. Asset management and retail are known as the *buy side*. On the sell side, brokerage firms earn substantial fees from corporate clients by offering their debt and equity securities (stocks and bonds) to institutional and retail investors. As a result, there exists a strong financial incentive for brokerage firms to recommend stocks and bonds to their buy side institutional and retail customers, creating an inherent conflict of interest between the brokerage firm's interest and the interests of institutional and retail clients. Brokerage firms generate fees by placing, trading, and investing in stocks and bonds on behalf of their clients. No investment banking or corporate finance fee is generated by the use of an index instrument, and especially one that focuses on investing outside of traditional stocks and bonds. This structure of the brokerage industry, whereby the buy side feeds the sell side, has evolved over decades and is hard-wired into the practices and habits of the professionals who work in the investment brokerage industry. Even many independent buy-side firms are impacted by this structure. For example, investment management firms are given a strong financial incentive to place clients' stock and bond trades through brokerage firms offering a special fee arrangement known as *soft dollar* commissions. When the asset management firm trades a security, the brokerage firm charges a high commission fee, which is passed directly to the client of the asset management firm. The brokerage firm then redirects a portion of the commission directly to the asset management firm as a reward for using the brokerage firm. This soft dollar commission is often in the form of an expense reimbursement, typically applied to offsetting a portion of the asset management firm's research, data acquisition, technology, or other operating expenses. To invest using an expanded universe of index instruments requires the investor to work outside of the high commission–oriented structure of the brokerage industry.

Asset allocation, as practiced today, is largely based on modern portfolio theory (MPT). MPT evolved from a series of academic studies published in the 1960s and 1970s. The principal idea behind MPT is that there exists a natural trade-off between risk and return. Consequently, only by assuming more risk could an investor expect higher returns. Risk is measured as the standard deviation, or volatility, of investment returns over time. Central to MPT is the notion of the capital market line, as illustrated in Figure 8.4. The x axis represents risk, as measured by the expected standard deviation of investment returns over the long term. The y axis represents return, as measured by the expected long-term compound annual return. M represents the risk/return plot of the overall stock market. R_f represents the risk-free rate of

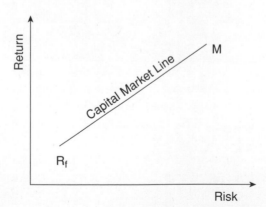

Figure 8.4   Capital Market Line
SOURCE: Courtesy of Windward Investment Management.

return, or the long-term return one might expect from investing in U.S. 90-day Treasury bills, considered the least volatile single investment. The line connecting M and R_f, known as the *capital market line,* identifies the expected risk and return profile of a series of portfolios created by combining stocks and cash (T-bills) in various proportions.

Adding bonds to this mix results in a new set of risk and return profiles, shaped in a curve known as the *efficient frontier,* as illustrated in Figure 8.5. Each point on the efficient frontier represents the mix of stocks, bonds, and cash that generates the highest possible expected return for each designated level of risk. Any point on the graph that is below or to the right of a point on the efficient frontier represents a suboptimal portfolio because for that given risk level, a lower investment return is expected. Therefore, the main idea behind MPT is to first determine the level of risk you wish to tolerate, and then create a portfolio of stocks, bonds, and cash that matches the point on the efficient frontier consistent with your risk level.

Earlier, we discussed the benefits of expanding your universe of candidate investments beyond stocks, bonds, and cash. Figure 8.6 compares the efficient frontier using stocks, bonds, and cash versus an enhanced efficient frontier using the entire set of market indices listed in Figure 8.3. As Figure 8.6 clearly demonstrates, expanding your investment universe greatly increases

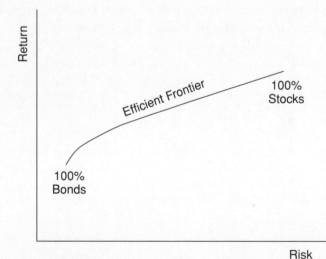

Figure 8.5   Efficient Frontier
SOURCE: Courtesy of Windward Investment Management.

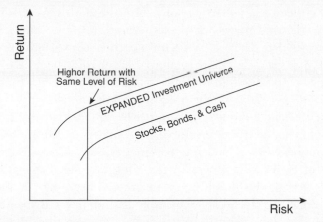

Figure 8.6   Efficient Frontier with Expanded Asset Class Universe
SOURCE: Courtesy of Windward Investment Management.

your expected investment return at each level of risk. Therefore, incorporating market indices as diverse as emerging market bonds, commodities, real estate, TIPS, European bonds, gold, and others into your investment strategy can add significant value to your investment portfolio.

Strategic asset allocation is the most common form of asset allocation practiced today. In this context, the term *strategic* refers to the fixed, or static, nature of a portfolio's asset allocation across investments. For example, if 10-year Treasury bonds were targeted to represent 15 percent of a portfolio's total market value, the investment manager practicing strategic asset allocation would maintain a fixed 15 percent allocation to 10-year Treasury bonds for the life of the portfolio, regardless of changes in the economy, changes in market outlook, or any other external reason. The rationale behind keeping the allocations fixed is based largely on the efficient market hypothesis (EMH). EMH states that because all important information is known to market participants at the same time, it is not possible to predict the direction of the markets consistently. Therefore, all market movements result from unpredictable news events, rendering the behavior of market prices to resemble random walks. According to EMH, if the markets move randomly, then there is no basis for making changes to a portfolio's asset allocation (except for a change in a client's risk tolerance).

Because so many of the investment industry professionals are specialists within a given asset class (for example, stock pickers, bond managers, or currency traders), there exists so much competition within each asset class that it is extremely difficult and rare for any of these professionals to sustain an edge over their market benchmarks over the long run. Over time, the evidence has been very strong that EMH applies within each asset class because the vast majority of professionals fail to match their market benchmark index. However, the competition in investing *across* asset classes is relatively scarce, leaving open the possibility that with less competition, investing across asset classes is less efficient, creating opportunities to exploit relative mispricings.

Over the last several years, investment researchers, aided by increasingly powerful computer-based modeling techniques, have seriously challenged the validity of EMH as it applies to analyzing the global capital markets. Rather than treating the global capital markets as behaving randomly, it is possible to model the global capital markets as a nonlinear, dynamic system, meaning that the global capital markets change through time in a complex, but somewhat predictable way. Scientists and engineers model complex systems like the weather successfully by carefully analyzing and depicting the interrelationships among each of the system's components. When the efficient market hypothesis was developed, simplistic assumptions were made because the computer modeling capability required to model the markets in a more robust, complex manner wasn't available at the time. By applying advanced computer modeling techniques practiced in scientific and engineering disciplines to the global capital markets, it is possible to outperform purely fixed or strategic asset allocation strategies over time.

A hybrid efficient frontier that combines elements of a dynamic, or tactical, asset allocation approach combined with a strategic asset allocation approach can, when correctly implemented, provide a set of portfolios with an even more attractive range of risk and return characteristics than strategic asset allocation alone. As a result, one's expected investment return, at each risk level, can be substantially enhanced.

CONCLUSION

In managing your personal portfolio of publicly traded securities, where you have no control over individual company performance, it pays to diversify extensively. Rather than focusing your time on selecting individual stocks or bonds, your rewards will be much greater if you instead focus your attention on how your portfolio is allocated across a variety of asset classes and then buying highly cost-efficient and tax-efficient index instruments to implement your strategy. Your opportunity to earn higher risk-adjusted rates of return is significantly enhanced if you expand your candidate investment universe beyond stocks, bonds, and cash to include market indices such as emerging market bonds, commodities, real estate, TIPS, European bonds, and gold. Furthermore, you can achieve substantial advantages by employing elements of a dynamic, or tactical, asset allocation strategy designed to exploit relative mispricings across asset classes.

Notes

1. Brinson, Gary P., Brian D. Singer, and Gilbert L. Beebower. "Determinants of Portfolio Performance II: An Update," *Financial Analysts Journal,* May/June 1991.
2. The author would like to thank Susan Luvisi for her work on the graphics in this chapter.

Additional Reading and Resources

Bernstein, Jake. *The New Prosperity: Investment Opportunities in Long-Wave Economic Cycles.* New York: New York Institute of Finance, 1989.

Berry, Brian J. L. *Long-Wave Rhythms in Economic Development and Political Behavior.* Baltimore: The John Hopkins University Press, 1991.

Browne, Harry. *Why the Best-Laid Investment Plans Usually Go Wrong and How You Can Find Safety and Profit in an Uncertain World.* New York: William Morrow, 1987.

Forrester, Jay W. Industrial Dynamics. Cambridge, MA: MIT Press, 1961.

Forrester, Jay W. *Principles of Systems.* Cambridge, MA: Wright-Allen Press, 1968.

Gleick, James. *Chaos: Making a New Science.* New York: Viking Penguin, 1987.

Goldstein, Joshua S. *Long Cycles: Prosperity and War in the Modern Age.* New Haven, CT: Yale University Press, 1988.

Grant, James. *The Trouble with Prosperity.* New York: Times Books, 1996.

Hagstrom, Robert G. *Investing: The Last Liberal Art.* New York: Texere, 2000.

Institute for Private Investors (IPI), 74 Trinity Place, New York, NY 10006.

Kosko, Bart. *Fuzzy Thinking: The New Science of Fuzzy Logic.* New York: Hyperion, 1993.

Milsum, John H. *Positive Feedback.* London: Pergamon Press, 1968.

Ormerod, Paul. *Butterfly Economics: A New General Theory of Social and Economic Behavior.* New York: Pantheon Books, 1998.

Peters, Edgar E. *Chaos and Order in the Capital Markets.* New York: John Wiley and Sons, 1991.

Peters, Edgar E. *Fractal Market Analysis.* New York: John Wiley and Sons, 1994.

Soros, George. *The Alchemy of Finance.* New York: Simon and Schuster, 1987.

Van Loggerenberg, Bazil J., and Stephen J. Cucchiaro. "Productivity Measurement and the Bottom Line." *National Productivity Review: The Journal of Productivity Management,* Winter 1981–1982.

Waldrop, M. Mitchell. *Complexity: The Emerging Science at the Edge of Order and Chaos.* New York: Simon and Schuster, 1992.

Zweig, Martin E. *Winning on Wall Street.* New York: Warner Books, 1986.

Author Background

Steve Cucchiaro is president and founder of Windward Investment Management and general partner of Windward Global Strategies L.P. with overall responsibility for investment performance. Steve has conducted over 25 years of research on the global capital markets. He earned a BS in Mathematics at M.I.T. in 1974 and an MBA in Finance at The Wharton School in 1977. Upon graduation, Steve held positions in management consulting with Coopers & Lybrand, Data Resources (as a senior economist) and CSP International (now part of Booz-Allen Hamilton) as managing director of strategy consulting. In 1984, he became president and co-founder of Datext, Inc., which was successfully sold to Lotus Development Corporation. As general manager at Lotus, his group was responsible for the commercial introduction of Lotus Notes. Subsequently, as president of ICAD, Inc., he helped position the engineering automation software provider for IPO and subsequent sale to Oracle Corporation. In 1990, Steve launched his proprietary model of the global capital markets and started Windward Investment Management.

Chapter 9

Developing an Investment Policy Statement

Ramelle M. Hieronymus

In any major undertaking in life, a plan is critical to success. This is particularly true in the investment world where emotions, rather than logic, can often drive the decision-making process. Having a formal written investment plan enables you to concentrate on long-term investment goals and avoid some of the short-term temptations many investors face. It can minimize the likelihood of your overreacting to short-term market fluctuations and will help in your evaluation of the ongoing success of the plan.

Key factors you should consider in developing an investment plan are time horizon, risk tolerance, and liquidity needs. Investment goals with a long time horizon (10+ years) generally will have more aggressive investment plans than those with shorter time horizons. With long time horizons, the ups and downs of the market will offset one another, giving riskier asset classes such as stocks a chance to prove their value. With shorter time horizons it becomes more critical not to lose money, so investments like short-term bonds tend to be favored.

An investor's risk tolerance can be difficult to quantify, but it basically translates into your ability to sleep at night. Some people have to know constantly how their investments are doing, checking their stock prices daily, if not more frequently. They become overly concerned when prices drop and find it hard to concentrate on other aspects of their life. These investors have a low tolerance for risk, and it may be in their best interest to have a more conservative investment plan.

Liquidity refers to the ability to convert assets quickly to cash. Liquid assets are important when you need periodic cash withdrawals from your assets to support general living expenses or other needs. In the past, people tended to invest in income-generating securities like bonds and high-dividend stocks to meet their cash flow needs. Today, however, many individuals (and most institutional investors) take a *total return* approach to investing. They concentrate on maximizing the total earning power of their assets (both income and capital gains), recognizing that most investments can be sold relatively quickly to meet cash flow needs. However, if your cash flow needs are great or very uncertain, you should limit investments in illiquid asset classes such as real estate and private equity.

The investment policy statement is the means of documenting your investment plan. An investment policy statement addresses such issues as investment objectives, spending guidelines, asset allocation, and selection and evaluation of managers. The second half of this chapter consists of a sample investment policy statement.

INVESTMENT OBJECTIVES

Your objectives for your assets determine how the investment plan will be structured. If you are saving for a teenager's college education, the investment plan will be fairly conservative and short-term oriented. On the other hand, if you are a 30-year-old saving for retirement, you can have a much more aggressive investment program.

The investment objectives section of the investment policy statement describes the purpose and goals of your investment plan. You may have many goals for your assets, including supporting daily living expenses, providing trust funds for your children, and making grants to favorite charities. You may find it useful to segregate assets for these various purposes and develop specialized investment plans for each.

Inflation is often a key component of your investment objectives. Over time, inflation will eat away at the purchasing power of your assets. For example, at

3 percent inflation levels, you will need twice as many dollars 24 years from now to buy the same basket of goods and services as you can buy today. As a result, many investors have as a goal to earn a return at least sufficient to offset inflation.

Taxes, investment expenses, and withdrawals also are a drain on your assets's value. To maintain the full corpus in purchasing power terms, you need to earn a sufficient return to offset these costs. Taxes and investment expenses can easily run 2 percent to 3 percent of the asset value. Combine that with inflation and you need a minimum return of 5 percent to 6 percent to keep your assets whole, *before any spending.*

SPENDING GUIDELINES

Spending levels and asset allocation are integrally linked. To support a higher level of spending, you need to generate a higher investment return, and a higher return requires a more aggressive asset allocation. Table 9.1 illustrates the relationship between asset mix and supportable spending levels. The table assumes stocks earn 10 percent, bonds earn 6 percent, and inflation is 3 percent. It also includes a 15 percent tax rate[1] on all earnings and a 0.8 percent investment management fee.

As the table shows, for each additional 10 percent commitment to the equity markets, you can increase spending by 0.3 percent to 0.4 percent. This analysis presumes that the goal is to protect your assets from inflationary erosion. If this is not the case (e.g., if you want to "die broke"), then you can justify higher spending levels. Nonetheless, for most long-term investment plans you should consider the effect of inflation on future needs.

Asset values tend to rise and fall from year to year due to volatility in the investment markets. As a result, if you set a spending guideline that just depends on the prior year's asset value, your withdrawals can vary significantly from year to year. For example, in the years 2000 to 2002 you would have experienced steadily declining withdrawals from your assets. To avoid this, you can attempt to smooth out the ups and downs in the market by

Table 9.1

Stock %	0	20	30	40	50	60	70	80	100
Bond %	100	80	70	60	50	40	30	20	0
Maximum spending %	1.4	2.0	2.4	2.7	3.0	3.4	3.7	4.0	4.7

applying a moving average. Many endowments and foundations, for example, will apply the spending percentage to the average market value over the past three- to five-year period.

An alternative to the percentage spending rate approach is to set a specific dollar amount of withdrawals and grow that each year by inflation. Although this is simple and has intuitive appeal, you need to be careful that you are continuing to preserve the purchasing power of your asset base.

ASSET ALLOCATION

As discussed in other chapters, asset allocation is the most important decision you will make. According to academic studies,[2] an investment fund's mix of assets explains over 90 percent of its return. The asset allocation decision should be long-term in nature and should be structured to have a high probability of achieving your objectives. It should be an allocation you can live with through good and bad markets, one you will not be tempted to change in reaction to market moves.

It is human nature to want to time the market, that is, get out at peaks and buy in at troughs. The problem is that few, if any, experienced investors have been successful at doing this. As an example of how difficult this is to do, consider the investor who 30 years ago bought an S&P 500 Index Fund. By year-end 2002, each $1.00 investment was worth $20.91. If, however, he had missed out on the 12 months with the best performance in that 30-year period, his $1.00 investment would only have grown to $5.54.

The investment guidelines document your long-term target allocations to each asset class and the percentage ranges in which they will be allowed to vary. They also show the market indices that the managers are expected to outperform. The role of the ranges is to keep the risk exposure of your investment funds within tolerable ranges. In setting ranges, you want to allow for enough variation so that you do not have to constantly sell positions (and incur taxes) to bring allocations back to target. Conversely, if they are too large, risk exposure can exceed desired levels, as many investors discovered in the late 1990s.

It is important to understand the role each asset class plays in the overall structure. Some asset classes like bonds provide stability, while others like stocks protect against inflation by providing real growth. Other asset classes serve to provide liquidity (cash) and to reduce risk (hedge funds, real estate) through low correlations with traditional asset classes. By understanding the role of each asset class, you are less likely to overreact in volatile markets.

REBALANCING

Because different asset classes will have different returns, your asset allocation will drift away from its target over time. If your allocation moves outside its allowable range, it is time to rebalance. This involves taking money from the asset class that exceeds its range on the upside and giving money to the class that is farthest below its target. In essence, this is selling your "winners" and buying more "losers," something that many find difficult to do. However, if you think of it as selling high and buying low, it may be more palatable.

Because security sales often generate a tax bill, it is important to keep the number of rebalancings to a minimum. Techniques to reduce the need to rebalance include directing any new contributions, including income and dividend payments, to the underweighted asset classes and taking withdrawals from the most overweighted asset classes. To minimize taxes, you may be able to realize losses in some portion of the portfolio to offset gains in another.

The goal of rebalancing is to have each asset class within its allowable range to keep your risk exposure at desired levels. It is not necessary to bring all asset classes back to target allocations, nor is it even necessary for a class outside its range to be returned to target. As long as all classes are within the stated ranges, further rebalancing is not required. Because of the tax consequences of rebalancing, you may wish to give yourself some "wiggle room" on when to rebalance. However, it is important to remember that rebalancing forces you to take some money off the table and helps avoid the late 1990s phenomenon of riding the market up only to give it all back in the market downturn.

MANAGER SELECTION AND EVALUATION

Once you have decided on your asset allocation, you need to determine how to implement your plan. It is difficult to find one firm that does a good job of managing all asset classes, so generally you are better served by looking for managers who specialize in a particular asset class. As a result you may end up with five or more managers with specialties in such areas as small-cap growth stocks, international developed markets stocks, municipal bonds, and equity long/short hedge funds.

There are many sources of manager information from national databases (Morningstar, Nelson) to financial consultants to recommendations from friends and family. Whatever the source, it is important to have a structured selection process. Look for firms with strong, *consistent* performance records, good risk and diversification controls, a well-elucidated investment philosophy and process, stable staff, and a good record of client service. On the tax front, look for an active tax management strategy. Year-end tax planning is not sufficient; the manager should be looking every day to reduce taxes by realizing losses and minimizing gains realization. One way to see if a manager is serious about tax-efficient management is to ask if he or she can provide after-tax rates of return.

Although most managers actively buy and sell securities, some firms offer what are called *index* funds. The goal of these funds is to provide the investor with the returns of selected market indices (S&P 500, Russell 2000 Small Cap Index, etc.) by basically replicating the index holdings. Fees for these funds are considerably lower than for active management. Also some index funds, like those tracking the S&P 500, can be very tax-efficient because they generally buy and sell securities only when the composition of the index changes; this is not true, however, of all index funds. The performance of index funds generally is competitive with active managers in the more widely researched (efficient) segments of the markets like large-capitalization stocks and domestic bonds. In less efficient areas like small- to mid-capitalization stocks and international stocks, however, there is a strong case to be made that active managers can add significant additional return over the indices.[3]

Managers may offer a variety of ways to access their capabilities, depending on the size of your investment. Larger sums of money can be managed in a separate account, one managed specifically for you and subject (within reason) to your investment guidelines. Smaller sums will often go into some type of commingled vehicle like a mutual fund where your assets are commingled with those of other investors. For a taxable investor, separate accounts offer more control over your tax liability since you can request that the manager realize losses or gains as your needs dictate. In commingled accounts you have little control over the tax management, and unless specifically billed as a tax-sensitive fund, there may be no tax management. It is also the case that if you wish to move your commingled assets elsewhere, you will be taxed on your entire unrealized gain. The benefits of commingled accounts are that they can provide greater diversification of assets due to the larger asset base, and they generally are cheaper overall because the fee includes custody of the assets. For a separate account, you will need a custodian bank to hold the assets and settle trades for you. Custody for international portfolios can be very expensive so accessing the international markets through commingled vehicles is generally the most cost-effective approach.

Once you hire investment managers, you should monitor their progress on at least a quarterly basis. This involves measuring their investment performance against stated return expectations. Two types of measures are generally used: a market index representative of the manager's investment approach and a universe reflecting the range of returns of other similar managers. In addition, you should look at the structural characteristics (PE, yield, etc.) of the manager's portfolio to make sure that they are consistent with its stated style.

It is not reasonable to expect a manager to outperform its benchmarks each and every quarter. There may be some periods when the manager's approach is out of favor. For example, managers who did not invest in technology stocks had poor relative performance in the late 1990s, only to look like superstars when the tech market crashed. Generally, a manager should be given a three- to five-year time period to prove his or her worth. Of course, if something changes at the firm such as the departure of a key decision maker, more immediate action may be required.

Ideally, you will want to evaluate your manager after all expenses, including management fees and taxes, have been removed from the account. Most managers, however, report returns gross of these expenses, and virtually all peer group universes are gross returns. Manager evaluation is an area where a financial consultant may be able to assist you by providing good comparison data.

LIMITATIONS AND RESTRICTIONS

This section of the investment policy statement allows you to set out restrictions on how your assets are invested. This can apply only to your separately managed accounts; for commingled/mutual funds a prospectus usually governs the investments. Typical restrictions can include a limitation on the size of individual holdings and quality constraints on the fixed-income holdings. You also can preclude investment in particular stocks, such as those in which you already have significant holdings. Some people use restrictions to support their social goals by prohibiting investment in tobacco companies or weapons manufacturers.

There is a balance that needs to be achieved in setting restrictions. You want to ensure that your portfolio properly reflects your risk tolerance. On the other hand, too many restrictions can unduly hamper your manager and result in subpar returns.

COMMUNICATION AND REPORTING

Communication is key to a successful investment relationship, but unfortunately not all firms are good it. At a minimum your investment manager should provide you with monthly statements of your account, showing the holdings and any transactions that have occurred. He or she also should notify you of any major events at the firm such as key personnel departures or changes in investment approach. Many firms also provide a quarterly review of results and discussion of their current investment strategy. If the firm is experienced in dealing with individual investors, your manager also may be willing to meet with periodically to discuss the portfolio. Before hiring a manager, make sure that his or her standard reporting package is sufficient for your needs, especially with regard to tax filings.

Commingled/mutual and hedge funds are a different matter when it comes to reporting. You will receive a monthly or quarterly statement showing your investment in the fund and any transactions. Depending on the type of fund, you may receive semiannual or annual reports discussing the fund's strategy. Many hedge funds do not disclose their holdings or other information on the fund structure like the degree of leverage. Although there is increasing pressure for greater hedge fund disclosure, change is slow in coming. For more information on mutual funds, Morningstar is a good source. They provide return and structural information along with periodic analyst reviews.

SUMMARY

Your investment policy statement lays out the components of your investment plan for all interested parties. You should share it with your investment managers, custodian bank, and any financial advisors you retain. While it is a long-term plan, you should review it at least annually to ensure that it continues to have a high probability of achieving your objectives.

SAMPLE STATEMENT OF INVESTMENT OBJECTIVES, GOALS, AND POLICY GUIDELINES

I. INVESTMENT OBJECTIVES

These assets are intended to support the XYZ family and their activities. The main objective for the assets is to provide suitable cash flow throughout the life of each family member, while protecting the corpus from inflationary erosion. The portfolio has a blended growth and income objective with disciplined longer-term strategies that will accommodate relevant, reasonable, or probable events.

In order to accomplish the main objective, it is necessary to achieve a net total return (income plus capital change, net of taxes and fees) that will preserve and enhance the fund assets in real dollar terms. Additional objectives are to minimize taxes, control risk, and provide competitive returns relative to peers and market indices.

II. Spending Guidelines

It is anticipated that the family spending requirements will be in the 3.5 percent range. Actual spending levels will be computed by taking the spending percentage times the average total fund market value over the past 12 quarters. The family will review the spending percentage periodically and will communicate any changes in cash flow requirements to the investment managers and custodian.

III. Asset Allocation

The selection and weighting of asset classes is the primary determinant of investment return and volatility. Diversification of assets (combining asset classes that do not move in tandem) serves to minimize risk and enhance returns over time. Asset class selection and weightings reflect the family's investment objectives, liquidity needs, risk tolerance, and time horizon for intended use.

The fund is to be structured for long-term growth with a broadly diversified mix of asset classes and styles. The domestic equity segments are intended to provide protection from inflation and provide real growth. The international equity segment serves to enhance return and control risk by reducing the fund's reliance on domestic financial markets. The role of the alternative assets segment is to enhance returns and reduce risk through the addition of investments with low correlations to traditional asset classes. The domestic fixed income segment is intended to provide protection from deflationary environments and to provide a source of money designed to meet cash flow requirements.

The asset choice has been carefully considered by the family, in accordance with a systematic allocation process derived in consultation with their advisors. The allocation will be reviewed at least annually to ensure that it continues to provide a high probability of achieving desired goals. Approved asset classes and policy target ranges are noted in Table 9.2.

IV. Rebalancing

Varying investment returns from each asset class segment will cause the actual asset mix to vary from the target allocations. To the extent possible, cash flows should be utilized to keep the fund's allocation close to target.

Table 9.2

Asset Class	Target	Range	Index Benchmark
Total equity	55%	45%–65%	
Large-cap. core U.S.	20%	15%–25%	S&P 500 Index
Mid-small U.S. growth	10%	7%–13%	Russell Mid-Cap Growth Index
Mid-small U.S. value	10%	7%–13%	Russell Mid-Cap Value Index
International equity	15%	10%–20%	MSCI EAFE Net Index
Total alternatives	25%	20%–30%	
Equity hedge	10%	7%–13%	CSFB Equity Long/Short Index
Absolute return	5%	2%–8%	CSFB Event Driven Multi-Strategy
Private equity	5%	2%–8%	Venture Econ. US Private Equity
Real estate	5%	2%–8%	NAREIT Index
Total fixed income	20%	15%–25%	
Municipal bonds	20%	15%–25%	LB Municipal Bond Index

Investments will be reviewed at the end of each quarter to determine if rebalancing is necessary. Changes in the allocation to the asset class segments or subsegments will be considered at any time the quarterly weighting is outside the established weight range as defined above. Tax liability will be a consideration in the magnitude and timing of rebalancings.

V. MANAGER SELECTION AND EVALUATION

Investment managers will be appointed following a systematic search for those with demonstrated quality in the style desired. Utilization of tax-minimization strategies will be a key factor in the selection process. Investment managers have full discretion to buy and sell securities and to vote proxies for the securities in which they invest.

Manager portfolios will be evaluated on a quarterly basis. The quarterly review will address fund performance versus benchmarks, portfolio structure, and risk characteristics. The review will confirm that the portfolio structure is consistent with the manager's stated style and that performance is on track to achieve the desired objectives.

Measurement of performance against policy objectives will be computed on a net total return basis (total return net of management fees, taxes, and transaction costs). Market indices will be adjusted for taxes for comparative purposes. The following criteria will be used to evaluate manager performance:

- Active managers will be expected to achieve an annualized net total rate of return over a five-year period that exceeds their after-tax market index rate of return, as indicated in Section III.
- Passive or index managers will be expected to provide an annualized net total rate of return and risk characteristics that closely track the designated index.
- The managers will also be expected to consistently achieve a total rate of return that is equal to or above the median return in a universe of peers with comparable investment styles.

VI. LIMITATIONS AND RESTRICTIONS

The total fund will be broadly diversified both across asset classes and within individual portfolios so as to minimize risk. To this end, the following restrictions will apply to separately managed accounts:

- Not more than 5 percent of a manager's portfolio may be invested in the securities of any one issuer, with the exception of the U.S. government or its agencies and other sovereign government issuers. Index funds and the family's investment in XYZ Corporation are exempted from this restriction.
- Fixed-income investments rated below BBB by Standard & Poors or a comparable rating service are limited to not more than 15 percent of the fixed-income assets. Fixed-income securities denominated in foreign currencies are limited to 20 percent of the fixed-income portfolio.
- Use of derivatives or leverage is allowed only with the family's written approval.

To the extent mutual or other pooled funds are utilized, they will be bound by the prospectus guidelines.

VII. COMMUNICATION AND REPORTING

The manager is responsible for free and open communication with the family in all significant matters pertaining the management of fund assets, including but not limited to (1) major changes in the investment manager's investment outlook, investment and tax strategy, and portfolio structure, and (2) significant changes in the firm's ownership, organizational structure, financial condition, or senior personnel.

The manager will provide the family and other designated parties with monthly reports detailing each security's cost, market value, number of shares, and anticipated annual income. In addition the manager will provide a summary of all transactions including the gain/loss realized in the trade and the associated transaction costs.

Notes

1. Federal tax rate in effect from 2003 through 2008 under the Jobs & Growth Tax Relief Reconciliation Act of 2003. Higher tax rates would require a reduction in spending levels.
2. Brinson, Gary P., L. Randolph Hood, and Gilbert L. Beebower, "Determinants of Portfolio Performance," *Financial Analysts Journal,* July/August 1986.
3. See Frank Russell Company's manager performance universe data compared to index returns as evidence that active managers can add significant additional return over the indices in the less efficient asset classes.

Additional Reading and Resources

Ellis, Charles D. *Winning the Loser's Game,* 4th ed. New York: McGraw Hill, 2003.
Schneider, William, Robert DiMeo, and D. Robinson Cluck. *Asset Management for Endowments and Foundations.* New York: McGraw Hill, 1997.
Williams III, Arthur. *Managing Your Investment Manager,* 3rd ed. Irwin Professional Publishing, 1992.
www.financiallearning.com. A website sponsored by the GE Center for Financial Learning dedicated to investor education.
www.vanguard.com. The Planning and Advice section of Vanguard's Personal Investor website offers help in developing an investment plan.

Author Background

Ramelle Hieronymus is a Principal at Prime, Buchholz & Associates, Inc., an international investment consulting firm based in Portsmouth, NH. Prior to joining Prime, Buchholz she was a Principal and Practice Leader of the Boston-office investment consulting practice of William M. Mercer and previously a Vice President at Boston Safe Deposit & Trust Company. Ms. Hieronymus has over 20 years of investment experience. She has consulted to corporations, wealthy families, public funds, endowments, and foundations. She specializes in investment strategies for taxable entities, including nuclear decommissioning trusts, non-qualified plans, and post-retirement benefit trusts.

III

Investing for the Long Term

Chapter 10

Selecting Investment Managers

Paul Greenwood

Perhaps it has happened to you. You interview someone for a job opening whose resume looks great. The person has achieved a lot in a short time and has a superb education pedigree. You hire the candidate.

But somehow things do not work out as they should. All those achievements that looked so good on paper do not translate into meaningful accomplishments at your company. It's not entirely the new employee's fault. After all, your company is different, requiring a different skill set. You looked at the job candidate's past when you should have tried to ascertain the person's potential for the future and for your company. So it is with hiring a professional investor to manage your money.

After all, when you entrust your money to a professional investment manager you are hiring a person, not simply buying a product. That person needs to have specific skills and you need to assess them. The task is an important one because the impact on your portfolio of a less skilled manager compared with an accomplished one can be significant.

Yet selecting such a person can be a challenging task. So much so that it pays to conduct intensive analysis of the factors driving the performance of investment managers. Research shows that this year's hot managers seldom

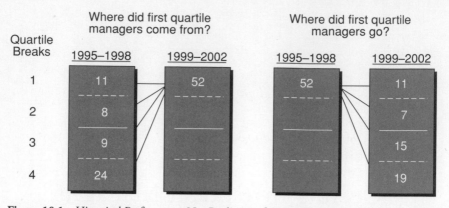

Figure 10.1 Historical Performance Not Predictive of Future Performance

NOTE: Universe consisted of 208 institutional managers in Russell's Growth, Market-Oriented, and Value universes with 8 years of history (excess of style benchmark) ending December 31, 2002.

EXAMPLE: Of the 52 managers in the top quartile for year 1995–1998, only 11 placed in the first quartile in years 1999–2002.

SOURCE: Courtesy of Russell Investment Group.

sustain their results to be next year's top performers. For example, as shown in Figure 10.1, of the 52 managers who were in the top quartile for 1995 through 1998, only 11 placed in the first quartile during 1999 through 2002. Predicting who will become the best investment manager for any future year simply on the basis of performance, therefore, becomes almost as futile as predicting how stocks will perform next year based on this year's performance.

Furthermore, you are likely to hire an investment manager not just for one year, but for many. You are looking for consistency as well as ability. At times, investment management firms change their investment staff, possibly replacing an experienced investment professional with a relative newcomer. Clients of these firms are often unaware of this until some time after the event, but the change can dramatically affect their portfolios.

The challenge of picking investment managers is illustrated by the pattern followed by most of those who enjoy intense but brief public adoration as elite market strategists. These celebrity investment sages initially spring into prominence as a result of a good market call. A strategist may predict, for example, that stocks will soon tumble bringing the bull market to an end. If the event does indeed occur, the strategist—soon dubbed a guru—is seen as someone who knows something that few other investors know. Before too long, the first good call is followed by another prediction that proves accurate and for a while it seems as if the strategist can do nothing wrong. Investors hang on every word. The market reacts immediately to any comment the strategist makes as investors seek to become wealthy off the predictions.

Few such prognosticators, however, can survive more than two or three good (perhaps lucky) calls. The next major prediction inevitably proves disastrous. The market reacts in the opposite way to the prediction and before too long the disgraced guru disappears from the limelight.

An example of how even the brightest managers can quickly go from hero to goat is the case of Long-Term Capital Management (LTCM), an investment company that managed hedge funds. In the late 1990s the firm became well known in elite circles on Wall Street for its all-star investment team, which included two Nobel laureates, and its exceptionally strong investment performance. But after a default in Russia led to a global financial crisis in mid-1998, LTCM's investment strategy proved fallible and performance collapsed. The result was a disaster that rocked global financial markets. It also cost LTCM's clients most of their invested capital.

The example illustrates what can happen to one degree or another with any investment manager regardless of pedigree. Those who have proven to be excellent stock or bond pickers in the past may not be excellent pickers the next time around.

So how do responsible advisors and investors select investment managers? Russell Investment Group has conducted many years of research to develop a system of investment manager selection designed to select above-average money managers and consistently produce good results for clients.

Russell's research and evaluation process is complex and involves aspects that are proprietary. But let's look inside this evaluation process to better understand how it might help you in your endeavors to select an investment manager who will stand the test of time.

ACTIVE OR PASSIVE?

The investment manager you select will depend partly on how you plan to implement your asset allocation. You may choose a passive (or indexed) strategy or an active (or actively managed) strategy.

In a passive strategy you invest in mutual funds that closely mirror the way in which stock or bond indexes move. For example, you may choose a mutual fund that mimics the performance of the Russell 2000 Index, the Russell 3000 Index, or the Standard & Poor's 500 Index.[1]

To create such funds, managers buy all, or nearly all, of the securities in an index in amounts that reflect the same proportional weight as the securities held in the index. The result is an investment product that will deliver returns that are always close to the performance of the index.

Index funds are usually less expensive than actively managed funds because the investment managers do not have to spend a lot of time selecting the securities for their funds. They simply buy the issues in the indexes and tinker with them only when the composition of the index changes. In many asset classes index funds at times have performed better than the average active manager. Thus, using passive strategies is a fairly low-risk approach to achieving average or slightly above average returns.

The lure of active management stems from its potential to perform better than an index fund. Indeed, within the United States alone thousands of investment managers use a myriad of approaches to find undervalued securities. The intense competition to find these securities means it is difficult, but not impossible, to consistently produce returns that are better than those of the index. But the evidence is strong that enough inefficiencies (or systematic mispricings) exist in capital markets for talented investment managers to add more than enough value to justify active management. Of course, the big trick is to find those investment managers.

Selecting an investment manager for a passive index fund is considerably easier and less labor-intensive than selecting active investment managers. Because almost all major index providers do a good job of closely tracking market indexes, the primary point of differentiation is not the performance they deliver but the fees they charge. Accordingly, it is generally worthwhile to compare the pricing of several index providers. Other factors, such as client reporting and client service, are also worthy of consideration, and should be discussed in advance with the investment manager.

Selecting active managers, on the other hand, is a demanding task, even for experts. But the most challenging aspect of manager selection is unrelated to investment expertise or knowledge and has a lot to do with psychology.

Far and away the most difficult challenge in selecting investment managers is avoiding the siren song of past performance. This task is more difficult than it seems. After all, we are only being human when we say, "Hey, this fund has a great track record; I'm buying it." At the same time, placing your hard-earned money in the hands of someone who has shown dismal results in the last few years feels foolhardy for most of us. Yet, so often hindsight shows you would have fared best had you pushed aside the top performer of previous years and gone with the loser. Next time around, of course, it may be different.

Indeed, we have all seen the disclaimers stating that past performance is not an indication of future results, yet few of us take this message to heart. In most vocations, be it baseball or dentistry, past performance and future results are strongly related; those who have done better in the past tend to do better in the future. Unfortunately, when it comes to investment management, this relationship breaks down.

The sober reality is that using past performance as an important factor in selecting an investment manager is far more likely to result in poor performance than good performance. Market research firm Dalbar Inc. studied individual investor performance from 1984 through 2002. Their analysis showed that while the average equity mutual fund produced a 12.2 percent annualized return over this period, the average investor in these funds achieved a 2.6 percent annualized return. This gaping disparity is a result of investors continually investing in funds that have done well and selling those that have done poorly. Such tail-chasing behavior is the biggest threat to the development and maintenance of a successful investment program.

If you take away nothing else from this chapter, understand that when it comes to investment management, the past is not prologue. Why should this be? Can't a good investment manager be expected to be a good investment manager year after year? Why are investment managers so different from other achievers? Understanding the answers to these questions can help you avoid painful mistakes.

The truth is factors other than investment insight can contribute to an investment manager performing better or worse than an index. For example, if the stock market produces a 10 percent return in a given year and an investment manager delivers a 30 percent return, the total difference in performance is rarely a function of the investment manager's brilliance. Indeed, even if the investment manager is highly skilled, it is more likely that perhaps 2 percentage points of the 20 percent performance differential can be attributed to skill. The rest is a function of factors unrelated to skill. Among those factors are investment managers' style of investing, the size of the companies in which they invest, exposure to particular economic sectors, and even luck. Over time these factors do not add or subtract much from performance, although over shorter periods they explain much of most investment managers' results and lead people mistakenly to attribute much of the performance to skill.

Another reason past performance is of little help is that the world around us is changing constantly. A talented baseball player has to face different opponents, a variety of field conditions, and other factors that may affect his ability to perform well. He often will learn to adapt to these situations, enabling him to play consistently well. But investment managers face a wide array of changing circumstances to which they find it difficult to adapt and which are hard to anticipate. Capital markets are fluid and continually influenced by an ever-changing mix of information and investor sentiment.

Not only that. Investment management firms tend to change as well, in the same way that a baseball team's make-up may change, making it difficult to assess their future chances of winning. When an investment firm loses one or more key professionals, this change may have serious implications for near-term performance. More often, the changes experienced by investment managers are subtle and their impact becomes apparent only across a longer period of time. Sometimes a key person's influence on investment decisions changes slowly.

Even good performance itself can result in change. Let's say an investment manager specializing in small-capitalization issues produces great perform- ance over several years.[2] This performance attracts many new investors eager to benefit from the manager's apparent skills. As the assets under manage- ment swell, the investment manager finds it becomes increasingly difficult to buy and sell the same smaller-capitalization issues without having a meaning- ful impact on the price of those stocks.

Short of shutting the doors to new business in that fund (which does hap- pen), the investment manager is left with several choices. The first is to invest in more stocks. The problem with this investment approach is that investment managers find they can't be as selective when picking securities to fit their stra- tegy. Another option is to keep investing in the same stocks, but this dimin- ishes the investment manager's ability to trade quickly and inexpensively. A third option is to own the same number of stocks, but hold those issues that are larger in capitalization. This option runs the risk of pushing investment managers into new areas of the market, where they may have less expertise.

Often, when people fully understand how little guidance past perform- ance provides, they question whether it is even possible to identify invest- ment managers that will do well in the future. We are convinced you can. But the task is not easy. Selecting investment managers is labor-intensive and requires access to considerable amounts of quantitative data.

The key to successful manager selection can be found in specific attributes of investment managers. As is the case in other professions, successful invest- ment managers have many traits in common. In the more than 30 years of re- searching and evaluating investment managers, Russell has learned a lot about what these traits are. Some attributes can only be assessed qualitatively, pre- ferably through face-to-face discussions. Other times, quantitative tools can shed light on the effectiveness and wisdom of particular investment behavior.

Identifying whether an investment manager has these success factors requires access to the firm's key investment professionals. Not surprisingly, your access to investment managers tends to be closely related to the amount of money you have to invest. It helps, therefore, that Russell has many large clients and $100 billion in assets under management. A high degree of access is essential to the process of determining whether an investment manager has a good chance of not only producing above-average results, but also producing them at an acceptable level of volatility.

FOUR Ps

Four key areas to focus on in discussions with investment managers are people, process, portfolios, and performance. We believe two of these "four Ps," people and process, are responsible for whatever success or failure a manager experiences, while the other two, portfolios and performance, can help provide evidence that managers are implementing their investment processes effectively.

Evaluating investment managers means asking many questions. The best investment managers not only tend to have good answers, but also are least threatened by such inquiries.

PEOPLE AND ORGANIZATION

As in any other business, people are the key to success in the investment industry. It takes people with superior insights and skills to make consistently better decisions or to build better investment processes. It also takes talented people to build quality investment organizations.

When it comes to analyzing people and organizations, it is less important to have investment expertise than good judgment of people. This is because most of the attributes one should seek in an investment manager are either readily observable or easily discoverable. Ideally, discussions with investment managers allow you to answer questions like these to your satisfaction.

PEOPLE

- Are the people impressive?
- Are they passionate about investing?
- How much experience do the key investment professionals have at the firm and in their current roles?

- Is their integrity unquestionable?
- Are they continually looking for ways to enhance their investment process?
- Do they have sufficient humility to readily acknowledge their mistakes?
- How have roles evolved over time?
- What have they learned over the years?

Of the many attributes to look for in evaluating a firm's professionals, several come to mind as being particularly important. An investment manager who is exceptionally passionate about investing and focused like a laser on producing good performance rates high on our list. A particular manager of our acquaintance typifies these traits. His firm has outperformed the market every year since the firm was founded. This investment success has provided him with a very large net worth, yet rather than become complacent, he continues to be more competitive and concerned about performance than almost any other manager in the industry.

ORGANIZATION

- Has the organization done a good job retaining key employees?
- Does the compensation reward good performance or business growth?
- Are there any organizational developments (such as a key person retiring) that are likely in the next three years?
- Do key employees have equity or equity-like interest in the company?
- How does compensation compare with industry averages?
- Will new business initiatives require significant amounts of key professionals' time?
- What does their Form ADV [a Securities and Exchange Commission (SEC) filing] say about any regulatory problems the firm has had?

Many investment managers have compensation schemes that do not encourage stability. One particular firm has suffered chronic turnover among its investment staff for nearly two decades. This turnover is not a function of the work environment or the other team members, as the firm rates well by those measures. The crux of the problem lies in the founder's reluctance to share equity ownership with the other key people. The result is an organization that is constantly hiring good people, seeing them mature and become major contributors, only to lose them when they begin to feel unappreciated and undercompensated.

Another investment manager had a different problem. A large component of variable compensation was based on the firm's average profits over the last three years. After the Internet bubble burst in 2000, the profits of many investment managers collapsed. This encouraged the firm's senior portfolio manager to leave the organization to receive future payouts based on the higher historical profits (because the payout formula in his contract would freeze upon his departure from the firm). Fully understanding how the investment professionals in a firm are compensated can dramatically reduce the risk of such unfortunate situations.

PROCESS

An investment manager's success is ultimately determined by its people and the investment processes they employ. The correct mix of people and process varies by manager, and it is critical to understand what this blend is for each. If the key to a firm's success is dependent upon simply implementing a highly structured investment process, the people are relatively less important. Of course, the reverse is true as well.

It is important to understand that not all investment processes are created equal. Some are inherently superior, while others stand little chance of success. Some are easier to implement, while others are more difficult. Every investment process has many aspects, and a major goal when talking with investment managers should be to answer some important questions in three areas:

SECURITY SELECTION PROCESS

- Does the investment process make intuitive sense?
- What are the premises underlying the investment process?
- What evidence supports these premises?
- What challenges does the firm face in implementing its investment process?
- Is the firm more reliant on people or process?
- What is the one thing that needs to go well for the firm's investment process to succeed and how can it be evaluated and monitored?

DECISION MAKING

- Is accountability clearly defined for all participants in the investment process?
- Are decisions made by one person or a group of people?

- If a group, how does the firm ensure accountability and the timeliness of decisions?
- Does the firm's decision-making model make sense in terms of how it is attempting to add value?

SELL DISCIPLINES

- Does the firm treat its holdings in a callously objective manner?
- Does it have recent examples of acknowledging mistakes?
- How actively does the firm trade? Has this trading enhanced or detracted from performance?
- How has the firm's approach to selling stocks changed over time?

One of the most difficult challenges every investment manager faces is that of knowing when to sell an investment. It is difficult to get right because human nature encourages us to do the wrong thing at the wrong time. We want to buy when everyone is ebullient and sell when things look the darkest. In reality, we should do the opposite.

Russell used to track an investment manager who appeared to have a great group of analysts that performed exceptionally thorough research. However, the lead investor found it so difficult to acknowledge any mistakes that few stocks were ever sold. The result was performance so bad that the firm is no longer in business.

PORTFOLIOS

Analyzing portfolios may be a more important part of the manager evaluation process than reviewing investment performance. The reason: You can gain insight into investment managers' thought processes by watching how the portfolios they build change over time.

Portfolio characteristics can shed light on the pattern of performance that should be expected from an investment manager. For instance, if it appears that a manager invests in companies with stable earnings, then it is likely that manager will perform best when the economy is slowing because investors tend to flock to companies with consistent earnings when they are concerned about economic growth. Such a manager's worst performance is likely to occur when the economy is rapidly accelerating because investors tend to look for companies with strong growth prospects rather than those with stable earnings.

Organizational and investment stress can also be reflected in portfolios. For example, a large change in the number of securities held (say, from 50 to 100 stocks) is typically indicative of a manager struggling to invest a growing sum of assets under management effectively, without having excessive impact on security prices. It also is consistent with a manager attempting to accommodate internal pressures to allow other investment professionals to have direct impact on portfolios. Insights into these issues can be acquired by seeking answers to questions such as:

- Does the size of each investment reflect the investment manager's risk and return expectations or does it simply reflect the past performance of the investment?
- Are the characteristics of portfolios, such as their price-earnings ratios, consistent with everything you know about the manager?
- How much do the characteristics change from period to period?
- What do the portfolios' characteristics say about performance volatility and the environments in which performance will be particularly good or bad?
- What systematic biases (such as always having relatively large exposure to technology stocks) are there in the portfolios? How do these impact performance expectations?
- How has the number of securities held in portfolios changed over time?

One investment manager used to hold roughly 60 stocks in small-capitalization portfolios. Over time, great performance and a tendency to hold on to successful stocks ultimately led to portfolios holding nearly 400 stocks, concentrated in mid- and large-capitalization issues. The portfolios did not necessarily become inferior, but clearly they were different than they once were. As a result, clients needed to reconsider their investments in the portfolios on the basis of the revised risk and return expectations.

PERFORMANCE

As already noted, past performance is a poor indicator of future performance. But past risk is a fairly good indicator of future risk. In other words, volatility is far more predictable than performance. Developing a sense for what performance to expect from an investment manager can only be achieved in the context of understanding performance volatility. The more volatile an investment manager's performance, the more often he or she will appear to be exceptionally gifted or hopelessly lost to investors. Of course, neither extreme is likely to be true.

One cannot generalize and say that investment managers with volatile performance are better or worse than investment managers with lower volatility. You can, however, state that the more volatile an investment manager's performance, the longer is the time horizon required to use the manager's services and be confident in the ultimate outcome. Therefore, volatile managers often require greater patience, as poor performance can extend multiple years, even among the best investors. When reviewing an investment manager's performance, you will need to get good answers to some additional questions:

- How has the firm performed in different market conditions?
- How does the performance volatility compare with that of the market?
- What level of volatility (both in absolute and index-relative terms) should one expect?
- What market conditions are hostile to the firm and which ones are conducive to good performance?
- How does performance compare with that of similar investment managers?
- Considering the market environment, has performance been consistent with expectations?
- How consistent has performance been on a quarterly and annual basis?

The red flag that reveals bigger issues is often an investment manager's performance that is different from expectations. Several years ago, when researching an investment manager that focused on small-cap growth stocks, we became concerned about performance. It wasn't that the firm had dramatically trailed the market. Indeed, it had actually exceeded the market index by more than 10 percent during the year. The concern arose because the firm failed to perform even better during a particularly friendly environment for its investment approach. On closer examination it was learned that an addition to their staff had adversely affected the way in which investment decisions were made. Without appropriate performance expectations, however, this connection would not have been made.

SUMMARY

People seeking investment management services have many options. Passive management offers the certainty of market-like returns, while active management, when done well, can provide above-average results, at the risk of falling short of market returns.

Active management is well worth the effort, provided you can tap into the pool of talented investment managers. Doing this is no small task. It requires a diligent, continuous effort, as well as access to large amounts of data and key investment professionals.

Analysis of an investment manager's people, process, portfolios, and performance is an essential element of the investment manager selection process. Leaning heavily on past performance is more likely to work against you than in your favor, because there is no strong relationship between past and future performance. Success can be achieved, but as in most elements of life, great success is seldom achieved without great effort.

Notes

1. The Russell 2000 Index® measures the performance of the 2,000 smallest companies in the Russell 3000 Index®, representative of the U.S. small-capitalization securities market. The Russell 3000 Index measures the performance of the 3,000 largest U.S. securities based on total market capitalization. The S&P 500 Index is an index, with dividends reinvested, of 500 issues representative of leading companies in the U.S. large-cap securities market. Russell Investment Group and Standard & Poor's Corporation are the owners of the trademarks, service marks, and copyrights related to their respective indexes. Indexes and/or benchmarks are unmanaged and cannot be invested in directly. Returns represent past performance, are not a guarantee of future performance, and are not indicative of any specific investment.

2. Small-company issues are subject to considerable price fluctuations and are more volatile than large-company stocks. Small-cap funds may involve considerably more risk than funds investing in larger-cap companies. Please remember that all investments carry some level of risk, including the potential loss of principal invested. They do not typically grow at an even rate of return and may experience negative growth. As with any type of portfolio structuring, attempting to reduce risk and increase return could, at certain times, unintentionally reduce returns.

Author Background

Paul Greenwood is Director of US Equity Investment Management & Research at Russell Investment Group, a global leader in multi-manager investing which manages $100 billion in assets and provides investment services for clients in 35 countries around the world. Paul is responsible for fund performance and quality of investment content in Russell's US equity group. He also oversees the company's research and evaluation of small capitalization and growth US equity managers. Paul joined Russell in 1989 as a research associate. He was promoted to research analyst in 1991 and senior research analyst in 1993. In 2002 he was named director of US Equity. Prior to joining Russell, Paul served as a pension consultant with Howard Johnson & Company in Seattle.

Note: Russell Investment Group is a registered trade name of Frank Russell Company, a Washington USA corporation, which operates through subsidiaries worldwide. Russell Investment Group is a subsidiary of the Northwestern Mutual Life Insurance Company.

Additional Reading and Resources

Publications

Christopherson, Jon, Zhuanxin Ding, and Paul Greenwood. *The Perils of Success.* Journal of Portfolio Management Winter, 2002.

Ware, Jim and Beth Michaels. *Investment Leadership: Building a Winning Culture for Long-Term Success.* John Wiley & Sons, October, 2003.

Organization

Institute for Private Investors *(IPI).* 74 Trinity Place, New York, NY, 10006.

Russell Commentaries

Ankrim, Ernie. *Past Performance Is No Guarantee of Past Results!* August, 1997.

Greenwood, Paul. *The Evolution of Investment Processes.* June, 1999.

Oberhofer, George. *Our Commitment to Qualitative Manager Research.* April, 1998.

Chapter 11

Risk: How Much Should You Take?

Paula Boyer Kennedy

There is a paradox in the psychology of investment risk. In choosing an investment advisor, people tend to focus on return—how to get this much capital appreciation or this much income—and they don't pay attention to how much they can lose. Yet, when asked if they would be happier to make a 50 percent return or more upset if they lost half of their money, most people say the emotional impact of losing money would be much greater than the positive impact of making the same amount. Logically then, people should focus on risk rather than return when making investment decisions.

Investing is the art of defining acceptable risk and building portfolios of investments that, as a whole, provide the desired level of risk. This is a good way to approach the investment process, and if you do this you will be a happier investor. However, to begin with, you need to understand risk. Periods of major market decline, whether in the equity or fixed-income markets, help clarify what is meant by risk and help you understand the appropriate level of risk for your investments.

Wall Street generally defines risk as volatility—how much the value of an asset fluctuates. This definition provides some value, but it is incomplete because it does not capture in concrete terms how much capital one can lose over time. Perhaps it is more useful to think of risk as a two-edge sword. In investing, you will always be making a trade-off between potential loss of capital and potential loss of purchasing power to inflation. These two will always be at odds, so it makes sense to think about the kind of risk you wish to take rather than whether or not to take risk. Even if you are invested in cash, you will be taking a risk.

The hedge fund industry, for all its faults, provides good alternatives for understanding risk. Hedge funds typically measure risk in terms of how much you can lose: *largest cumulative decline,* also known as *drawdown.* Hedge funds use additional measures to quantify how an investment does when markets are going down, and what the correlation is of that investment to others in declining markets.

Returns in the hedge fund world generally are risk-adjusted so that investments with very different characteristics can be compared to each other on a level playing field. For example, how can you compare an arbitrage manager whose strategy takes advantage of small price differences between currencies in different markets with a macroeconomic manager who tactically moves money from gold to bonds to equities? The simple answer is to adjust the returns of each of these managers for risk using measures like the Sharpe or Sortino ratios.

This can also apply to more traditional equity and bond managers. Adjusting returns for risk would have helped people understand that while many firms made huge returns during the Internet bubble, they were taking on a lot of risk and playing a dangerous game. People who gave the managers credit for smart stock picking learned the hard way that the majority of their returns came from simply being in the category that was doing well at the time. These huge returns (and subsequent huge losses) can be explained by the asset class's volatility characteristics.

Many people get upset with their investment advisors in bear markets, even though their advisors are performing in line or better than the broad category. In rising markets, investment advisors generally try to take credit for their good performance. They want their clients to think the returns are not driven by the overall index. However, in periods of decline, advisors frequently blame the overall market. How often do you hear, "The whole market is down ... all managers are down, you just have to ride it out"? These are not comforting words. However, once investors understand that their advisors are not likely to do much better than the *category* in which they are investing, they will be able to understand the risk characteristics and expected returns of their portfolios to a much larger extent.

How do you decide how much risk you want to take on? Many people experienced investment loss in the early 2000s. For those who had made large bets on equities during those years, the risk of owning equities now may seem to be unnecessarily high. It is important to limit your risk exposure in any one category, but there is another lesson to be learned. Individual asset categories make and lose money at different times. If you hold multiple categories of assets, however, you can minimize risk while maximizing return. The right response to a down market is to make sure your portfolio is properly diversified across asset classes. The wrong response is to sell whatever investment performed poorly last year.

This strategy of selling underperforming asset categories and buying hot ones is known in the trade as *buying high and selling low.* Obviously, it is not a good strategy for anyone. Yet many investors in difficult market times simply abandon the losing asset category and move money into what they consider to be a more stable one. They tend to go lower on the risk pyramid.

Figure 11.1 shows a sample risk pyramid. The investments on the bottom tend to be more stable, but also tend to return less over the long run. Those on the top tend to have higher long-term returns but with precipitous drops in down years.

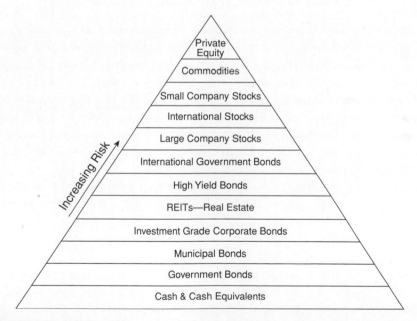

Figure 11.1   Risk Pyramid

NOTE: The risk (volatility) of these asset classes will vary at different times in the economic cycle and depending on market conditions. This graphic should give you a general idea of the relative risk of these asset categories. At any given time, one given category could be more risky than another. This graphic is for illustrative purposes only. No investment decisions should be made based on its content.

Which asset class is best for you? The simple answer is, all of them. It's the mix of asset classes that brings the greatest return for the least risk. This concept is called modern portfolio theory. It was introduced by Harry Markowitz in a paper called "Portfolio Selection," which appeared in the *Journal of Finance* in 1952. Merton Miller and William Sharpe helped to refine the theory. Thirty-eight years later, in 1990, Markowitz, Miller, and Sharpe shared a Nobel Prize "for their pioneering work in the theory of financial economics."

It is helpful to get a general idea of how risky an asset class is by itself, but it is more useful to combine this knowledge with an understanding of how each asset class relates to other asset classes. Investors make a common mistake when they pick one category, for example, bonds, whose risk/return characteristics make them comfortable, but fail to understand that it is the mix of categories that matters as much the categories themselves. Taking this example further, there are mixes of asset classes that provide the same type of return as a bond portfolio but with less risk.

RISKS OF SPECIFIC ASSET CLASSES

When talking about risk, there's a balancing act involved. If you make any investment other than cash in an insured bank account or government bonds that you hold to maturity, there is a risk of loss of capital. Something may happen to the market that results in your ending up with less money than you started with. So for the risk-averse investor, cash and government bonds may look very attractive. But these investments have another risk: loss of purchasing power. Investments you make in them may not keep up with inflation, especially after taxes are taken into account. Your portfolio decisions need to weigh and balance these two opposing risks.

Equities (stocks) have many different kinds of risks associated with them. All equities have exposure to the broad risk of the stock market, also known as *systematic risk*. Systematic risk comes from such things as recession, anticipated high inflation, or high interest rates. These typically are environments in which almost all stocks will do poorly.

Market risk cannot be diversified away, but many other types of risk can. *Company-specific risk,* also called *unsystematic risk,* for example, can be diversified away to a large extent. It is the unique risk associated directly with an individual company, so building portfolios consisting of many companies in different industries will do much to reduce company-specific risk. Unsystematic risk includes such things as management competence, product life cycles, and labor problems. It is often measured by beta, which we will discuss later under Measuring Risk.

The risk/return profile of stocks is less attractive than many believe. Over the 30-year period from January 1, 1972, through September 30, 2003,[1] the U.S. equity market (Wilshire 5000) returned 11.1 percent annualized with volatility of 18.1 percent and a maximum drawdown (highest point to lowest point) of –46 percent. Equities have done well over the last 30 years, but if someone had told the people who had 100 percent of their money in stocks that they could lose nearly half their assets in a three-year period, they might have been less surprised by the recent past, beginning in March of 2000.

Private equity and international equities share the above risks, and add some of their own. Private equity normally has liquidity risk and lacks the transparency normally associated with public company stocks. Since private equity is not traded on exchanges, liquidity generally comes with a transaction [sale, merger, or initial public offering (IPO)], so there is a good deal of uncertainty surrounding the timing of when you will get your investment back. If you need liquidity before a transaction occurs, you can sometimes get it, but typically at a very deep discount to the intrinsic value of your investment.

Since many businesses fail, especially in their early years, there is a higher degree of business risk than with public company equities, whose business models and markets have been validated. Valuation of private equity is very difficult to determine because private businesses frequently have short histories, and complex structures or accounting practices, or are in emerging parts of the economy where comparable companies are difficult to find.

For this reason, private equity investments are generally most successful when handled by professional investors with specific industry operating experience and contacts. It is generally accepted to think of private equity return targets in the range of 15 percent to 25 percent depending on the type of private equity you invest in and the market environment. But there are periods like the mid-1980s to early 1990s when private equity returns were much lower—in the single-digit range. Data on private equity is generally less easily accessible than public company data, so be careful of drawing too many conclusions from private equity statistics.

International equities, although generally quite liquid, share some of the accounting transparency issues of private equity. International equities as represented by the EAFE index had a compound annual return of 10.5 percent over the 30-year period mentioned above with a volatility of 19.2 percent and a maximum drawdown of –46.3 percent. Like U.S. public equities, private equity and international equities typically do well in periods of solid economic growth and low inflation.

Commodities, also called *real assets,* include precious metals, energy resources, livestock, grains, and other foodstuffs like coffee, sugar, and orange juice. They trade on their own special exchanges. They have a low correlation to investments like stocks but tend to be very volatile. By themselves, commodities are very risky, but when combined with other asset classes, the low correlation can make them a useful diversifier. Commodity prices are affected primarily by supply and demand, which manifest themselves through factors such as weather patterns and political situations, as well as the overall health of the underlying economy. Commodities tend to do well in periods of very strong economic growth and inflation.

To approximate the risk/return characteristics of commodities as a whole, one can look at the Goldman Sachs Commodity Index (GSCI), which represents the prices of commodities in the proportion that they are represented in the real economy (over half is oil and natural gas). Over the recent 30-year period ending in September 2003, the GSCI had an average annual return of 11.2 percent with a volatility of 21.4 percent and a maximum drawdown of –48.3 percent. The highly volatile nature of commodity prices scares off many investors, but the very low correlation with other asset classes should be enough to get people to take a second look.

Real estate investment trusts (REITs) represent a wide variety of different property types and capital structures, each with its own risk characteristics. They are generally considered to be a hybrid asset class with both equity and fixed-income characteristics. Despite the varied nature of different kinds of REITs, they do have some commonalities, namely, long-term leases and high debt loads. In the best case, the leases help cushion REITs to a certain degree from economic cycles because leases are carefully negotiated and rents have typically been locked in for multiyear periods.

Because REITs generally carry a good deal of debt, economic slowdown can impact them in two ways. On the positive side, their cost of borrowing generally goes down along with interest rates, and this acts as a cushion in an economic downturn. On the negative side, the downturn reduces occupancy levels and the ability to negotiate high rents when leases are renewed. Of course, if there is too much debt, an economic downturn can drive real estate assets within the REIT into bankruptcy. REIT returns over the aforementioned 30-year period have averaged 12.7 percent annually with a volatility of 15.3 percent and a maximum drawdown of –37.0 percent. Generally, REIT returns are in line with equities over long periods but with a lag, explainable in part by the long leases and sensitivity to interest rates.

Bonds have their own risks. These risks include default or credit risk, liquidity risk, inflation risk, and reinvestment risk. The safest bonds are Treasury bonds. All other bonds are generally priced relative to treasury bonds of the same maturity. Thus, as bonds get more risky, their yields increase relative to treasury bonds to compensate for that risk.

If you hold a bond to maturity and it does not default, you will get the bond's par value plus all of your interest payments along the way. For example, if you buy a corporate bond at par (face value) when it is issued, and hold it until it comes due, you will get the interest rate stated on the bond. When it matures, you will get the bond's face value. However, the company gets into financial trouble, there is a risk of default. The bond you hold could be worthless. That is called, naturally enough, *default risk*. Even if the company does not default, the bond will drop in value during the time that the company's financial stability is in question, so if you need to sell the bond before it matures, you may realize a significant loss of principal. It is hard to know what you will need for cash in 5, 10 or 15 years, so if you purchase a long-term bond, you should understand that you risk losing capital if you want your money back before the bond matures.

Even Treasury bonds have risks associated with them. Like all bonds, they have interest rate risk. If you buy 30-year bonds at low interest rates and then interest rates climb steeply over the next 30 years, your bonds will decline in value and you will realize a capital loss if you sell them before maturity. If you hold the bonds until maturity, you have no interim liquidity in that investment.

If you buy short-term bonds, preferring the liquidity they offer, you have more *reinvestment risk.* Your bonds come due more often, and the interest rates may be lower at that time, so you lose the ability to lock in a rate for a long time.

Inflation, or *purchasing power risk,* can be a big deal over the long run. If your investments don't keep pace with inflation, although they may look as if they're growing, you could be losing ground every year. In an inflationary environment, long-term bonds purchased when rates were low will suffer greatly. The rising interest rates that normally accompany significant inflation will reduce the value of the bonds, and you will be faced with either losing principal value if you sell early to reinvest in more attractive assets, or losing to inflation if you hold to maturity.

Figure 11.2   75 Year Returns of Various Asset Classes
Courtesy of CRA RogersCasey; Data Source: Ibbotson Associates.

Cash and cash equivalents are also affected by purchasing power risk. It can be difficult to obtain a positive return on cash, once inflation and taxes are factored in. But cash is a very attractive asset class when there is a great deal of geopolitical uncertainty or when interest rates are rising rapidly.

When you look at your investment portfolio, you need to take all these risk factors into account. You can have a portfolio that is entirely in bonds and therefore sheltered from any changes in the equity markets. But that portfolio may not keep pace with inflation over time and may experience periods when the principal declines more than 15 percent. Once taxes are factored in, an all-bond portfolio may cause you to lose ground in real terms every year.

In contrast, an all-stock portfolio, especially containing the type of technology stocks so popular in the late 1990s, can be extremely volatile, as those who were expecting 20 percent returns instead saw their portfolios decline sharply in the early 2000s. Over the long run, stocks tend to outpace inflation by a significant margin, but many people find the market swings hard to take.

As you can see from Figure 11.2, you'd be much better off over the long term if your portfolio had been entirely in small-capitalization stocks. But look at the periodic deep dives taken by that asset class. How many people have the stomach for a drop of over 50 percent, especially if you get invested at the wrong time?

MARKET TIMING

Some experts will tell you that market timing is the answer to the problem of market volatility. If you know when the market will decline, simply get out before it does. It turns out, however, that most experts are terrible at predicting market turns. That means there are huge risks to this practice. As an example, during the 912 months between 1926 and 2001 the S&P 500 had an average monthly return of 1 percent. But a great deal of that return was due to the best 64 months, or only 7 percent of the total, where the average monthly return was 11.7 percent. If you tried to time the market over this period and you missed the best months, your return per month was 0.02 percent instead of 1 percent.[2] So think carefully before you agree to a market timing strategy.

MEASURING RISK

We already have talked about how certain investments are more volatile than others. Economists and statisticians use certain standard techniques to measure that volatility. Some of the most common measures are beta, variance, and standard deviation.

Beta is calculated through regression analysis. It adjusts returns for risk. Stocks with a beta of more than 1 (more than the market) are more volatile, and those with a beta of less than 1 (less than the market) are more conservative. In a diversified portfolio, the beta of a stock is a good summary of its risk properties with respect to the systematic risk, or fluctuations in the overall stock market. A stock with high beta responds strongly to variations in the market, and a stock with low beta is less sensitive to market volatility.

Variance is another term used to describe volatility. If you have a set of data points, it will tell you how tightly all the points are grouped around the mean. Variance is the mathematical estimate of the average squared deviation from the mean. Its square root is called the *standard deviation.*

Figure 11.3 shows what is known as a *normal distribution*. The more spread out the bell curve is, that is, the greater the distance from end to end, the larger is the standard deviation. If you want a more stable portfolio, you want investments whose returns, when combined, form a tighter bell curve—a lower standard deviation.

In addition to standard deviation, financial analysts also use a measure they call *maximum drawdown*. This is the largest percent retrenchment from a performance peak to a performance valley. If you take the highest point an

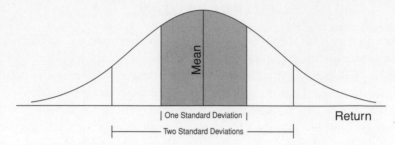

Figure 11.3   Normal Distribution Bell Curve
Courtesy of Windward Investment Management.

investment reaches before it begins to fall and follow it down to its lowest point, you have the maximum drawdown. Ask your investment managers what their largest cumulative drawdown (decline) has been since they started managing money, and this will give you an idea of the kind of risk you might be taking.

RISK-ADJUSTED RETURNS

The *Sharpe ratio* was developed by Bill Sharpe to measure risk-adjusted performance. To get it, you take the rate of return for a portfolio, subtract the risk-free rate, and divide the result by the standard deviation of the portfolio returns. The Sharpe ratio seeks to analyze whether the returns of a portfolio are because of good investment choices or exposure to excess risk.

The *Sortino ratio* is similar to the Sharpe ratio, except that it uses downside deviation for the denominator, where as the Sharpe ratio uses standard deviation. It was developed to differentiate between good or upside and bad or downside volatility.

Also important are up- and down-market capture. *Up-market capture ratio* refers to how much a manager participates in up markets. *Down-market capture ratio* refers to how much a manager participates in down markets. The goal, of course, is to capture as much up-market performance as possible while not participating fully in down markets.

The magnitude of the ratios may be deceptive if the returns are small. For example, an up-market capture ratio of 200 indicates that the manager captured 200 percent of the index's up market. If the market's return is 0.1 percent and the manager's return is 0.2 percent, the capture ratio is much less significant than if the index return was 10 percent and the manager's return was 20 percent.

When evaluating managers and thinking about how much risk you want to take, ask for these performance variables and compare them to the same measures of an appropriate benchmark over an identical time period.

TAX RISK

Another risk to be dealt with is the risk that the tax law will change after you have a strategy in place that fits the current law. Recently (May 2002), the United States signed into law broad cuts to the dividend and capital gains taxes. Such a change likely will result in more companies paying dividends or increasing dividend payout rates already in place, and might make some stocks as attractive as bonds for income purposes. It will also make holding stocks outside of retirement plans more attractive. You can't plan for tax law changes, but when a significant one occurs, it is certainly worth discussing with your accountant and financial advisors.

HOW DO YOU MINIMIZE RISK?

Most of us have a limited tolerance for risk, at least for downside risk. (No one seems too upset when the market goes up by 500 points.) We want to minimize risk and maximize return. What's the best way to do this?

All the research points to broad diversification. It is important to diversify because different asset classes perform differently in response to various economic conditions. For example, Treasury bonds typically do well in times of economic slowdown, equities in times of stable economic growth, hard assets in times of political uncertainty and U.S. currency devaluation, and cash when there's a credit crunch (either from very high interest rates in an overheated economy, or because banks are not willing to lend because the economy is so bad).

To minimize risk and maximize return, your portfolio should contain elements of many asset classes. Every asset class has a relationship to every other. The degree to which they relate, that is, move together in response to economic conditions, is measured by their *correlation coefficient*. When building a portfolio, you want to hold assets that do not correlate. That way, part of your portfolio will always be performing well, no matter what the market conditions.

	Wilshire 5000	U.S. 10-yr T-Bond	U.S. T-Bills	REITs	EAFE	Intl Govt Bonds	Gold	GSCI	U.S. Inflation
Wilshire 5000	1.00	0.17	-0.01	0.57	0.56	0.09	0.00	-0.02	-0.06
U.S. 10 yr T-Bond		1.00	0.02	0.23	0.16	0.32	0.01	-0.05	-0.11
U.S. T-Bills			1.00	-0.04	-0.05	-0.11	-0.06	-0.01	0.47
REITs				1.00	0.36	0.15	0.00	-0.01	-0.05
EAFE					1.00	0.28	0.19	-0.01	-0.10
Intl Govt Bonds						1.00	0.08	0.00	-0.08
Gold							1.00	0.26	0.10
GSCI								1.00	0.06
U.S. Inflation									1.00
Comp. Annual Return	11.05%	8.42%	6.52%	12.68%	10.51%	10.69%	7.11%	11.19%	4.86%
Annual Std Dev.	18.10%	8.48%	0.86%	15.25%	19.18%	13.82%	24.66%	21.35%	1.26%
Max Drawdown	-46.34%	-15.93%	0.00%	-36.97%	-46.30%	-24.04%	-61.69%	-48.25%	-0.46%

Figure 11.4   Correlation, Return, and Risk of Various Asset Classes (1/1/72 to 9/30/03)
Courtesy of Windward Investment Management; Data Source: Ibbotson Associates.

Figure 11.4 shows the correlation coefficients of the most common asset classes. The number 1 represents a perfect correlation. The more closely one asset class resembles another in its response to economic conditions, the closer their correlation will be to 1. You can see that while U.S. and international stocks are quite highly correlated with each other, they are not correlated with gold or other commodities. Bonds lie somewhere in the middle, as does real estate.

HOW DO YOU MAXIMIZE RETURN WHILE MINIMIZING RISK?

The key to constructing portfolios with the lowest risk for any given return lies in using what modern portfolio theory calls *The Efficient Frontier* (see Chapter 8). The efficient frontier is a concept developed by Harry Markowitz and Bill Sharpe, of Nobel Prize fame. The frontier is calculated by graphing rates of return and standard deviations for various securities and for the portfolios one can develop from them. The boundary of this collection of points is the efficient frontier. If you choose a portfolio on the frontier, you get, according to Sharpe and Markowitz, the best possible return for any given level of risk.

Where your portfolio should be on this frontier depends on your own tolerance for risk. If the ups and downs of the financial markets don't bother you, then put more of your portfolio (but not all of it) into more volatile assets. One of the most important research findings coming out of modern portfolio theory is that a mix of investments that are not perfectly correlated will provide a higher risk-adjusted return than any one of the investments alone.

The most efficient portfolios include assets that are as uncorrelated as possible but each with positive expected returns. In statistical terms, this effect is due to lack of *covariance*. The smaller the covariance between the two securities—the less correlated they are—the lower is the volatility of a portfolio that combines them.

TIME AND RISK

The likelihood of achieving expected return increases with time. Said another way, risk of loss relative to one's starting principal value tends to decrease with time, as demonstrated in Figure 11.5.

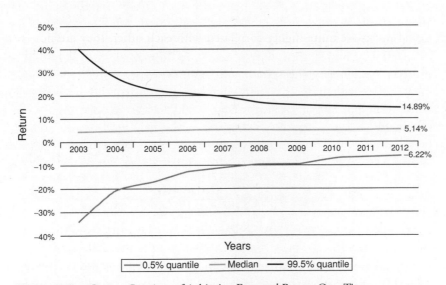

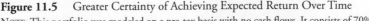

Figure 11.5   Greater Certainty of Achieving Expected Return Over Time

NOTE: This portfolio was modeled on a pre-tax basis with no cash flows. It consists of 70% Large Cap Equities and a 30% Aggregate Bond allocation. The simulation uses annual portfolio rebalancing to continue that original allocation. This simulation is for illustrative purposes only. No investment decisions should be based on its content.

Courtesy of CTC Consulting.

The financial markets have their peaks and valleys. Time gives those rough edges a chance to smooth out. Small-company stock prices, for example, can vary enormously from period to period. If you looked at those variances on a daily, monthly, or yearly basis, the chart would look like the Rocky Mountains, but back away a bit, and you can see that, however variable the short term, the long-term trend is sharply upward. In fact, over the past 75 years, through 2002, small-company stocks have outperformed nearly every other investment one could have made.

So why not just own small-company stock? Because modern portfolio theory shows that a mix of investments brings more reward for the same level of risk, or, if you prefer, the same level of reward for less risk; This also is true because, as noted earlier, the short-term ride is too bumpy for just about every investor. The psychic pain conferred by all the periods of downturn is too much to make up for the long-term gains. Remember, a 50 percent drop in value requires a 100 percent rise just to get to break even. If you have a stock worth $40 and it suffers a 50 percent decline to $20, it needs to have a 100 percent growth to return to $40. If you need to withdraw money in a period of downturn, it is all the more difficult to recover to the point where you started. For this reason, stocks and other more volatile investments are best suited for the long haul.

Investment professionals have generally recommended that those with the shortest time horizons keep money in cash, the least volatile type of investment. Those with an intermediate time frame can mix in bonds, while those with a time horizon of 10 years or more should have at least some of their money in the stock market. Taking this to the next level, if you add additional, uncorrelated asset classes to your investment portfolio, you can generally keep your risk level the same while increasing your expected return.

THE PSYCHOLOGY OF RISK

What's been covered so far is mostly statistics and logic. But investing has two parts, the *head* part and the *heart* part. The head part is relatively easy. You could look up mountains of statistics, and construct spreadsheets that could reach from here to Mars. You could have a computer make your investing decisions. But you will never be happy with your portfolio until it *feels* right.

What makes a portfolio feel right for you is a combination of many factors. How much education you have in the financial markets is part of it. The more you have, the more comfortable you'll be with investment decisions. This book is a good start.

But there are other things at play here. How was money and investing treated in your household growing up? Was it ever discussed? If so, what were the messages attached to it? Did your family feel anxiety about money? How has that affected you and your own relationship to it? Understanding these things can help you to make better decisions about your own financial future.

In the end, what makes a portfolio right for you? If you can't sleep well at night, you're not correctly invested, no matter what the books say. It's all about your comfort level. Your money needs to be invested in places that let you relax and enjoy life.

HOW MUCH RISK SHOULD YOU TAKE?

You've got to look at a number of factors. How you feel about risk is important. So is your knowledge level. Know the facts. Read each investment's prospectus. Make sure you know its performance history and, equally important, the risk statistics over the last year, over the past 5 years, and over the past 10 years? If your advisor makes promises about performance, get those promises in writing. If you take away anything from this chapter, it is to always look at performance in the context of the risk taken to achieve it.

Trust your instincts. If an investment sounds too good to be true, it almost always is. Remember that there is always a trade-off in any investment between risk of loss of capital and risk of loss of purchasing power. Which one of these two factors is most important to you?

You also need to look at your goals, your net worth, and your cash flow. Can you meet your goals under the current circumstances? If not, are you willing to invest more aggressively, change your goals, or wait longer to reach them? Which trade-offs make the most sense for your life?

Each one of us evaluates risk and reward every day. In your business, risk may have meant investing in an expansion or new project, taking on debt to do so. It may have meant entering into a partnering opportunity not knowing whether the other party could be trusted. In each case, you were putting your capital and reputation on the line. You understood the risks you were taking because you knew the business, so you could take risks that others would not.

As you make the transition from operating a business that you understand to owning a more diversified investment portfolio, you are encouraged to:

1. Initially take less risk than you otherwise might until you understand the investment industry and the investments you are making.

2. Diversify your investments as broadly as possible to protect against major declines and to benefit from some exposure to asset classes that will benefit in each phase of the economy. You have already won the game, so protect what you have made.

3. Figure out how much you are willing to lose, and let this drive your investment decisions. Balance this with the need to fund future financial obligations. Do not let your desired return drive the decision as much as your threshold for losses and your need to keep up with inflation.

4. Keep in mind that the categories you choose and the mix of those categories will drive your overall portfolio risk and your returns to a much greater degree than the specific security selection within the categories.

5. Insist that your advisors give you risk measures of the investments you are going to make relative to an appropriate benchmark. These should include largest cumulative decline, and the other measures laid out in this chapter.

The more carefully you think through your need to keep up with or outpace inflation and the more you consider your ability to withstand declines in your portfolio, the less likely you will be to change from one asset class to another and then to another, trying to capture the hot new trend or make up for a loss in one part of your portfolio or another. If you understand your emotional side and can translate this into the risk and return characteristics of the different broad categories, you will feel in control of your investing and empowered by it.

Notes

1. This 30-year-plus period is used because it begins at the time when central banks abandoned the gold standard, allowing currencies to float freely, setting the dynamics of the market we live in today. It is a period during which the world markets went through boom and bust, inflation and deflation, recession and economic prosperity, and high and low interest rate environments. In short, it is a good test period to judge how different asset classes react to varying economic climates.

2. Sources: Ibbotson, Roger G., and Rex A. Sinquefeld. "Stocks, Bonds, Bills and Inflation: Year-by-Year Historical Returns." *University of Chicago Press Journal of Business,* January 1976; Compustat; The Center for Research in Security Prices (CRSP®) and AllianceBernstein.

3. The author would like to thank Susan Luvisi for her work on the graphics in this chapter.

Additional Reading and Resources

Bernstein, Peter L. *Against the Gods: The Remarkable Story of Risk.* New York: John Wiley and Sons, 1996.

Lowenstein, Roger. *When Genius Failed: The Rise and Fall of Long Term Capital Management.* New York: Random House, 2000.

Taleb, Nassim Nicholas. *Fooled by Randomness: The Hidden Role of Chance in the Markets and in Life.* New York: Texere, 2001.

http://www.garp.com. The Global Association of Risk Professionals trains institutional financial risk managers. Their website has dozens of links to related sites.

http://www.financialengines.com. Financial Engines is a company funded by Nobel Prize–winning economist William Sharpe to help individual investors and institutions model the risks in their portfolios, and the likelihood of achieving specified financial goals.

Author Background

Paula Boyer Kennedy is a Certified Public Accountant, Personal Financial Specialist, and Certified Financial Planner™. She received her MBA in Finance and Accounting from Cornell in 1980. Paula specializes in serving the needs of high net worth families. She was named by *Worth Magazine* as one of the 250 best financial planners in America in 1999, 2001 and 2002. Paula has been featured on National Public Radio, PBS, CNN, and Reuters and has been quoted in such publications as *The Wall Street Journal, The Journal of Retirement Planning, Woman's Day, McCall's, Working Mother* and *Parents.* She is one of the authors of *Ernst & Young's Financial Planning for Women,* published by John Wiley & Sons in January of 1999.

Chapter 12

Fixed Income

Peter B. Coffin

This chapter seeks to answer the basic question I frequently hear from entrepreneurs: "Should I do it myself by building a bond ladder with a stock broker, or should I hire a professional manager to build and manage a bond portfolio for me?"

To answer this question, you'll need a solid knowledge of the bond market as a whole, its participants and how they interact, how bonds are valued, how bonds trade, and the basics of fixed-income portfolio construction.

To begin with, let's look at the overall bond market. In simple terms, the market can be divided into taxable bonds and tax-exempt bonds. Taxable bonds comprise over 90 percent of the over $20 trillion fixed-income market capitalization. These bonds include U.S. Treasury and Agency securities, corporate issues, mortgage bonds, and asset-backed bonds. For the most part, individuals participate in the taxable bond market to a much smaller degree than tax-exempt institutions such as endowments or pension funds. Individual investors purchase U.S. Treasury bills, notes, and bonds for extra safety and liquidity or may participate in the Treasury inflation-protected market (TIPS).

Callable Agency bonds (issued by government-sponsored enterprises such as FNMA or Freddie Mac) also are occasionally popular with individual investors because they offer slightly better yields than Treasuries with an implicit U.S. government guaranty. Less risk-averse investors may find opportunities in the corporate market, including high-yield corporate bonds, but are well advised to do their investing through funds in order to achieve proper diversity and oversight.

Individual investors put the vast majority of their fixed-income money into the tax-exempt municipal bond market simply because, after adjusting returns for taxes and risk, municipals offer a very significant yield advantage over taxable bonds. Calculating the advantage municipal bonds offer is accomplished by "grossing-up" the municipal tax-free yield to an equivalent taxable return. For example, using the current 35 percent top federal tax rate, this means a 4 percent municipal yield equates to a 6.15 percent taxable yield.[1] Although the size of the advantage municipal bonds offer will vary over time, it generally is quite significant and therefore, the remainder of this chapter will focus on the municipal bond market.

The question of whether to use a professional municipal bond manager or to buy bonds through a broker usually comes down an assessment of the value added through professional management versus the management fee. However, what investors often fail to recognize is that an unmanaged brokerage account can have very significant, albeit hidden, costs. These undisclosed costs include not just added mark-ups or missed opportunities, but also costs associated with improper exposure to unforeseen risks. Since an unmanaged brokerage account's performance is not reported and its risks are rarely analyzed, individual investors generally do not understand these costs fully.

The advantage of using a professional money manager begins with the added investment expertise—measured by both the depth of analytical and trading experience and the breadth of market knowledge. The potential for this expertise to add value is based on the view that the municipal market is very inefficient, and therefore municipal bonds are often mispriced. In addition, understanding the potential value added through professional management comes through recognition of the fact that a portfolio's structure matters. In other words, a process that actively manages and monitors risks related to credit quality, interest rate exposure, call (early redemption) risk, and portfolio liquidity should do better than one that accumulates bonds over time in a less deliberate fashion.

MUNICIPAL MARKET INEFFICIENCIES

A number of factors cause the municipal market's inefficiency. To begin with, it is an increasingly retail-oriented market. This trend has been influenced mainly by changes in the federal tax code, which have impacted demand within the market. Tax reform in the 1980s significantly reduced demand from banks and insurance companies. Meanwhile, demand from individual investors strengthened as alternative tax havens were eliminated.

Most individual municipal bond investors are buy-and-hold investors. This is because most individuals buy bonds in order to generate a tax-exempt income stream, not to achieve capital gains. After all, a gain only exists when a municipal bond was purchased at a higher yield than can be attained in the current market. Realizing that gain effectively converts the value of that future "extra" tax-free income into a current taxable capital gain, a trade most investors will understandably avoid.

The buy-and-hold nature of municipal bond investors limits trading volume in the municipal market. Less than one-third of the bonds outstanding in the market are likely to trade over a one-year period and most of what does trade is from recent new issues. As a result, there is rarely any meaningful price or transaction history for municipal bonds, making it difficult for investors to have a clear sense of what a bond is worth. Their ability to know the price at which a municipal bond should trade is further complicated by the fact that there are over 1.5 million different municipal bonds outstanding. In contrast, the corporate market, which is almost twice as large in dollar volume, has fewer than 180,000 bonds outstanding.

The large number of relatively small, infrequently traded bonds gets broken down into even smaller trades as they are distributed among individual investors. Over 80 percent of the trades in the municipal market are in positions of less than $100,000. The median trade size is only $25,000. Therefore, large blocks of municipal bonds are far more scarce than small blocks, so major dealers and institutional investors are often forced to "pay up" and accept lower yields if they want to hold sizable positions. The municipal market's fragmented nature frustrates major dealers—in some cases to the point where they have decided to substantially cut back their presence or even pull out of the institutional municipal bond market entirely. Although a number of large dealers continue to dominate major new issue underwriting and large block trading in the secondary market, hundreds of smaller, more regionally focused dealers continue to thrive in today's municipal market. Much of their success is tied to the market's inefficiency and resulting price disparities, which provide countless trading opportunities.

Trading is further limited in the market by the reluctance of dealers to carry a large inventory of municipal bonds. This is partly due to the fact that it is difficult for dealers to hedge municipal bond positions. Although a municipal bond futures contract exists, it is based on an index that—like most municipal indices—lacks credibility in the market. Dealers don't believe the contract accurately tracks the performance of the market and therefore are reluctant to use it as a tool for hedging. If dealers don't carry a deep inventory of bonds, liquidity suffers, and the spread between what someone is willing to pay to buy a bond and what someone is willing to sell the bond for can be wide.

Individuals choosing the do-it-yourself route are severely disadvantaged by the municipal market's fragmented and inefficient nature. Most individual investors work through just one or two of the hundreds of municipal bond dealers active in the market. Because there is no central exchange, this means they see only a fraction of the market's opportunities. It also means they are ill-equipped to know what a particular bond is worth. This is because buying a bond is a lot like buying a house. Rarely is there a quoted market or transaction history to rely upon in determining a fair price. Instead, value is recognized through comparisons to other market offerings and activity. In the real estate market, this process is facilitated by the multiple listing service (MLS). Unfortunately, the municipal market has no such central exchange. Moreover, unlike brokers in the real estate market, municipal bond dealers own the inventory they offer and their markups (profits) and commissions are undisclosed. The higher are the commission and markup, the more profitable are the sales and trading. Clearly, this puts the dealer's interests at odds with those of the client. In an inefficient market with limited price transparency, this makes individuals quite vulnerable.

It is important to recognize that when a professional manager uncovers a value in the marketplace, that value is passed along to the client's portfolio. There is no markup or "spread" added to the transaction.[2] A manager's only compensation comes from an asset-based fee. The best way a manager can ensure continuing to receive that fee is to add as much value as possible to the portfolio within the appropriate risk parameters. In this way, the manager's incentive is completely aligned with the interests of the client.

Professional managers can exploit trading inefficiencies in the municipal market by maintaining relationships with hundreds of municipal dealers. In fact, a manager's window into the market is potentially much wider than that of most dealers, who have less access to bonds simply because the vast majority of the municipal market is controlled by their competitors—other dealers. As an institutional customer, professional managers are given priority by dealers in access to new issues along with secondary market bids and offerings. Not only does this help ensure the best execution in trading, it also means the manager is extremely well positioned take advantage of market inefficiencies. When coupled with a high level of expertise, this offers the potential to add an enormous amount of value through security selection.

PORTFOLIO CONSTRUCTION

A well-structured portfolio will generate larger amounts of tax-free income with significantly less volatility when compared with a less thoughtfully built portfolio. It is difficult to create or maintain appropriate structure in an unmanaged account because individuals in retail accounts tend to accumulate bonds over time, frequently losing sight of their portfolio's overall structure. A managed portfolio, on the other hand, receives ongoing attention to ensure that all the securities work together to reflect a client's objectives, risk parameters, and state of residence. Furthermore, a managed portfolio minimizes credit and liquidity risk, balances interest rate exposure, manages call/ extension risk, and considers tax implications, all the time seeking an optimal balance between risk and return. Most individual investors lack the tools and/or the market access to monitor and manage these characteristics.

DURATION—A PORTFOLIO'S SENSITIVITY TO CHANGES IN INTEREST RATES

Investors often attempt to predict the timing and magnitude of interest rate changes. They rarely succeed with any consistency. There are simply too many variables that can influence short- and long-term moves in interest rates. Geopolitical and economic factors impacted by both market forces and policy makers with differing agendas drive interest rates and inflation. Thousands of sharp minds participating in the credit markets analyze these factors every day. All of this information is quickly distilled into a yield curve—the product of the market's collective wisdom. Rather than trying to second-guess the market, investors are better off trying to hedge and balance their interest rate exposure.

Since no one can really predict where interest rates will be from one year to the next, portfolios should avoid a concentration along any part of the yield curve. This is the premise behind building a laddered portfolio. Laddering—or having a certain amount of bonds coming due in each year—achieves this diversity and thus a more balanced interest rate exposure.

Active management of municipal bond portfolios does not reject the concept of laddering a portfolio. It simply attempts to improve upon it. The municipal market is inefficient and as such requires some measure of flexibility in constructing portfolios. Laddering is often too rigid and constrained—leading to missed opportunities. Improved portfolio management systems allow portfolios to be structured more opportunistically while still maintaining the degree of diversity and balance in interest rate exposure sought by a ladder.

The question then becomes how far to extend out the yield curve. Ordinarily, the longer a bond's maturity, the higher is its yield. This relationship compensates for the risk that rates will rise in the future, leaving the investor locked into a below-market rate of return and a loss in market value. Longer maturities are useful because they provide more yield and add stability to a portfolio's income stream—sustaining it through periods of low interest rates. Conversely, short-term bonds add stability to a portfolio's market value and a hedge against higher rates. A portfolio with a significant short-term bond allocation can take advantage of a rise in rates to build its income stream.

Although there is no one right answer, an average maturity of around five years usually represents an appropriate level of interest rate exposure for an individual portfolio. Five years happens to be generally viewed as an approximate length of an interest rate cycle. A portfolio with an average maturity of 5 years might include bonds maturing from 1 to 10 years, or slightly longer depending on factors such as tolerance for market volatility, need for income, or any potential need for liquidity in the foreseeable future. Investors who are tempted to buy very long-term bonds should understand they are locking in a return for a period beyond which one can reasonably predict inflation. This was the lesson learned in the 1970s, when bonds were nicknamed "certificates of confiscation" as inflation rose above yields at which many bonds were originally purchased. Conversely, those favoring a significantly shorter average maturity put the portfolio's income stream at risk by ignoring the threat of deflation—such as that experienced by Japan, where interest rates on 10-year government bonds hovered around 1 percent for more than a decade.

It is important to keep historical trends in interest rates in the proper perspective. Most investors focus too much on changes in nominal rates and, therefore, fail to understand underlying trends in real interest rates and inflation expectations. For instance, while nominal rates are currently (early 2004) at or near 40-year lows, real interest rates (nominal rates minus inflation expectations) remain well within a more normal range.

In evaluating a portfolio's interest rate exposure, maturity tends to be a pretty crude measure of when a bond is likely to pay back its principal. Bonds often have call features, sinking funds, or premium coupons, all of which may return capital prior to the stated date of maturity. In short, maturity is simply too broad a bucket. For example, consider the difference between a zero coupon bond with a 10-year maturity and a premium, high coupon bond with a 10-year maturity and 5-year call. Both bonds have the same maturity but very different levels of interest rate exposure. If interest rates rise, the zero coupon bond will decline in value much more rapidly than the premium, high coupon bond.

To better analyze interest rate exposure, one must analyze all of the bond's cash flow—not just its principal payments. This is achieved by calculating a bond's *duration*. Duration equals the weighted average life of the present value of a bond's cash flow. It provides a very useful measure with which one can analyze how a bond or portfolio will perform under different interest rate scenarios. Generally, for a 1 percent change in interest rates, the percentage change in a bond portfolio's market value will be equal to its duration. For instance, if a portfolio has duration of four years, a 1 percent rise in rates would cause its market value to fall by about 4 percent.

A municipal portfolio's maturity/duration structure should take into consideration the relative value of municipals along the yield curve. Normally, as shown in Figure 12.1, municipal yields offer an advantage over taxable bonds that increases as maturities extend. There are two primary reasons for this. First, it is a reflection of the fact that buying municipal bonds involves some speculation on future tax rates and their continued tax-exempt status. The longer the maturity, the greater are that uncertainty and risk. Higher yields relative to taxable bonds are offered to compensate for that risk. The second reason has to do with a persistent technical imbalance of supply and demand in the market. Municipal borrowers prefer a level debt service structure (not unlike a home mortgage), which means principal payments on their bond issues are weighted towards longer maturities. Yet buyers of municipals, primarily individual investors, tend to prefer short or intermediate bonds. The

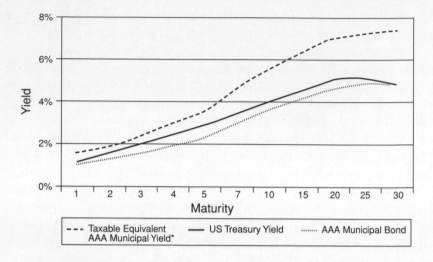

Figure 12.1   Yield Comparison—Municipal vs. Treasury (9/30/03)
*Assumes a 35% Federal Tax Rate
Courtesy of Breckinridge Capital Advisors; Data Sources: Municipal Market Advisors, Bloomberg.

result is that prices are bid up for short and intermediate bonds, whereas longer bonds must offer higher yields to attract sufficient demand.

LADDERS VERSUS BARBELLS

The optimal maturity structure of a bond portfolio will be impacted the steepness of the yield curve. Generally speaking, in a normal yield curve environment, the curve is quite steep in the first 10 years, after which time it begins to flatten out. This means that in the earlier years, an investor receives greater compensation for owning longer-maturity bonds. As one moves further out the yield curve, the incremental gain in yield typically becomes less and less attractive given the additional risk, although this is not always the case. If the expectation is for the shape of the yield curve to flatten, as is the normal trend during an economic recovery—with short rates rising more than long rates—investors may prefer a more barbelled maturity structure favoring a combination of long-term (although longer than 15 years is not recommended) and short-term maturities. In this scenario, the intermediate part of the yield curve has historically experienced a greater rise in yields than long-term bonds—so much greater that, in fact, the decline in market value of intermediate-term bonds has actually exceeded that of longer-duration, higher-yielding bonds. Thus, a barbelled structure has often proven more defensive during this phase of an interest rate cycle. Conversely, an investor will do better with a laddered portfolio, overweighting intermediate maturities, during periods of economic weakness when the yield curve steepens.

CREDIT QUALITY AND DEFAULT RISK

Credit quality is of paramount importance to municipal bond investors. The market's reputation for safety has been established over more than 150 years, through wars and depressions, with municipal bonds proving to be a highly resilient investment. Municipal bonds are safe mainly because municipalities rarely go out of business. In fact, no state has defaulted on its general obligation debt since 1840. The issuers of general obligation bonds or essential service revenue bonds effectively have perpetual monopolies with an exclusive franchise and complete rate-setting and/or taxing authority. It also is important to note that municipal credit quality is not the result of astute management or immunity to economic cycles. In fact, in both cases the reverse is more often true. A municipality's financial performance may vary widely over a business cycle, but ultimately bondholders are extremely well protected. This has been demonstrated on countless occasions, most recently with Orange County, California. Despite terrible mismanagement resulting in multibillion-dollar losses and the county's bankruptcy, it is a little-known fact that all bond holders received all payments of principal and interest when due. According to a recent study by Moody's, between 1970 and 2000, there were no permanent defaults of investment grade (Baa-rated or better) general obligation or essential service revenue bonds.[3] During the same period, only 0.12 percent of other investment-grade municipal bonds issuers defaulted.

Although the municipal market continues to grow, its expansion is limited by restrictions on issuance at the state and local level and by limitations by the Internal Revenue Service (IRS) on what constitutes a valid public purpose and is eligible for tax-exempt financing. These factors provide a healthy restraint on the amount of indebtedness incurred by state and local governments because municipalities generally do not issue debt beyond their means to service it. Therefore, traditional municipal issuers have remained extremely safe investments.

Over the past 30 or 40 years, however, there have been numerous changes in the municipal market. Many new types of issues such as hospital, housing, industrial revenue, lease revenue, and project-based financings account for a significant part of today's market volume. Most of these issuers tend to have characteristics that make them more like a business than a municipality. The security of their bonds is therefore impacted by management, competition and the success of their enterprise. Although there are high-quality bonds in these sectors, much greater caution and more careful analysis is required. For this reason most individual investors should limit their portfolios to general obligation and essential service revenue bonds.

Analyzing municipal credit quality should begin with an assessment of the degree to which the issuer/obligor enjoys a monopoly. Investors should then evaluate the stability of the issuing state's economy and demographics, among other factors. It also is important to measure an issuer's debt burden in relation to its resources and operating budget. For general obligation bonds, total debt service in excess of 10 percent of a municipality's expenditures is usually cause for concern. Likewise, total outstanding indebtedness should generally not exceed 3 percent of a municipality's tax base. Financial performance should be monitored, but periodic deficits are inevitable and alone should not be cause for avoiding a particular issue. Opportunities present themselves when investors shy away from certain bonds based on over-hyped news or rumors. Careful analysis can uncover the chance to buy or sell at a favorable price. An example of this might include announcements that a certain state or municipality is going into financial crisis. As investors avoid or sell these bonds without first doing the analysis of the sources of cash flow supporting a particular issue, unwarranted price dislocation can occur.

RATINGS AND BOND INSURANCE

Credit risk is often addressed by buying insured municipal bonds. However, not all AAA bonds are the same. The market sees through bond insurance and other credit enhancements, and prices bonds accordingly—lower. Professional account managers offer many collective years of experience and an understanding of fundamental credit analysis that can look beyond the ratings and appropriately analyze each security to avoid credit risks an individual may overlook.

Most municipal bonds are rated by Moody's, Standard & Poor's, or Fitch. Ratings are useful tool and enhance a bond's market value and liquidity. However, there are substantial inconsistencies in ratings between sectors. It is important to note that municipal bond ratings are not comparable to those in the corporate market. In fact, Moody's concluded in a recent study that virtually any performing general obligation bond or essential service revenue bond would be rated at least Aa3 on a corporate scale.[4] Within the municipal market, ratings are useful only for measuring relative risk with in a sector. For instance, an A-rated general obligation bond will often trade at a lower yield than a AA rated hospital bond—reflecting the market's view that the hospital has more risk regardless of its higher rating. Rating agencies acknowledge this inconsistency.

Ratings should not be relied on exclusively because most municipal bonds are rated AAA because of some form of credit enhancement—usually bond insurance. Bond insurance certainly offers additional protection to investors. Insurers carefully analyze bond issues before pledging their capital to guarantee timely payment of principal and interest. Rating agencies assign insured bonds a higher rating, usually AAA, and thus, insurance enhances a bond's liquidity and market value. Nonetheless, the municipal market makes a significant distinction between insured bonds of different sectors and underlying credits. In fact, investors have grown increasingly cautious about bond insurance. The amount of each insurer's capital in relation to the total amount of guaranteed debt has always been small (about $1 per $150 par guaranteed). Recently, the adequacy of some insurers' capital has become a greater concern as they have moved beyond their traditional municipal business into other fixed-income markets such as asset-backed bonds. These new markets have far less history than the municipal bond market, and thus, the level of risk is less certain. This is not to say that bond insurance should be avoided. To date, there is no evidence of problems. Investors simply should not depend exclusively on bond insurance. It is an enhancement to the credit, not the credit itself.

PRE-REFUNDED/ESCROWED MUNICIPAL BONDS

Investors can come closest to the security of owning U.S. Treasury obligations by purchasing *pre-refunded* or *escrowed* municipal bonds. These bonds are created when a municipality decides to refinance its bonds in advance of a call or maturity date. To accomplish this, the municipality takes the proceeds from a new bond issue and purchases an amount of U.S. Treasury obligations that is sufficient to fund all principal and interest payments on the original high coupon bonds. The U.S. Treasuries are then held in escrow and pledged exclusively to repayment of the now pre-refunded bonds.

HIGH-YIELD MUNICIPAL BONDS

On the opposite end of the risk spectrum, there are significant opportunities in high-yield municipal bonds. However, investors are generally better off investing in this sector through high-yield municipal bond funds or partnerships. Most individuals and many professionals do not have sufficient expertise to analyze and monitor lower-quality issuers. In addition, it is difficult to achieve adequate diversity in an individual portfolio. Finally, high-yield municipal bonds have very limited liquidity under the best of circumstances. Most issues do not trade often enough or with sufficient size to justify a dealer assigning an analyst to follow the issuer. If problems with an issue's credit quality become apparent, investors are unlikely to find any support in the market for the bonds. The choice then becomes selling at a very distressed price or holding the position and hoping for a turnaround.

PREMIUM VERSUS DISCOUNT BONDS

Bonds are often purchased at significant premiums or discounts to par. If a bond is purchased at a premium, income is calculated by charging off a portion of the premium (amortizing) against the coupon each year. For instance, if straight-line amortization were used, a 10-year bond with a 5 percent coupon purchased at a price of 110 would produce a return of approximately 4 percent each year because special 1/10 of the premium or 1 percent would be charged against a 5 percent coupon. If after five years the bond was sold at 105, there would be no gain or loss because by that time 5 points of the premium would have been amortized, leaving the bond with an adjusted cost base of 105. What is most important to note with premium bonds is the fact that some portion of the coupon (equal to annual amortization) always represents a return of capital.

With discount bonds accretion is simply the reverse of amortization. Just as a premium bond's cost is adjusted over time, so too is that of a discount bond. Thus, for a 10-year 5 percent bond purchased at a price of 90, each year 1 percent is added to the coupon to produce a return of 6 percent. After five years, the bond would have an adjusted cost basis of 95. The important issue with discounts is how the accreted income is treated for tax purposes when the bond matures or is sold. This will depend on whether the bond is a *market discount bond* or an *original issue discount* (OID) bond. As the name suggests, OID bonds are bonds that were originally issued at a price below par. When they are sold or mature, the cumulative amount of accreted income is tax-exempt. In contrast, market discount bonds are bonds that are trading significantly below their original issue price. When they are sold or mature, the accreted income is fully taxable as ordinary income.

Since a portion of the return on a market discount bond is taxable, the market demands a higher yield versus other bonds whose income is fully tax-free. To accomplish this, the price of a market discount bond is reduced by an amount equal to the present value of the future income tax that will be owed at maturity, using the top marginal tax rate. In actual fact, it's likely that the bond's price will be reduced even further so as to offer a higher after-tax yield as incentive for investors to purchase it. The additional yield is warranted since market discounts are less liquid and more volatile than their fully tax-free counterparts. Institutional investors recognize this, and thus try to avoid owning bonds that are likely to become market discounts by purchasing bonds at substantial premiums.

Similarly, an individual's account should also be sensitive to tax issues, and seek to avoid market discount bonds that often carry with them undesirable capital gains and limited liquidity. Such an account should seek out premium bonds, which typically trade more easily, are less volatile, and present less risk in a rising interest rate environment.

CALL (EARLY REDEMPTION)

A substantial number of municipal bonds can be redeemed prior to maturity. There are four different kinds of redemption features: *optional redemption, mandatory redemption, special redemption,* and *extraordinary redemption.* Individual investors frequently overlook call risk, and their portfolios suffer accordingly.

OPTIONAL REDEMPTION

Optional redemption is when the issuer has the right to call the bond, which means prepay it at a specified price (usually par or a slight premium) and date. When buying a callable bond, investors must value both the bond and the call option. In effect, the investor is buying a bond and selling a call. An investor should be paid for the call by earning more yield than he or she would earn in owning a similar noncallable bond. Assessing how much to get paid is the difficult part. Option pricing models value the call by attempting to determine the probability of it being exercised—a function of time, volatility, and current price. The convention in the municipal market is much simpler. Bonds are traded *yield-to-worst,* which simply means if the call is *in the money* (usually when the market yield is sufficiently below the coupon), the presumption is that the issuer will exercise it and refinance the bond. Thus, the call date becomes the effective maturity date. This practice has a tendency to overestimate the probability of a call being exercised and thus creates opportunities. Often a high coupon bond can be purchased and held beyond its call date, meaning an investor earns a higher coupon for longer than expected.

MANDATORY REDEMPTION

Mandatory redemption is typically associated with sinking fund payments. Bonds with sinking funds pay off a predetermined amount of principal over a number of years. The actual selection of individual bonds (usually in $5,000 denominations) occurs by Depository Trust Company (DTC) lottery. Investors should avoid paying a premium for bonds with active sinking funds unless the position is large enough—at least $100,000—to enable accurate calculation of its average life.

SPECIAL REDEMPTION

Special redemptions typically are calls that occur due to prepayments on the underlying mortgages of housing bonds. Again, investors should avoid the paying a premium for bonds with special redemption features unless there has been a thorough analysis of the issue.

EXTRAORDINARY REDEMPTION

As the name implies, extraordinary redemption occurs under unusual circumstances. For instance, most bond indentures have provisions whereby bonds are prepaid with the proceeds from insurance payments due to damage or destruction of a facility.

CONCLUSION

Individual investors' tax-exempt bond portfolios generally suffer from neglect, whereby risks are ignored or not understood, and opportunities are missed. Most brokerage clients don't know how their portfolio is structured, what risks they are taking, or their execution costs. Because the municipal market is fragmented, not centrally traded, and relatively illiquid, most investors (and some professionals) lack the analytical tools and market access to construct a portfolio that appropriately meets their specific needs. A proactively managed account with oversight from an experienced portfolio manager, however, offers investors the market access, security selection, and—most importantly— suitable portfolio structure to achieve a safe, reliable tax-free income stream while preserving capital and minimizing risk.

Notes

1. Although valid for federal tax purposes, this example does not represent a true yield calculation and does not take into account state income taxes, if applicable.
2. Some advisors are also dealers (i.e., wolves in sheep's clothing).
3. Lisa Washburn. *Moody's U.S. Municipal Bond Rating Scale.* New York: Moody's Investors Service, 2002.
4. Ibid.

Author Background

Peter Coffin is president and founder of Breckinridge Capital Advisors, Inc., an investment advisory a firm that specializes in municipal bonds with over $2 billion currently under management. Prior to founding Breckinridge, he was a Senior Vice President with Massachusetts Financial Services (MFS) where he managed a number of municipal bond funds and served on the firm's Fixed Income Policy Committee, which oversaw the management of close to $20 billion in bond portfolios. Peter began his career in municipal bonds as an analyst at The Connecticut National Bank and Aetna Life, & Casualty. He received a BA with honors in Classical Studies from Hamilton College in 1982. He is a member of the National Federation of Municipal Analysts and the Boston Municipal Analysts Forum. Peter also recently served a three-year term on the Municipal Securities Rulemaking Board (MSRB). He has spoken at a number of conferences on topics related to the management of municipal bond portfolios. His comments on the developments in the municipal market have been reported in publications including *The Wall Street Journal, The New York Times, Forbes, The Los Angeles Times* and *Business Week.*

Chapter 13

Global Investing

Lindsey A. Richardson

THEORETICAL BENEFITS
OF NON-U.S. INVESTING

Twenty years ago, U.S. institutions swallowed whole—largely from hungry EuropeZan money managers looking to extend their mature domestic client base—the idea of allocating parts of their pension plans to overseas equities. These money managers backed up their arguments with impeccable academic credentials. Since international markets' correlations were low, diversification into international markets could lower the overall risk of a plan, they claimed, citing Markowitz's modern portfolio theory. More than that, it could also improve return—and here these money managers would triumphantly flourish efficient frontier diagrams. The major problem confronted by our intrepid Europeans at the time was to overcome the U.S. institutions' skepticism of any marketplace other than their own: unfamiliar stocks, irregular settlement practices, over-regulation, radically different accounting methods, and domination—verging often on outright market manipulation—by local brokers and investors.

Compelling as such arguments seemed at the time, it is interesting to assess their relevance in today's world. With the benefit of hindsight, how useful are they?

FORCES OF GLOBALIZATION

First and foremost, the fear factor has largely disappeared in the wave of globalization that has overtaken the world in the last decade. The rise of the multinational giant that derives much of its revenue from economies other than its own has been aided by the relaxation of trade and political regulation. Some of the more prominent international companies have infiltrated the U.S. market so successfully that 90 percent of U.S. consumers may believe them to be American in origin—Nokia and Bridgestone Tire come to mind as good examples. In fact, the line between domestic and international companies is becoming hopelessly blurred. Honda's plants in the United States will soon be manufacturing all the models needed to satisfy its demand in this country; by 2004 it has plans to build models in the United States and re-export back into the Japanese market. How does one categorize the huge multinational oil companies like BP Amoco? Can BP truly be said to have a British identity when it accounts in dollars and has operations all over the world?

The structure of professional money managers began to reflect the changing global complexion some years ago, when analysts began to cover stocks on a global sector basis rather than splitting up their coverage by geography or market. As the world's major economies became steadily more intertwined, it became clear that the best means of anticipating the evolution of U.S. sectors was to look at competition overseas rather than to focus exclusively on the domestic variety. For example, a U.S.-based analyst might have anticipated that Motorola's toughest competition was likely to come from Nokia and Ericsson rather than AT&T; Eastman Kodak's, from Fuji Photo Film rather than Polaroid.

AMERICAN DEPOSITORY RECEIPTS
VERSUS LOCAL STOCKS

Given this background, it certainly is true that more information flow has led to developed international markets gaining in efficiency and becoming less costly for investors. Greater liquidity and transparency have been the by-products of a wave of deregulation that, in the 1990s, embraced open competition. For example, moves to denationalize industries often involved the sale of many government stakes in the large incumbent European and Japanese telephone companies.

These improvements have clearly encouraged U.S. investors to adopt the arguments noted above. Back in 1990, the number of companies with American depositary receipts (ADRs)—essentially a listing on one of the U.S. exchanges (generally the NYSE, NASDAQ, or AMEX) that enables an overseas company to be traded in the United States in dollar terms—stood at around 700. In early 2004 the number was around 1,850. U.S. investment in all non-U.S. equities, including ADRs, was estimated at over $2 trillion from under $200 billion in 1990.[1] From the point of view of the individual investor, the arguments as to whether to buy ADRs or to purchase local stocks directly have evolved significantly. Because ADRs trade and settle in the same way as U.S. stocks do, they are still less expensive and more convenient administratively, particularly for smaller portfolios, than their local equivalents.

Meanwhile, the expansion of the ADR universe affords a wider opportunity than before—albeit one dominated by large-cap companies, but there is at times misunderstanding over their use. Although quoted in dollar terms, they do not protect the U.S. investor from currency fluctuations. Instead, foreign exchange risk is essentially embedded into the ADR's price. For example, if the price of a stock on a local exchange rises by 10 percent and at the same time the currency in which it is denominated appreciates by 2 percent against the dollar, then the ADR should also reflect a 12 percent rise. Handling currency risk in this way may be easier and cheaper than considering it separately; however, as we discuss later, it also denies the opportunity to manage currency actively as a source of added return.

ADR liquidity is another issue that varies widely from stock to stock. The liquidity of an ADR may be superior to that of the local share when there is a high proportion of U.S. ownership; however, the reverse also may be the case.

The question of liquidity can be particularly critical when we consider the large proportion of emerging markets (especially Latin American) companies with ADR listings. ADR investors should not assume that a U.S. listing automatically implies more efficient trading. A number of other assumptions are equally dangerous.

Most obviously, including within an international portfolio companies domiciled in emerging markets introduces political risk of a completely different magnitude from the risk/return trade-off implicit in a discussion of developed equity markets. Political risk can often be difficult to quantify and even more so to anticipate. Although returns from emerging markets can be attractive at times, capturing them can be hard. Even for ADR-listed companies in this category, liquidity can be thin at times and the basis of their accounting statements opaque, to put it politely. Trading directly in the local market may sometimes overcome the problem of liquidity but may give rise to additional expenses, particularly administrative ones: Settlement times in many of these markets are dauntingly long.

Recent corporate accounting scandals illuminate other misperceptions. ADR-listed companies are required to report under U.S.-style generally accepted accounting principles (GAAP) accounting conventions, a practice that until recently was meant to reassure and protect investors otherwise skeptical of overseas standards. In the case of the emerging markets stocks mentioned earlier, it is certainly true that U.S. GAAP accounting requires many of these companies to abide by standards of corporate governance not required in their domestic markets. But the mere application of GAAP alone clearly does not protect the investor from corporate managements determined to manipulate accounting conventions to suit their own interests.

In the aftermath of Enron and other scandals, it is ironic that the International Accounting Standards (IAS), Europe's equivalent of Financial Accounting Standards Board (FASB), are now considered by some as in some areas—acquisition accounting, for example—potentially fairer than those of the United States. The truth of the matter is that neither GAAP nor IAS is better than the other, nor should the submission of an international company to GAAP reporting be considered a proof of its blue-chip nature. Once again, the rule is *caveat emptor*.

DIVERSIFICATION AND RETURNS

The original point of moving into international markets—to diversify away risk and potentially add return—is arguably still moot. As Figure 13.1 shows, international returns have been frustratingly elusive to capture over time, particularly when compared to the alternative of staying at home.

Of course, other forces are at work in mapping these relative returns. The impact of currency is a major one. The inclusion within the Morgan Stanley Capital International's Europe, Australasia, and Far East Index (EAFE) Index of Japan, the world's worst-performing developed market over the last 20 years, is another. Nonetheless, confronted by this pattern of volatility, U.S. investors have traditionally regarded international investing as a higher-risk complement or satellite allocation within a larger portfolio.

Earlier claims of lower correlation are also subject to dispute, as Figure 13.2 shows. It is interesting to see that, although correlations appear to be rising, this does not preclude either the U.S. or the international asset class from each having good years.

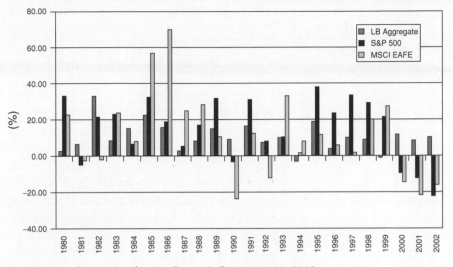

Figure 13.1 International versus Domestic Returns, 1980–2002
Courtesy of State Street Global Advisors.
Data Sources: Lehman Brothers, Standard & Poors, Morgan Stanley Capital International.

Like all statistics, correlation numbers can be argued over *ad nauseam*. One explanation of heightened correlations in the last five years may be the common effect of the valuation bubble across the global telecommunications and tech industries at the height of the market in 2000. Greater convergence in terms of monetary policy by the world's central banks since then is another.[2] It certainly seems probable that the culmination of the late 1990s rally—and conversely, the extreme bear markets since the bursting of the tech valuation bubble—might have contributed to markets behaving in similar ways. It is ironic to note that, just when investors prudently diversified across global equity markets might have expected the forces of diversification to work their benefit, and just when they needed it most, the bear market of 2000–2003 provided little or no respite. Markets have fallen indiscriminately in impressive if unfortunate synchronization.

However, common sense tells us that if international economies have become more closely linked over time, it is no surprise that the correlation of major international developed markets has also been rising. Mention has been made elsewhere in this book of the "deficient" frontier and its drawbacks. Even today the correlation argument is trotted out as a reason that individual investors should consider buying international stocks. If one does indeed believe that globalization is here to stay in both its welcome and unwelcome aspects, it seems dangerous to argue that markets will diverge rather than converge over time.

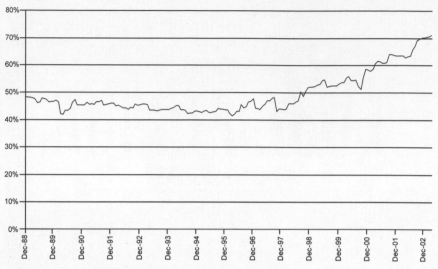

Figure 13.2 Correlations EAFE—U.S. over Last Ten Years
*Each data point represents the correlation of 120 months of the MSCI EAFE Index and the S&P 500 Index relative to each other.
Courtesy of State Street Global Advisors.
Data Sources: Standard & Poors, Morgan Stanley Capital International.

One way round this problem is to include smaller-capitalization stocks and/or an emerging market element in an international allocation. Either of these two have been found to result in a dramatically lower correlation to the U.S. market.[3] However, as we mentioned earlier, the characteristics of these two sub–asset classes can be idiosyncratic and certainly require different disciplines to manage successfully. Successful investors in emerging markets generally focus on country-specific politics first and stocks second. The vagaries of small-capitalization stocks require a deep understanding of each and every individual company selected.

OPPORTUNITY SET

Where, then, is a more sustainable argument for introducing international stocks into a portfolio? Quite simply, the answer may lie not in quantitative confirmation, but in pointing out the expanded opportunities available. The United States now represents around 57 percent of the total capitalization of the world's capital markets as shown in Figure 13.3.

Some of the best companies in the world are headquartered overseas. In an era of borderless investing, why would investors confine themselves to

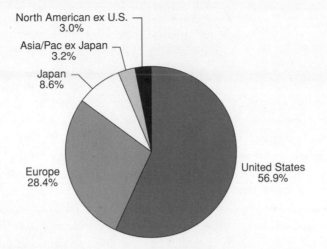

Figure 13.3   MSCI World Regional Make-up (as of 3/31/03)
Courtesy of State Street Global Advisors.
Data Source: Morgan Stanley Capital International.

old-fashioned geography and be deprived of an opportunity to buy some of these world-class companies? There are equally compelling strategic reasons for investing beyond the borders of the United States. Particularly in Europe, corporations have gone through a painful decade or more of cost cutting, aided by the liberalization of previously sclerotic labor markets in some economies. The benefits of this stringency, while showing up in steadily improving returns on capital, have yet to be rewarded in higher stock market multiples. At the time of writing, many world-class companies are trading at multiples equivalent to a 20 percent discount to their U.S. counterparts. Meanwhile, the business environment has changed significantly. Merger and acquisition activity in Europe in 2002 exceeded that in the United States for the first time, with the trend continuing through 2003. Pension reform in some of the major economies, including France and Germany, implies that the local demand for equities over the long term will increase.

GLOBAL MANDATES

The idea of a portfolio consisting of the world's best companies or "best of breed" is stark in its simplicity, yet a logical extension of this idea. For an individual investor in particular the concept of a one-stop shop money manager is appealing in terms of both costs and convenience. For actively managed portfolios that rely heavily on stock selection for their superior returns, a global mandate is even more compelling. After all, if the research function of many professional money managers is organized along global sector lines for the reasons described above, surely it makes more sense to develop one discrete portfolio to reflect the analysts' preferred picks directly.

It is interesting to note that many countries and investors outside the United States came to this conclusion some time ago. Particularly in small, open, and advanced economies—the Netherlands, the United Kingdom, Australia, and New Zealand are good examples—the preferred option for overseas investment tends to be a global brief. Holland's largest investment funds and pension plans were among the first to embrace the concept of global investment many years ago, for obvious reasons. Clearly, there is a great deal more natural reluctance to move overseas if your domestic bias lies in the deeply liquid U.S. market, as opposed to, say, the tiny New Zealand market, in which liquidity is concentrated in relatively few bellwether issues and stocks.

This is the argument that informs many years of discussion in the United States over how much to allocate to overseas markets to achieve optimal diversification. Many of the larger U.S. institutions appear to have allocated around 11 to 12 percent of their assets internationally; some of the endowments and foundations allocate more, reflecting their greater independence of U.S. interest rate–related liabilities.[4] Given that the United States accounts currently for just over 50 percent of the world's developed market capitalization, you could argue that a more rational allocation overseas would approach that order of magnitude after adjusting for domestic investor bias, liquidity, or so-called investibility issues.

Indeed, the definition of *international* investing as meaning *the rest of the world outside the United States* is a uniquely North American concept developed by the institutions. The individual entrepreneur, however, has the luxury of operating from a world where the old institutional traditions need not apply. The application of a global mandate avoids having to justify the appropriate level of overseas diversification for a given level of risk. It is hardly surprising that the most enthusiastic adherents of a global approach have so far come from the individual arena.

CURRENCY

Currency is a major component of international equity returns, as Figure 13.4 shows. Currency exposure and how to manage it are critical elements of investing internationally. These elements sometimes are overlooked, or minimized, by equity managers focused on their core competency—whether this be selecting stocks or overweighting sectors of the equity market to produce return. Contrast this with international and global fixed-income investing, where managers have long recognized that the currency decision often drives returns.

Why are attitudes so different? The far higher volatility of equities over bonds, enabling the impact of currency to be obscured, is an obvious reason. Less obvious is the problem that currency fluctuations, although they can be spectacular, are frustratingly elusive to capture. The foreign exchanges have evolved a long way from the days when fundamental analysis alone, involving theories of purchasing power parity and trade flows and notions of relative under- or overvaluation, could hope to reflect accurately future movements. As many of the equity markets have globalized over the past two decades, so foreign exchange transactions now reflect predominantly speculative rather than trade-influenced investment.

The price behavior of currencies is certainly very different from that of bonds and equities. Although currencies appear to trend in one direction

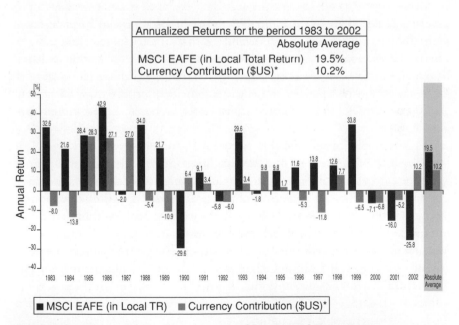

Figure 13.4 Currency is a Major Component of International Equity Returns
*Currency Contribution = MSCI EAFE Index (in $U.S. Total Return) − MSCI EAFE Index (in Local Total Return).
Courtesy of State Street Global Advisors, Data Source: Bloomberg, as of December 31, 2002.

over long periods of time, near-term capture of interim moves can be baffling. Referring to these trends and despairing of capturing near-term ones, some believe that currency moves are a zero-sum game that equals out over time. This argument is used to support the idea of leaving currency unmanaged over time. Academic battles rage as to whether currency markets are the most inefficient in the world or conversely whether they are the most efficient, constantly self-correcting with the addition of each new piece of information. For these reasons many investors regard currency as a separate asset class in and of itself, recognizing once again that the skills involved in active management of currency can be very different from those of a good stock manager.

What is the best solution for an investor looking to move into the international markets? The answer lies in the details of that investor's overall allocation and, as ever, his or her tolerance for risk. Some of the larger institutional plans prefer to use a currency overlay manager who will oversee the different exposures of many specialist managers to ensure that the currency exposure agreed in advance by the plan is adhered to. In contrast, some professional money managers actively manage the currency element of the portfolio, hedging (eliminating nondollar exposure) through forward foreign exchange contracts or futures contracts. The extent to which currency can be manipulated in this way is infinite. For example, hedging may be undertaken either opportunistically (i.e., to defend against an anticipated weakening of the underlying currency) or on a more permanent basis—hedging all exposures, all the time. At the other extreme, the manager can decide to leave all currency exposures open, or to hedge to some proportion—say, 50 percent or 100 percent of the portfolio. The last option tends to be the more popular solution.

As always, the benefits of this exercise can sometimes be outweighed by the costs involved. The cost of a forward hedge can be expressed as the interest rate differential prevailing at any one time between two currencies. Assume that an investor enters into a contract today to sell dollars spot for euros and buy them back three months forward at an agreed rate. If three-month U.S. rates are at 1 percent and euro rates are at 2.5 percent, the cost of putting on the hedge will equal 1.5 percent. Our investor is protected against any fluctuation in the exchange rate, but at a cost. Should the interest rate differential narrow inside three months, the investor's opportunity cost will increase—meaning that the investor would have been able to put on the hedge at a lower cost at that point.

Nor does a 100 percent hedged strategy necessarily mean that the impact of currency moves can be ignored. Neutralizing currency exposure can protect returns when the dollar is strengthening against other currencies, but can deny investors the opportunity to reap the translation benefits of a weaker U.S. unit when overseas holdings are translated back into dollars. What a fully hedged international strategy does provide is access to a different opportunity set of overseas assets, be they stocks or bonds, stripped of the volatility potentially conferred by open currency exposures.

SELECTING MANAGERS

The decision to hire a manager for international or global equity raises in lights some of the thornier issues discussed above. U.S. money managers as a group generally are used to running domestic and international strategies discretely; managers with a separate and distinct global product are few and far between, in the United States at least.

Potential investors also need to consider whether the organization of the manager is appropriate for their particular style. For example, an active international manager holding mostly large-cap stocks may claim legitimately that increased information flow allows adequate research coverage from a centralized location in the United States. In contrast, a competitor specializing in the less efficient small-cap international arena should certainly be able to point to significant research resources across the globe in different regions. This is even more the case for managers covering truly emerging economies, given the idiosyncrasies of local markets. Only recently, for example, settlement in the Indian market could take up to a year; even this time frame looked hopelessly optimistic a while back when a fire in the back room of the Bombay Stock Exchange destroyed all existing paper stock certificates.

Given these (not atypical) problems, it is critical for any manager covering these more arcane markets to have a local presence in the area and knowledge of trading practices and administrative minutiae. From the investor's point of view, the question of whether to choose a manager who favors centralization versus local input thus depends largely on style. Beyond this, in practice both management philosophies have advantages as well as drawbacks: Centralization may lead to focus or myopia, local input to original research or dislocation of thinking.

Perhaps the most dangerous trap of all in the context of selecting an international manager lies in the increasing tendency to break down individual asset classes into distinct styles. In recent years, the dreadful absolute performance of international markets as a whole has led consultants and institutions alike to extend the concepts of value and growth into the international arena in an attempt to avoid the whipsaws seen over the period from 2000 (when markets and many growth managers peaked) to 2003. The problem here is that the methodology used to do so has been crude at best. The Morgan Stanley Capital International (MSCI) EAFE index is widely used among international managers as a proxy for world non-U.S. developed equity market returns. MSCI also splits this index into value and growth subindices purely with reference to price-to-book metrics: The top 50 percent of the stocks with the highest price-to-book ratios are deemed *growth* and the lower 50 percent, *value.*

The extraordinary volatility of international markets witnessed in the last three years has emphasized the shortcomings of these classifications. As value stocks have appreciated and growth equivalents sold off, a number of companies have migrated between value and growth indices without their underlying characteristics necessarily changing. Consider a company like Vodafone, the U.K. telecom company that many would classify as one of the world's quintessential growth stocks. On the strength of its lower price-to-book ratio, this is now classified as a value stock.[5]

Why should this matter to potential investors? First, migration of stocks between style indices may give rise to a convergence of return among managers with supposedly different styles at precisely the time when complementary approaches are needed most. The straightforward classification of a manager as growth or value may give investors less help in evaluating how that manager is likely to perform in certain environments in the future than other, more basic characteristics. Other factors, such as credit quality or particularly capitalization biases, may weigh more heavily on a manager's returns over certain time periods.

CONCLUSION

What is the entrepreneurial investor to make of all of this sometimes conflicting information? If one accepts that the concept of globalization is irreversible, it seems that a process of simplification along the following lines would help:

1. Abandon old-fashioned notions of country or region. Consider consolidating large-cap exposure under one single global management mandate. After all, the professional skills required to identify truly dominant companies should vary little, given the convergences seen over the last number of years, among the major developed markets. For a manager espousing a global outlook, one super-portfolio should represent the culmination of this process. It is vital that consistent thinking inform

stock selection in this type of mandate, and thus one centralized approach to decision making is preferable.

2. For less efficient areas of investment such as the emerging markets or international small-cap stocks, a specialist manager may be a better route. Successful investment in these markets still needs analytical personnel on the ground in the various investment centers. Operations structured in this way may be found among a number of the smaller niche boutiques or occasionally within a large group that has dedicated resources to this type of specialist investment approach.

3. Beyond these recognized asset classes, over the next decade or so there are likely to be other emerging opportunities even more difficult to capture by direct investment, yet potentially even more lucrative. China's recent acceptance into the World Trade Organization is just one step of many marking its steady emergence as a world economic power. Other high-growth centers, mainly in Southeast Asia, also are worth considering. Although accounting practices there remain opaque or nonexistent, a small allocation via a third-party investment such as a closed-end fund may be appropriate for the higher-risk investor.

4. Given the challenges of capturing currency upside, a more practical approach may be to accept the role of currency in diversifying returns from the domestic market. Leaving the currency element unhedged saves the individual investor time and money (in terms of manager selection and accounting headaches) if one is prepared to accept some opportunity cost over the medium term.

Notes

1. Sources: Salomon Smith Barney, Bank of New York. Estimates of US investment in local markets overseas are notoriously imprecise and difficult to pinpoint; but the relative growth of the trend is clear from Salomon Smith Barney's collation of data from 1990 onwards.

2. For a more thorough discussion of these arguments, see Fender, William E. "Why International Equities Belong in a Diversified Investment Portfolio," *Journal of Investing,* Winter 2002.

3. See Sinquefield, R.A. "*Where Are the Gains from International Diversification?*", *Financial Analysts Journal,* January/February 1996.

4. Source: Greenwich Associates. Given that endowments and foundations are obligated to distribute a certain percentage of their income as grants each year, they can often afford to adopt a more pragmatic approach to asset allocation than pension plans wedded to more actuarial assumptions.

5. For a more thorough discussion, see The Style Turnstyle, internal research published by State Street Global Advisors. This presentation demonstrates how the
flawed definition of style benchmarks leads managers to follow stocks based on
somewhat arbitrary characteristics, including ones far removed from the
underlying company fundamentals. It concludes that a more effective assessment of portfolio risk is required to predict returns more accurately, and
approves the segregation of beta into three component pieces to do so following a concept originally developed at Prudential Securities.

Additional Reading and Resources

Feinberg, Phyllis. "International Growth Looks More Attractive As Managers See
Turnaround on the Horizon." *Pensions and Investments,* March 17, 2003.
Fender, William E. "Why International Equities Belong in a Diversified
Investment Portfolio." *Journal of Investing,* Winter 2002.
Keefe, John E. "Style Search." *Plan Sponsor,* February 2003.
Keefe, John E. "International Equity: The Rethinking of International Investing."
Plan Sponsor, April 2003.
Sinquefield, R.A. "Where Are the Gains from International Diversification?"
Financial Analysts Journal, January/February 1996.
Solnik, Bruno. *International Investments,* 5 ed, Boston: Pearson Addison-Wesley,
July 11, 2003.
http://www.FT.com. This website has numerous articles on the growth of the ADR
market.
http://www.msci.com. This website has updated statistical information on the
MSCI international indices.

Author Background

Lindsey Richardson is a Principal of State Street Global Advisors and a portfolio
manager on the International Growth Opportunities team within the Global Fundamental Strategies group. Prior to joining SSgA, Lindsey was a Director at Barclays
Global Investors' New York office, where she formed part of the portfolio management and marketing teams responsible for two fundamental closed-end country
funds quoted on the New York Stock Exchange: the Asia Tigers Fund and the India
Fund. She was formerly a Director in charge of marketing for the global fixed income
and international equity products at Lazard International Investment Management.
Preceding this, Lindsey was affiliated with the British money manager NatWest
Investment Management Ltd., where she headed the Multi-Currency Asset Management Group, which was responsible for the investment of international and global
bond portfolios. Lindsey started her investment career at S.G. Warburg where she
worked for four years. She has been working in the investment management field
since 1979.

Chapter 14

Real Estate

Nicholas Bienstock with Laura Corwin Burkhart

Looking for an avenue for creating and preserving wealth? Interested in how others have done it? First, look at *Forbes* magazine's "Forbes 400" list. Seven members of the list found their fortunes in Wal-Mart. Five members found theirs in Microsoft. Twenty-seven members—the largest group other than inheritance—found their fortunes in real estate. Great fortunes are made and preserved in real estate.

Academic theory also supports a level of investment in real estate based on the risk-return balancing benefits of diversification. Professor Harry Markowitz's modern portfolio theory, for which he won the Nobel Prize for Economics in 1990, argues that investment strategy should be based on combining investments with varying risk-return profiles, or diversification, rather than on betting on the performance of individual assets. Because private real estate performance historically has shown little correlation with the stock and bond markets, it is an excellent avenue for portfolio diversification. And, because real estate's approximately $3.5 trillion of assets has represented between 10 percent and 20 percent of the total stock, bond, and real estate capitalization in developed countries in recent times, ample diversifying opportunities to balance an investor's portfolio exist in real estate.

The goal of this chapter is to give readers a practical introduction to real estate investing. We begin by discussing the rationale for investing in real estate, why it makes a good investment, and what makes values appreciate. Then, we introduce the various classes of real estate assets, the real estate products in which to invest, and the characteristics of each type of investment class. Finally, we discuss the different channels available to invest in real estate and which channels are most appropriate for which investors.

Given the complexity of investment and ownership of real estate, many investors may neglect to diversify their portfolios with adequate investments in real estate. This chapter hopefully provides a base of knowledge to give readers the confidence to increase the real estate portion of their portfolios, to the make an initial investment in real estate, or to explore the topic further.

WHY INVEST IN REAL ESTATE?

MARKET INEFFICIENCIES PRODUCE OPPORTUNITIES

Real estate investments are everywhere: the condo your neighbor owns, the suburban office building down the street, the retail strip mall where you get groceries, the residential apartment building at the end of the block, and the open piece of land that you drive by each day on your way to work. The market for these real estate investments is just as diverse: homeowners who no longer want to pay rent, individual investors who want to see, touch, and control their investments, groups of investors looking for specific returns, corporations that sometimes forget they own these assets, and institutions such as pension funds and insurance companies who simply want a predictable, long-term investment in hard assets. The wide diversity of real estate investment opportunities and the divergent investment needs, skills, and interests of the buyers and sellers of these opportunities create great inefficiency in real estate markets and therefore create great opportunities for building and preserving wealth in real estate.

The homeowner who needs to sell his or her house immediately creates an opportunity for the buyer who can close quickly. The local government that wants to sell off abandoned industrial buildings that they have acquired through foreclosure to put them back on the tax roll creates an opportunity for a real estate developer who will clean up and redevelop the properties. A downsizing corporation selling off superfluous office space creates an opportunity for an investor who will purchase the space and lease it another tenant. Because reliable, centralized, and widely available information about individual opportunities does not exist, opportunities are presented to buyers who get there first or see something others don't see.

Each real estate asset is unique. Each property is defined by a specific and unique combination of characteristics: location, quality of construction, age, and design, for example. Even identical apartments in a condominium building feature slightly different views and have experienced different levels of wear and tear. The calculus of assigning a dollar value to each of these characteristics to produce a value for each property is equivocal—and often subjective. In other words, translation of the needs of the many, many users of real estate into a market value for a specific property can produce different answers. If an investor believes that the office workers in a certain market will pay more for larger windows in an office space, he may think that a certain property is worth more than the investor who believes office workers are indifferent with respect to windows. Because the market value of a specific property, based on its unique combination of characteristics, is often ambiguous, opportunities are presented to investors who see that a certain set of property characteristics will satisfy the needs of a certain set of users.

LEVERAGE MULTIPLIES RETURNS

Because the useful life of a real estate asset is many, many years, financial institutions will lend a large percentage of the asset's value to the buyer; the loan is secured by the asset. This use of financial leverage not only puts relatively large real estate purchases within reach of many investors but also creates an opportunity for investors to increase the returns on their equity investments exponentially. For example, if an investor buys a $1 million apartment building, borrowing 80 percent of the purchase price, and the building increases in value at a rate of about 3 percent per year, the building will be worth $1,160,000 after five years. If the property is sold and the mortgage debt is repaid, the investor will realize a profit of $160,000 on a $200,000 investment. Thus, a 3 percent annual increase in asset value equates to a 12.5 percent annual leveraged return.

TAX BENEFITS

Because federal and state governments have an interest in individuals' buying and maintaining property, the federal government provides significant tax benefits to real estate investors. Categories of benefits, for homeowners, include mortgage interest deductions and capital gains exemptions; for investors, benefits include the right to defer tax liability from property divestment indefinitely, annual deductions for all real estate investment expenses, and annual deductions for depreciation.

Homeowner Benefits

A number of tax benefits are available to homeowners. First, the federal government gives homeowners the ability to deduct the interest portion of their mortgage payments (up to a mortgage amount of $1.1 million) from their taxable income. This creates a very low after-tax cost of mortgage debt. For example, if a homeowner borrowed $1 million at 6 percent, his or her interest payments would be $60,000 per year. If the homeowner is in the 40 percent tax bracket, he or she would realize a tax savings of $24,000 (40 percent of $60,000). The after-tax cost of the mortgage would be $60,000 − $24,000 = $36,000, or 3.6 percent of the $1 million face value of the mortgage. This is the cheapest borrowing that is available in the market. Property taxes may likewise be deducted from taxable income. Finally, within certain limits, gains from the sale of a personal residence are tax-exempt.

Passive Investor Benefits

Another set of tax benefits are available to passive investors, classified by the Internal Revenue Service (IRS) as those who derive income from rental activities. First, for the purposes of calculating taxable income from rental activities, investors may deduct both operating expenses (property taxes, insurance, water bills, and other costs associated with operating the property) and depreciation (a loss based on property's purchase price and the IRS metric for the property's useful life). Second, selling expenses can be deducted from the purchase price for the purposes of determining the investor's gains from the sale, and these gains are treated as capital gains, usually taxed at a lower rate than ordinary income. Finally, tax-deferred exchanges (rolling the proceeds of the sale of a real estate investment into another real estate investment) give investors the option of deferring tax liability from property divestment indefinitely.

Of course, investors should consult their tax advisors to understand the specific tax implications of an investment in real estate.

OPPORTUNITIES TO CREATE VALUE IN A REAL ESTATE INVESTMENT

Opportunities to create returns beyond the average levels are often available in a real estate investment. Think of the conversion of that vacant warehouse at the end of the street to an apartment building, the under-construction housing development on a formerly overgrown field, or the improvements a landlord makes to the kitchens of his rental apartments. Each of these examples represents an effort by the real estate owner to increase returns by creating value in a real estate asset. Opportunities for creating value consist of enhancing the property's net income stream—increasing revenue or decreasing expenses— or decreasing the risk associated with the property's income stream.

ENHANCING NET INCOME

Increasing revenue and decreasing expenses are two ways investors may create a more valuable income stream. Increasing revenue can be accomplished in a number of diverse ways, some directly controlled by the investor and some a product of the environment and changing market forces:

Physical Changes

Renovating an office lobby or upgrading the kitchens and bathrooms in an apartment building may allow the owner to charge higher rents. More dramatically, changing the use of a piece of property—think of the converted empty warehouse or the new, high-end housing development—creates a rental income stream where none previously existed. In each case, physical changes to a property may improve the appeal of the property to users and thereby increase the income stream.

An Improving Location

The value of some real estate will rise simply due to its location in an improving neighborhood. The rate of property appreciation over time is typically dictated by supply and demand. Growth in jobs and income generally signals an increase in demand for housing, office space, and hotel rooms. As long as supply (new housing developments, new office buildings, new hotels) does not keep pace with demand, the value of existing properties will rise.

Investors may also increase a property's net income by decreasing the costs of operating the property. Examples include implementing more efficient property management, successfully appealing for a reduction of real estate taxes, and negotiating lower-cost insurance.

CREATING A MORE PREDICTABLE REVENUE STREAM

In addition to increasing the projected revenue stream through physical improvements and location within a developing neighborhood, investors may make changes to reduce the risk associated with the revenue stream.

Acquiring Higher-Credit Tenants

Even though the building's lease states that XYZ tenant will pay $12,000 per year to occupy its space, if XYZ goes out of business and cannot pay its rent, investor returns will be damaged. Thus, tenant credit quality determines the predictability of the revenue stream and therefore the value of the property. Therefore, even if rent does not increase, an investor can increase the value of the property by trading a tenant with subgrade credit for a tenant with excellent credit.

Stabilizing the Asset

Other factors, in addition to the credit quality of the tenants, affect the perceived risk associated with the property: high vacancy rates or major deferred maintenance may adversely affect value. To improve the property's appeal, investors may lease empty space or make selective capital improvements to create a more stable asset that has predictable cash flow.

REAL ESTATE ASSET CLASSES

Investors in real estate may choose from a wide variety of asset classes, each with its own set of risk and reward characteristics. In addition to risk preferences, an investor may select an asset class based on personal interests and tastes. An overview of the major asset classes follows.

RESIDENTIAL

Residential real estate—apartment buildings and single-family houses—is often considered the most stable investment asset class. Because people always need somewhere to live, housing will always be in demand. Moreover, as the U.S. population, fueled further by immigration, continues to grow and as the supply of available land for new housing developments depletes, net demand for housing is growing. And, because the risk of an investment in a large residential property is spread across multiple tenants, investor risk is significantly less than in other asset classes. An apartment building investment may hold hundreds, even thousands, of tenants, each with a separate lease. Therefore, investors' exposure due to any single tenant's default is minimal. The performance of a residential real estate investment often tracks the economic performance of the local market: If the local economy performs—if jobs are being created—local residential real estate will also perform.

RETAIL

The same factors that contribute to the stability of residential real estate—long-term overall population and job growth—also contribute to the stability of retail real estate. And the nature of retail real estate—store-front retail, strip centers, regional malls, retail pad sites, and super-regional malls—creates attractive opportunities for investors. First, because leases for retail tenants are often 10 years or more, vacancy risk, leasing commissions, and ownership expenses associated with tenant turnover are smaller relative to many other types of assets. Second, because large tenants act as magnets that attract other tenants to retail centers, securing one large magnet tenant facilitates leasing and mitigates vacancy risk. Third, these magnet tenants often reduce credit risk: Large, national retail companies will likely pay their rent, reducing credit risk for investors. Finally, because retail tenants typically design and build their own spaces to match their consumer brands, major cash outlays to cover improvements to the space are typically the tenants' responsibility, not the owners'. Predicting the performance of these retail assets is similar to that of residential real estate: It generally tracks the performance of the local or regional economy.

OFFICE

As the service economy continues to grow, demand for office space also grows. Notwithstanding the many forays into telecommuting, videoconferencing, and other technology-enabled "work anywhere" strategies, face-to-face interactions and meetings, and the space in which to facilitate them, will always be an important component of doing business. However, office investments, including central business district towers, suburban low-rise space, and "flex" buildings, for example, often present greater complexities and risks than residential and retail asset classes.

First, because office tenants may consist of companies from IBM to Amazon.com to ABC Printing Services, tenant credit quality is sometimes difficult to evaluate. Office investment returns are directly tied to tenant performance, and a single questionable tenant poses a significant risk to the performance of the investment. Next, office leases typically include large capital improvement budgets to configure the space for the tenant; these capital improvements are funded in part by the owner at the outset of the lease. Thus, office investments not only require large amounts of capital beyond the purchase of the building but also expose the owner to significant risk. If the owner spends $100,000 before the tenant moves in to build space for ABC Printing Services and if ABC goes out of business early in its lease, returns will be significantly damaged. The additional risks posed by office investments are often offset by higher projected income per square foot than that for retail or residential investments.

INDUSTRIAL

Industrial real estate, although probably not as familiar to the average investor, is an integral part of the local and national economy. Industrial investments include important subtleties: They require not only a tolerance of the risks associated with a limited number of tenants but also a sophisticated understanding of the dynamics of an industrial building and its users. Industrial real estate investment opportunities—warehouses, distribution centers, single-tenant specialty spaces, and industrial plants, for example— typically have fewer than five tenants; therefore, risk of default is greatly concentrated. And, unlike residential, retail, and office investments, to which the investor may bring personal experience as a tenant, industrial investments often are not intuitively accessible to the average investor. That is, an investor may understand, based on his or her experience as a user, what makes a particular building a good place to live or a nice place to work. However, he or she may not know that, in an industrial building, the required floor load is 100 pounds per square foot or that the optimal ceiling height is 40 feet to accommodate stackable pallets. To invest in industrial properties, an investor must understand the needs of users and be prepared to deal with the risks associated with a few tenants that are in specialized businesses. As with office investments, the risks inherent in industrial investments may be compensated with higher projected returns.

HOTELS

"Hotels aren't real estate" is a common quip from the real estate professional. The idea is that a hotel acts more as an operating business, in which returns depend on the expertise and operating efficiency of the management, than it does as a real estate investment, in which returns depend on predictable inflows and outflows of cash based on stable, long-term leases. The success of investment in a hotel often depends more on the success of the management company in operating the hotel than the bricks and mortar that make up the hotel's real estate. Hotel investment opportunities include tourist (MGM

Grand in Las Vegas), boutique (Ian Schraeger hotels), limited service (Best Western), and luxury (Four Seasons). A real estate investor interested in hotels should look for an opportunity in which a proven hotel brand (called a *flag* in the hotel industry) has a long-term lease on the property and can demonstrate proven cash flow.

In addition to the major asset classes discussed above, other, specialized assets, such as senior housing, medical facilities, mixed-use buildings, and research and development facilities, are available to real estate investors. Because each real estate asset class has specific and varying risks and rewards, prospective real estate investors can match both their risk preferences and personal interests and predilections with the appropriate asset class.

REAL ESTATE INVESTMENT OPTIONS

Now that we have discussed the various classes of assets, we discuss how an investor may participate in each of these asset classes. How should you approach an investment in real estate? Where do you begin? Choosing an appropriate vehicle for your investment depends on your investment objectives, skills, risk tolerance, and personal interests and inclinations. Specific investment options for individuals include:

- Home ownership
- Purchasing shares in a real estate investment trust
- Investing in a real estate private equity fund
- Partnership in a syndicated real estate deal
- Direct purchase of investment property

This section describes each opportunity, discusses the pros and cons of each, and points interested investors in the right direction to learn more.

BUYING YOUR OWN HOME

The simplest and lowest-risk form of direct real estate investment is the purchase of your own home. Overall, as long as you can hold (you can, if necessary, avoid selling) for three to five years, and you have the cash to cover your down payment, closing costs, and mortgage payments, purchasing a home historically has been a solid investment. Why? First, a mortgage payment is at least a partial replacement for a cost that you already may be incurring: the cost of renting. Rather than handing your monthly rent over to a landlord, you are building equity each month in your own investment. Second, the federal government's mortgage interest deduction means that your after-tax monthly cost (mortgage and taxes) will be significantly lower than the mortgage payment. Sometimes, buying is cheaper on a monthly basis than renting. Finally, many types of homes in certain neighborhoods are available to purchase—not to rent. You may find that in order to have the house or apartment that you want, you will need to buy it.

Example: You currently pay $2,000 each month in rent. The purchase price of a comparable residence is $600,000. A simple comparison of your options reveals that renting, on an annual basis, is about 30 percent more expensive than buying. (See Table 14.1) Moreover, if the value your property rises just 3 percent a year (roughly the rate of inflation), at the end of four years it will be worth about $675,000. After paying off your mortgage balance and other selling expenses, you would take home about $200,000, a 66 percent gain on your initial $120,000 investment, over and above the annual cash flow savings.

How to Buy a Home

The best way to investigate the purchase of a home is by using the local brokerage community. Good brokers are invaluable, serving a vital role between buyers and sellers in creating transactions that are acceptable to both sides. A good broker can help buyers and sellers understand the state of the market, can facilitate negotiations and smooth over the issues that often arise, and can

Table 14.1

	Year 1	Year 2	Year 3	Year 4
Rent				
Annual rent payments	$24,000	$24,000	$24,000	$24,000
Tax savings	—	—	—	—
Equity gained	—	—	—	—
Net cost to rent	24,000	24,000	24,000	24,000
Buy				
Mortgage payment*	34,500	34,500	34,500	34,500
Tax savings**	11,300	11,300	11,300	11,300
Reduction of loan principal	5,900	5,900	5,900	5,900
Net cost to buy	17,300	17,300	17,300	17,300
Net annual savings	**$ 6,700**	**$ 6,700**	**$ 6,700**	**$ 6,700**

*Based on 20 percent down payments and a 30-year fixed-rate mortgage at 6 percent.
**Based on 39.6 percent tax bracket.

recommend attorneys, architects, contractors, mortgage brokers, and housing inspectors. In most cases, the seller pays the buyer's broker's commission.

You should see a wide array of houses or apartments before you purchase and should ask the broker to provide you with a list of 10 to15 comparable sales—similar properties that have recently sold. By reviewing these "comps" with your broker and comparing each one to a specific house that you are considering purchasing, you can develop a view on the property's value and its relationship to the asking price. The broker should show you examples of houses that are both above and below your price range to help educate you on what you are getting for the money.

Words of Caution

As mentioned above, the easy availability of high loan-to-value mortgage financing (70 to 90 percent) on attractive after-tax terms creates an opportunity to realize significant returns on the equity you invest in your home—provided that the value of your home has gone up when you are ready to sell. The danger is that if you are forced to sell your home at a time when the value is lower than when you purchased, the same modest decreases in value each year will disproportionately eat into your invested equity. Thus, a buyer looking to increase his or her chances of realizing solid returns on the home purchase will follow two general rules:

1. *Purchase in a proven location.* Good-quality real estate in established neighborhoods tends to increase in value over time, at least in pace with inflation. Fringe, or developing, neighborhoods are susceptible to fluctuations in value that may hurt a homeowner forced to sell at the wrong time.
2. *Be prepared to hold over a long period of time (at least three years).* Planning to hold over a shorter period of time (three years or fewer) increases the possibility that the homeowner will get caught in a short price correction period and get hurt by short-term decreases in value that disproportionately reduce the owner's equity investment. Planning to hold over a longer period of time enables the homeowner to capitalize on the long-term upward trend.

REAL ESTATE INVESTMENT TRUSTS

Real estate investment trusts (REITs), pools of real property assets owned by a company and run by that company's management team, allow investors to participate in real estate markets while maintaining a maximum degree of liquidity and flexibility. Although most REITs invest in a particular asset class across a wide geographic area, some REITs have a fairly narrow investment focus. For example, whereas Equity Residential Trust invests in apartments in major markets across the United States, S.L. Green Realty Trust invests only in Class B office buildings in Manhattan. Although some REITs are privately owned, most are publicly traded investment vehicles.

The advantages of investing in a REIT are similar to those of investing in many funds. First, the investors enjoy liquidity: REIT shares trade on the stock exchange and can be bought and sold like traditional stocks. Second, because the value of the REIT is derived from multiple properties that are often located across different regions of the country, REITs represent an opportunity to diversify risk across multiple assets and multiple markets. Third, REITs are typically run by teams of professional real estate investors and operators, which both contributes to quality control and relieves the investor of any management responsibility. REITs also offer benefits not available through many funds. REITs are required by law to distribute 95 percent of their funds from operations—the REIT equivalent of net income. As a result, they tend to pay high dividends relative to equities. In addition, because most REIT income derives from rent from tenants under fairly long-term leases on fixed contractual terms, the income streams they produce tend to be fairly steady and predictable. Thus, REIT prices are not as volatile as those of many other classes of equities.

How to Invest in Real Estate Investment Trusts

REITs are tracked by the analyst and banking communities and a wide variety of information is publicly available to evaluate individual REITs and to assist investors in making decisions about which to invest in. In addition, various "fund of funds" of REITs exist. These function as mutual funds of REITs, allowing an investor to broadly invest in a preselected cross section of the REIT universe. Investors should look for REITs that are well managed and demonstrate successful track records over a long period of time. Investors should be wary of smaller, less established REITs. Any stock broker can facilitate an investment in a REIT.

Words of Caution

The disadvantages of REIT investment parallel those of other fund investments. REIT investment performance may be closely correlated with that of the stock market. In addition, because an investment in a REIT is an investment in a wide portfolio of properties, the potential for very high returns, inherent in a single asset investment, is reduced.

REAL ESTATE PRIVATE EQUITY FUNDS

Wealthy investors also may invest in a broad cross section of private equity funds that focus on real estate. Unlike REITs, these funds often do not invest in cash-flowing stable assets with long-term leases in place. They are usually higher-risk, higher-return vehicles that invest in value added real estate deals or turn-around situations. These investment vehicles are established by seasoned real estate investors with a demonstrated track record of years of successful investing. They are typically structured as partnerships or limited liability companies (LLCs), and their investors come from a cross section of institutional investors (pension funds, endowments, life insurance companies, etc.) and high-net-worth individuals. Although the size of these funds varies, most are in the $50 to $500 million range. These vehicles can target a specific asset class (regional shopping malls in the United States or Japanese office buildings, for example), or they can be established with broad investment parameters that allow them to invest in any type of real estate in any location.

Investing in a private equity fund offers many of the same benefits of REIT investment and participating in a syndicated real estate deal. First, a private equity fund offers top-tier management with a proven track record. Because the managers of these funds have the opportunity to make a lot of money, they tend to attract very talented, sophisticated, motivated real estate investment professionals. These managers are highly focused on identifying, securing, and delivering very profitable real estate transactions for their investors. The managers' track record, detailed extensively in the offering memoranda, simplifies an individual investor's due diligence and offers investors peace of mind. Second, these professionals often bring investors access to transactions that often are not available to the general public. Third, because these fund tend to focus on value-added transactions, returns can be far greater than the average returns produced by simply investing in stable, cash-flowing real estate assets. Most real estate private equity firms try to generate returns in excess of 20 percent per year on the value-added assets that they invest in. Finally, these funds spread investments over many assets in many locations. The investor in the fund benefits from this diversification and therefore has less exposure to a single bad investment.

How to Invest in Real Estate Private Equity Funds

The typical fee structure of private equity funds is similar to the leveraged buyout fund or venture capital fund structure. Usually, it is a "2 and 20" structure. This means that the managers of the fund often collect an annual fee of 2 percent of funds under management, and they receive an override equal to 20 percent of the profits once all the investors receive a return of capital plus an amount of distributed cash equal to a 10 percent internal rate of return. Given the large size of many funds, the override provides the management of the fund with the opportunity to make a lot of money if their fund is successful. Investors are required by law to be *qualified* and *sophisticated.* This means that they have to be able to understand the risk/reward trade-off of the investment and must be able to lose the money they invest without a risk that their lifestyle will change.

There are many real estate private equity funds; several are associated with banks or other financial institutions. Examples of real estate funds include Whitehall (Goldman Sachs), Blackstone, Blackacre Capital Group, The Praedium Group, Alex Brown Realty Partners, Clarion/ING, and Angelo Gordon.

Words of Caution

One disadvantage of these funds is that the minimum investment is usually $1 million or more. Obviously, this puts participation out of the reach of most individual investors. It is a big sum of money to invest if the fund is not successful. Also, for all practical purposes, these funds, once invested, are totally illiquid. Most of the funds have a five- to seven-year investment horizon, and the investor cannot access his or her money until the fund pays out to investors or is dissolved. The nature of the real estate private equity world is that these funds tend to focus on riskier transactions in order to make the returns that they have targeted. These risks are real, and there are plenty of situations in which the risks are larger or more problematic than anticipated. If several large investments in a fund go bad, it can have a profound effect on an otherwise successful series of investments and will have an impact on the returns of the entire fund.

On balance, if an investor has a large portfolio and can afford to part with the minimum investment during the five- to seven-year investment horizon of the fund, these vehicles are an excellent way to invest in real estate with the most talented people in the business and secure an excellent chance of generating superior returns in real estate.

PARTICIPATING IN SYNDICATED REAL ESTATE DEALS OR JOINT VENTURES

Investors who like the idea of seeing and touching their investments but are not prepared for directly purchasing investment property may want to participate in syndicated real estate deals or other joint ventures. Arranged by professional real estate investors or developers, called *syndicators,* syndicated real estate deals enable investors to purchase property as an investing member in a small partnership or LLC. As with direct investment, the investor enjoys annual returns, equity buildup, tax benefits, and leveraged returns. The difference is that the syndicator takes a percentage of profits in exchange for finding the deal, arranging the financing, and managing the asset once it is purchased.

The control inherent in these types of investments gives the investor significant advantages. First, an investor may review each opportunity on a deal-by-deal basis and decide to invest or not; an investor may decide to invest in those he or she believes to be good deals and pass on bad ones. Second, the investor may often negotiate both the amount of his or her investment and the terms of the deal: A savvy investor whose investment represents a large portion of the deal will negotiate low management fees and secure a high percentage of the upside, especially if dealing with a syndicator that needs equity and does not have many options. Third, the single asset exposure nature of these deals ensures that if the deal succeeds, investor returns may be quite high. Finally, if ownership is structured as an LLC, as is typical, an investor's liability with respect to ownership of the property is limited to the amount of his investment.

How It Works

Real estate syndicators are often small operations with little mass exposure; the best way to find them is by asking friends, brokers, investment advisors, and bankers. A syndicator will find an appropriate deal and present it to investors. If the investors like the deal, the syndicator and investors will form a partnership or a LLC to purchase and own the property. The LLC is run according to a specific operating agreement, outlining the rights and responsibilities of each partner; terms are negotiated by the syndicator and the individual investor. Usually the syndicator serves as the managing member or managing partner of the deal. The agreement usually specifies that the syndicator is responsible for management of the deal and operation of the property; investors' responsibilities include capital contributions and may include decision making about capital events such as sales or refinances, major leases, or capital investments. The agreement also outlines how profits are distributed; generally, returns are distributed to investors proportionate to their equity investment, usually a return of invested capital plus a certain hurdle rate return. Then, returns are split between investors and the syndicator; the syndicator takes a larger share of the returns over the hurdle rate than his pro rata investment. The agreement also includes terms such as fees charged by the syndicator for managing the deal and how the managing member would be replaced.

Words of Caution

Unlike investing with established REITs or real estate private equity funds, there is no measure of credibility associated with real estate syndicators. Anyone can try to throw together a real estate deal, pull in investors, and put himself or herself in business. This means that an investor has to do substantial due diligence to assess the ability and credibility of not only the investment itself, but also the syndicator. Investors need to be careful because the water contains many sharks who may not have the best interests of their investors at heart. Single asset exposure can be another disadvantage: If the deal does not succeed, there are no other investments to counter the downside.

Often, people who invest in syndicated real estate want to be more active investors than those that invest in REITs or real estate funds. They enjoy the process of evaluating individual deals, tracking their progress through the investment cycle, and maintaining a relationship with one or more syndicators. An investor who develops a good relationship with a syndicator will be on the "inside track" when a good deal comes along and will get the first call. If, on the other hand, an investor does not want to be bothered, then this is probably not the best form of real estate investing.

Direct Purchase of Investment Property

Direct purchase of investment property—a small apartment or office building, a neighborhood strip center, etc.—also is an opportunity for an individual investor. As long as the possibility exists to hold the property over the long term, the investor can benefit from (1) annual leveraged returns on his or her equity investment, (2) positive net income after debt service, (3) tax benefits, and (4) leveraged returns on his or her equity at the time of sale. Unlike most other investment options, the investor buying real estate directly has control over each component of the investment: researching the market, selecting the property, arranging the financing, managing the investment, and choosing when to sell. Moreover, unlike other investment options, in which profits are shared between the investor and the fund manager, the individual investor enjoys all of the profits from the operation and sale of the property.

How to Buy an Investment Property

An investor looking to invest directly must undertake significant research and "legwork" to collect the information necessary to make a wise investment. First, the investor must truly understand the local market in which he or she will invest. Who are the users in this market, what are their needs, and what will they pay for space? What are the local transportation options and where are they located? What industries drive the economy? Working with real estate brokers who specialize in commercial, or investment, property, an investor may scour the market looking for deals. Once a property is identified, the investor must develop a plan. If the plan is to hold the property with minimal upgrades, the investor needs to understand the property's operating costs and predict when and at what rate rents will escalate. If the plan is to renovate or change the use of the property, the investor must understand how the local zoning ordinances affect the plan, the necessary approvals and costs associated with the renovation, and the projected rents the renovated property will command. The best way to collect this information is to talk to experts: local real estate brokers, local zoning and planning officials, contractors, etc.

Words of Caution

Direct investment of this sort is analogous to purchasing a business: It requires active, informed management to succeed. Investors considering a direct investment should recognize that operating the property is a day-to-day activity: Toilets in an apartment building may leak in the middle of the night, retail tenants may file a lawsuit if the landlord does not maintain the roof, and industrial tenants may complain about noxious odors emitting from another tenant's space. Although some investors enjoy solving these day-to-day problems, others will consider them an enormous headache. And, if the investment strategy involves direct purchase of multiple investment properties, these day-to-day management activities become overwhelming. In addition to time-consuming hassles, property management requires a knowledge base—knowledge about mechanical systems and other bricks and mortar issues and local laws, for example. Moreover, investors who choose to invest directly take on the liability associated with owning the property. To mitigate these challenges, investors may choose to partner with an experienced manager or to hire a management company.

INVESTMENT OPTIONS' RISK/RETURN TRADE-OFFS

The various investment options, as noted above, have different characteristics: different levels of investor involvement, various minimum investments, etc. Each option has a different level of risk and expected return. The comparative levels of risk and return of the real estate investment options we have discussed, as well each option's typical target rate of return, are illustrated in Figure 14.1.

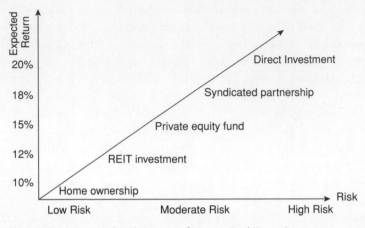

Figure 14.1 Expected Risk/Return of Various Real Estate Investments

CONCLUSION

To achieve a balanced, diversified portfolio, investors must consider an investment in real estate. Additionally, regardless of portfolio diversification theory, the benefits of investing in real estate, including attractive opportunities due to market inefficiencies, the compounding effects of leverage, and tax benefits, make real estate an attractive investment. As discussed, real estate's many asset classes, including residential, retail, office, and industrial, as well as the many investment channels, including homeownership, direct investment, participating in a syndicated deal or joint venture, REIT investment, or investment in a private equity fund—all provide opportunities for the investor to find the best real estate investment.

To take the first step, ask yourself: What are my needs, preferences, and investment objectives? Would I like to remain actively involved in the operation of the property or would I prefer to leave the management to an expert? Would I prefer to keep my investment liquid or am I happy to invest over the long term in exchange for potentially higher returns? Am I interested in evaluating individual deals myself or would I like to leave that to a fund manager? In answering these questions, the investor can begin to identify which real estate investment best suits him or her. Regardless of the channel you choose, the potential exists to create and preserve significant wealth over the long term through real estate. Just think of the Forbes 400.

Note

1. The author would like to thank Susan Luvisi for her work on the graphics in this chapter.

Additional Reading and Resources

Brueggeman, William B., and Jeffrey D. Fisher. *Real Estate Finance and Investments*. New York: McGraw-Hill/Irwin, 2001.

Jaffe, Austin J., and C.F. Sirmans. *Fundamentals of Real Estate Investment*. 3d ed. Upper Saddle River, NJ: Simon & Schuster, 1995.

Miles, Mike E., Gayle Berens, and Marc A. Weiss. *Real Estate Development: Principles and Processes*. 3d ed. Washington, DC: ULI—the Urban Land Institute, 2000.

Poorvu, William J., with Jeffrey L. Cruikshank. *The Real Estate Game*. New York: The Free Press, 1999.

Thomsett, Michael C., and Jean Freestone Thomsett. *Getting Started in Real Estate Investing*. New York: John Wiley & Sons, 1994.

Author Background

Nicholas Bienstock is a Managing Partner of Savanna Partners. Nick has worked on the acquisition, financing, restructuring, and sale of over $3 billion of real estate throughout the United States. He oversees the ongoing marketing and leasing of Savanna's investments. Prior to joining Savanna in 1999, Nick was a Vice President at Capital Trust, Inc. (NYSE: CT) in New York where he worked on a wide variety of real estate principal investment and advisory transactions, including the purchase of equity interests in various properties, the negation and structuring of mezzanine loans, single asset and portfolio sales, asset management, debt and equity private placements and REIT IPO advisory work. Prior to Capital Trust, Nick worked for Chemical Bank's Real Estate Investment Banking Group. He is an Assistant Adjunct Professor at Columbia University, where he teaches a seminar in Real Estate Finance.

Laura Corwin Burkhart is Founder and Principal of Slate Capital, LLC, a real estate syndicate focusing on urban redevelopment projects in northern New Jersey. Prior to founding Slate, Laura worked in construction and project management for Zander, LLC, a redeveloper of historic residential properties in Harlem, New York City. Laura received a Masters of Science in Real Estate Development from Columbia University and an AB, cum laude, in Politics from Princeton University.

Chapter 15

Private Equity

Sallie Shuping Russell

Private equity is a very broad category of investments. It includes transactions from equity in small local businesses to holding private debt in multinational corporations. There are three basic characteristics of private equity:

1. No public market exists for the transactions, and therefore it is more illiquid relative to other financial investments.
2. Prices are set purely by the auction process—that is, the selling price is whatever amount someone is willing to accept in order to part with the asset, and the purchase price is whatever one is willing to pay for that same asset. There is no predetermined price, nor are there market makers, who are going to help support the price at a certain level, as there are in the public stock market.
3. The investment generally has a higher risk than other asset classes, and usually takes several years to mature.

TYPES OF PRIVATE EQUITY INVESTMENTS

As with all investments, long-term success in private equity investing requires diversification. Although an investor can profit substantially from a single holding at a given period of time, it is unlikely that an investor will continue to reap profits by investing in that same type of company time after time over a decade or more. The recent example of the tech stock bubble provides an example. For about six years investors profited mightily from making private investments in companies related to the Internet. Then, in March 2000 the bottom fell out of that market, and today it is almost impossible to find a buyer for those kinds of Internet-related stocks.

This being said, one can be very successful investing in private equity using a portfolio strategy, that is, investing in several companies over a period of time. However, the form that this diversification takes can vary. Often investors break private equity into three categories: venture capital, leveraged/ management buyouts, and distressed securities and use these for diversification. Because such categorization is based on type of financing rather than stage of a company's operations, however, it can leave a portfolio over- or underexposed to attractive parts of the private markets. A preferred method is to diversify across stages of a company's life cycle: (1) beginning or early stage companies, (2) expansion or growth stage companies, (3) mature companies, and (4) distressed securities. Early stage companies are the domain of venture capital, as are many growth company investments. Mature companies are the domain of leveraged buyouts, although some later stage growth companies may use debt for capital growth and, in such cases, are known as *growth buyouts*. Finally, distressed securities are usually investments in companies that have been overleveraged and cannot continue operations without a restructuring of their debt. Each of these is discussed in detail below.

EARLY STAGE COMPANIES

This is what most people think of when they hear "venture capital"—that is, a new company that has just started, perhaps transferred out of university laboratories or developed in someone's garage. Early stage companies have a technology, but may not have yet fully developed a product. They may have revenues, but they do not have profits. Management is usually not fully fleshed out, and may not even exist beyond a founder or initial CEO. These companies are indeed venture capital, and they generally represent the earliest stages of such investments. They usually take the longest to mature and have the highest risk of capital loss associated with them. Consequently, they also are expected to have the highest rate of return among the various asset classes. More on this later.

EXPANSION STAGE COMPANIES

Generally, these are companies that have a product and management and are at or near profitability. They still do not have much free cash flow because all capital is being redeployed in the company to fuel its growth. However, this is not enough. The company is growing faster than revenues can support; without additional outside capital the company will miss opportunities to obtain market share, acquire competitors, etc. Depending on the availability of credit, the capital provided to these companies may be either equity or subordinated debt. If interest rates are low enough and the company's growth prospects are strong, a layer of subordinated dept may be the optimal capital structure. Investors may choose to invest in a debt instrument, which will be junior to bank debt but senior to the equity classes. Such investments are less risky than equity, but they also will have a slightly lower return. Overall, investments in expansion stage companies will be quicker to mature than early stage deals, less risky, and also lower in expected return. Nevertheless, these assets can be very attractive for individual investors. They frequently are the last round of private capital that goes into a company before it goes public. As such, when the initial public offering (IPO) market is robust, expansion stage investments can be particularly attractive.

MATURE STAGE COMPANIES

These companies are similar to those in the expansion stage, but they do generate free cash flow and the business has sufficient assets and cash flow to support substantial debt. This is the traditional *leveraged buyout* category. Mature stage companies are usually substantially larger than those in the previous two stages. They also are often in more traditional industries because the high growth required for early stage and expansion stage firms requires redeployment of working capital rather than allowing accumulation of current assets to support debt. The late 1990s saw an attempt to preempt this rule, when young telecommunications companies were debt financed and buckled under that burden when sales fell and inventories soared. The early 2000s are showing a return to buyouts in many industries because public market prices have fallen to levels that undervalue either the assets or future growth prospects for the firms.

DISTRESSED SECURITIES

The telecom example above provides a nice introduction to this investment stage. Distressed securities arise usually from companies that have been over leveraged and risk bankruptcy without some debt relief and equity infusion. Investments in these securities can take the form of high-yield debt, negotiated purchase of bank debt, super-preferred equity, etc. In almost all cases the security will be structured so that it is senior to other investors or lenders. Opportunities in the distressed security area are cyclical. They tend to follow periods when credit is cheap and banks tend to overcommit. When banks begin to call nonperforming loans and take advantage of other creditor tools, that often is a cue that distressed security investing is coming into favor.

WHO WILL INVEST MY MONEY?

Because diversification in so critical to successful long-term private investing, unless the investor has significant assets to deploy in this area, it is advisable to use a commingled vehicle of some sort. These can be large or small, professionally managed or not.

Professionally managed funds are usually structured as limited partnerships or limited liability corporations (LLCs), depending on tax and other issues. Here, the investors provide most of the capital while the investment professionals identify, select, and manage the transactions that go into the fund. This is no small task. Unlike public companies, where decisions are basically to buy or to sell a security, private investment managers select the company, help formulate strategy, hire executives, and move the company through to an exit event (sale or merger of the company, or IPO if conditions are appropriate) so that investors make a return on their capital. In return, the professionals are paid a disproportionate amount of the return relative to the amount of money they invest. To protect investors from egregious allocations to the manager, most funds require that investors receive their capital back before the investment manager receives any of his carried interest.

Professional investment partnerships can be structured as either as a *blind pool*, in which an investor commits a certain amount of capital to be invested and returned over a limited time period (usually 10 years) but does not have any choice in the investments made, or a *pledge fund*, which is similar, but here the investor gets to review each transaction and decide independently whether to invest or not in that particular deal. Most professional funds are structured as blind pools. Pledge funds are generally recommended only if you have an expertise in the types of companies targeted by the partnership, or if you have a lot of time to devote to conducting independent due diligence.

Another form of professionally managed accounts is the *Fund of Funds*. Here, the investor invests in a single vehicle; however, the fund invests in a series of separate private equity partnerships, usually across stages. This allows individuals to have a diversified private equity portfolio without the administrative burden of selecting and monitoring an array of partnerships. It is imperative, however, that the investor understand the strategy the fund of funds manager is deploying and how it is weighted vis-à-vis venture stages and buyouts. It also is important to examine the underlying partnerships in which the fund will download individual's dollars. If these are not stellar performers, there is little value the fund of funds manager can provide to offset this. Investors also must realize that, with a fund of funds manager, they are relinquishing the asset allocation decision. Asset allocation—or the percentage of your funds invested in early stage venture, growth capital, buyouts, etc.—is an important part of a successful private equity portfolio.

Funds that are not professionally managed but are popular in many areas include investment clubs and "angel groups." These are groups of individuals, often entrepreneurs or technical persons, who commingle their resources and meet periodically to evaluate particular private investment opportunities. Some clubs are large enough to have an administrative staff. Unlike traditional blind pools or pledge funds, which have a specified life, investment clubs and angel groups are often evergreen, redeploying distributed returns back into new private investments.

COMMON TERMS AND CONDITIONS

CARRIED INTEREST

As mentioned above, the investment manager usually receives as compensation a disproportionate amount of a fund's profits, relative to his investment. This is to reward him for his direct involvement with the investments' outcome. Most partnerships require the investment manager/general partner to invest at least 1 percent of capital commitments and receive 20 percent of the profits. Usually, this allocation comes after all investors have had a return of their invested capital. Details on these terms are discussed later. It is important for investors to be very clear on these conditions prior to finalizing their partnership.

Later stage venture funds, buyouts, and distressed investments often have an added feature that early stage partnerships lack—a *preferred return*. This is a minimum return on investment that must be paid to investors prior to the manager/general partner getting any carried interest. Such terms are reasonable in these areas because the investments mature much sooner than early stage ventures. Thus, all parties in the partnership—investors and managers—usually get their capital back sooner. The amount of the preferred return varies. Later stage venture partnerships' preferred return usually ranges from 5 percent to 8 percent. Buyouts, which often are a significantly larger pool of capital, have ranges between 8 percent and 15 percent. Often, new firms trying to attract capital for the first time will have a higher preferred return relative to their peers in order to attract investors.

Different private investment stages may have different carried interests and terms. Overall, the standard terms are a 20 percent carried interest and a management fee of around 2.0 percent, with no preferred return. The logic to this is that early stage venture investments take a long time to mature relative to other private equity types. Partners in early stage firms usually work years before they reap any direct profit from their efforts. To require that they pay investors a preferred return prior to their receiving anything can make the payoff to the managers too far off to be meaningful. The result can be turnover among the partners, which is generally not in the investors' interest. Carried interests for later stage venture are most likely to be 20 percent also, but they will have additional terms (such as a preferred return and full return of capital prior to any payment to managers) that cast a larger burden on managers before they participate in the carry. The carried interest for buyout firms and distressed managers is sometimes lower, around 15 percent, although premier buyout funds generally reap 20 to 25 percent carry. These investments usually do not require the high level of hands-on oversight that venture investments do and, as such, managers are not quite as highly compensated. Furthermore, buyout and distressed investment funds are usually substantially larger than venture capital partnerships. This allows the general partners to make significant profits from a 15 percent carry, while the smaller-sized venture funds often require a 20 percent rate.

Another important term for investors to understand is whether their partnership will provide a *clawback,* which ensures that the manager/general partner does not receive more than the 20 percent (or 30 percent, etc.) carried interest stipulated in the partnership agreement. A clawback requires a manager to return to investors all capital in excess of what's due to him or her under the carried interest formula. Because investments in commingled vehicles usually are made over a three- to four-year period, initial investments may mature before the final committed capital is invested. Usually managers/general partners will take their 20 percent carried interest from each deal, once the cost of the transaction has been returned to the investors. If early investments are more successful relative to later ones, it is possible at the end of the fund for the manager/general partner to have received more than 20 percent of total profits. This is the scenario under which the clawback applies. If a partnership does not have a clawback provision for investors, it is important that the partnership does not allow managers/general partners to receive distributions unless the capital accounts of the investors are significantly greater than invested capital. Terms frequently seen as such are capital accounts exceeding 120 to 135 percent of invested capital prior to any distribution to the manager.

MANAGEMENT FEES

In addition to the carried interest, management fees are also an item of negotiation in partnerships. The common fee for venture funds is 2 to 2.5 percent of capital, often declining in the later years of a partnership. Buyouts and distressed investments usually carry fees of 1.5 to 2 percent committed capital. Again, since these latter partnerships are significantly larger in capital commitments, they can run their businesses on smaller percentage fees.

Firms that have many sequential private equity partnerships under management should have lower management fees because they are drawing fees from multiple funds. Newer firms have greater reason to insist on higher percentage fees. Smaller firms also need to have higher management fees relative to larger ones in order to cover certain fixed costs that exist regardless of fund size. For example, a 2 percent fee on an $85 million fund provides less capital for overhead, etc., than a 1.5 percent fee on a $500 million fund.

OTHER CONSIDERATIONS

There are several other provisions within partnership terms and conditions—too many to cover here. Some of these include *key man* provisions for certain key employees of the investment firm, how partnership agreements are amended, whether there is an advisory board of investors that approves valuations and resolves conflicts that may arise, and when the manger/general partner can raise another fund.

It is always important to know how much negotiating strength you have before agreeing to sign the partnership legal documents. Negotiating strength does not only come from dollars invested. Often, partnerships want to list prestigious investors among their LPs. If there are terms in the draft partnership agreement that you would like changed, do not hesitate to try to negotiate these changes into the final documents. Limited partnership documents often are very fluid until the final hours of a close.

PORTFOLIO EXAMPLE

As mentioned at the outset, a key to successful private equity investment is diversification. Allocations should depend on investors' risk tolerance, liquidity needs, and age. The first two are probably obvious: People who do not like wide swings in their investment performance or need liquidity should stay away from early stage venture investing. Older investors, in general, also may want to stay away from early stage venture, tilting their portfolios toward shorter-duration investments. This is because swings in early stage venture capital can be so wide it can take years to make up losses.

Below are examples of possible portfolio allocations, based on variables cited above. Please note that these percentages apply to the private equity portion of your portfolio. Private equity, in total, should be a relatively small percentage of your entire investment portfolio. The most astute, risk-tolerant institutional investors seldom have more than 15 percent of their total funds invested in private equity.

- *For risk-tolerant investors:* The portfolio should be weighted toward early stage venture and distressed securities. Generally, these are the highest-returning groups, although liquidity may not occur until after five years from the initial investment. One should also consider have some holdings in mature stage/buyout companies. The early stage venture and buyout sectors have some countercyclicality to them so it is advisable to have some of each to reduce volatility.
- *For risk-averse investors:* The portfolio should be weighted toward later stage venture and buyouts. These will generally provide liquidity sooner than the other categories and the likelihood of having the underlying portfolio companies go totally out of business is much smaller. Consequently, the risk of losing your invested capital is lower. A portfolio mixed with later stage venture and buyout opportunities should also be less volatile in any given year.

CONCLUSION

Private equity is an exciting investment area, one where exceptional managers are especially important. Of course, should you choose to invest directly in private companies, it is important to stay focused on those areas you know.

In all investments, diversification is the key to control risk and reward. Private equity is no exception. Although many investors consider private equity as a diversifying tool for their overall portfolio—and it is—too often they do not understand the importance of diversification *within* the private portfolio itself. This chapter has tried to set forth the various strategies that investors in private equity should consider.

Table 15.1 summarizes key characteristics of the four major private equity categories. These are broad generalizations, and specific managers will vary. Expected internal rate of return (IRR) figures represent returns over the life of a partnership (usually 10 years) and assuming normalized conditions (i.e., assuming neither technology bubble period nor technology slump).

Table 15.1

Type of Private Equity	Expected IRR (%)	Carried Interest (%)	Management Fee (% committed capital)
Early stage	20–25%	20–30%	2.0–2.5%
Later stage	18–20%	15–25%	1.5–2.0%
Mature stage	15–23%	15–25%	1.5–2.0%
Distressed	18–25%	15–20%	1.5–2.0%

Author Background

Sallie Shuping Russell is a General Partner at Intersouth Partners. She has been part of the venture capital and entrepreneurial communities for nearly 20 years. Sallie joined Intersouth in 2001 as its third General Partner. She focuses on investments in life sciences and information technology companies. Prior to her career at Intersouth, Sallie spent 15 years at Duke University. She was a founding member of Duke Management Company, the entity which oversees the university's endowment and other investment funds. As Vice President and Director of Private Investments, she was responsible for Duke's holdings in venture capital, leveraged buyouts, restructurings, oil & gas and timber. Prior to her career at Duke, Sallie was a Consultant at Cambridge Associates. She was also a Vice President at McMillion/Eubanks, a money management company in Greensboro.

Chapter 16

Hedge Funds

DeFred G. Folts III

People often have misconceptions about hedge funds. Moreover, it is hard for even wealthy and sophisticated investors to find high-quality hedge fund managers. Despite the difficulty of evaluating and accessing good hedge funds, they continue to be the most rapidly growing area of the investment industry. Investors should investigate and understand the world of hedge funds, not because it will continue to experience dramatic growth, but because hedge funds can provide clear benefits to high-net-worth investors.

By including hedge funds in an overall asset allocation, there exists the potential to add meaningful levels of true diversification to investment portfolios while enhancing investment returns. Hedge funds usually exhibit low correlation to traditional markets. They do not march in lockstep with either stocks or bonds. As most of us learned, yet again, during the bubble and subsequent burst in the equity markets beginning in March of 2000, diversification is still the cornerstone of portfolio risk management.

In addition, hedge funds offer investors an opportunity to have their assets invested by some of the most talented investment managers in the industry. Many top managers have migrated to the hedge fund platform for the freedom to invest as they choose and the ability to share directly in the profits that they generate.

In the past decade, hedge funds have grown from a cottage industry of eccentric genius into a well-organized profit generator for the major global investment firms. In 1991, there were less than 1,000 hedge fund mangers. By the beginning of 2003, the number had grown to over 6,000. Hedge fund assets grew correspondingly from less than $50 billion to over $600 billion.

So what are hedge funds? Are they private partnerships providing higher risk and higher return? Or are they truly hedged strategies, damping down investment volatility and seeking above-average risk-adjusted return regardless of market direction? The answer is that they can be either. Hedge funds as a category are not homogeneous. There are many different approaches, all with different risk and return objectives, spread across the entire hedge fund investment universe.

Hedge fund investment strategies belong in the category of *alternative investments.* Just as private equity, venture capital, and private real estate partnerships represent the private and illiquid side of alternative investments, hedge funds have come to dominate the public securities side.

Hedge funds are typically private investment partnerships, often structured as limited partnership vehicles and therefore only sold as private placements to accredited investors and qualified purchasers. Because they are private placements and not registered as securities, these funds are to a large extent unregulated. They typically invest in traditional assets such as stocks, bonds, and derivatives, but they employ nontraditional strategies. For example, a typical equity hedge fund will invest in common stocks, but do so using both long *and* short positions. Furthermore, hedge funds will often employ investment leverage, thereby investing more than 100 percent of the fund's capital. They are offered with a different fee structure than traditional investment management and typically charge not only a fee for assets under management, but also share in a portion (typically 20 percent) of the profits generated by the fund manager. Finally, the hedge fund manager almost always has a material percentage of his or her personal liquid net worth invested in the strategy alongside the other investors.

INDUSTRY CHARACTERISTICS AND BACKGROUND

The hedge fund industry evolved initially from the work of Alfred Winslow Jones, who is seen as the father of the modern-day hedge fund. In 1949, Jones developed an investment strategy that featured the use of long equity positions hedged through short selling, combined with investment leverage to enhance potential returns. Jones enjoyed success with this strategy, which was the prototype of the modern long-short equity hedge fund.

Jones's approach was fairly simple:

- Incorporate short positions in the portfolio
- Utilize leverage
- Receive a performance fee of 20 percent of the profits

Hedge funds also owe part of their genesis to the evolution of commodity trading advisors (CTAs), such as John Henry & Co., and the managed futures industry. CTAs trade in the futures market in a variety of ways, use leverage, and are familiar with hedging strategies. For example, they might employ highly quantitative models to exploit often very small and short-lived price inefficiencies in the commodities market, or provide liquidity to physical commodity producers wishing to hedge their exposure to one or more commodities.

In the 1990s, hedge funds emerged fully into the mainstream due to the very public successes of global macro hedge fund managers like George Soros and Julian Robertson. These managers became famous in financial circles as they demonstrated the potential for hedge funds to provide outsized investment returns for their well-heeled clients. Today, a large percentage of the hedge fund industry, and in particular the newer hedge fund managers, have come out of large Wall Street firms, where they managed those firms' own capital on the proprietary trading desks. Although not identified as such, Wall Street firms remain large players in the hedge fund industry as they make trading bets with their shareholders capital.

Technology also has played a key role in the expansion of the hedge fund industry. It has enabled smaller hedge fund boutiques to gain the same instantaneous access to market and financial data that only used to be available to the large Wall Street proprietary trading desks. Furthermore, technology has provided these smaller firms with the same computing power as their Wall Street brethren to run the quantitative models, simulations, and stress tests that drive their complex approaches. The proliferation of hedge funds can also be attributed to the ever-expanding universe of securities available to implement their specialized strategies.

DIFFERENT TYPES OF HEDGE FUND STRATEGIES

Too often, hedge funds are described as though they are one asset class, offering the same approach and exhibiting the same risk and return characteristics. It may seem obvious, but it is important to understand that not all hedge funds are alike. In fact, hedge funds should not be viewed as an asset class at all, but rather as an investment structure within a broad range of asset classes. Joe Nicholas, in his book *Investing in Hedge Funds* (Bloomberg, 1999), describes it this way: "In the past, the term hedge fund described both an investment structure—a commingled fund (private partnership) and a strategy—a leveraged long portfolio of stocks "hedged" by short sales (the strategy developed by Jones back in 1949). Today, it really only describes the structure." However, hedge funds do provide risk and return characteristics not easily obtained from investments in other asset classes, and for this reason some firms refer to them as an asset class. However, it is important to recognize how difficult it is to categorize hedge funds, because the managers may employ more than one strategy at the same time, and may switch among different strategies in pursuit of investment opportunities over time.

In simple terms, hedge funds fall into two broad investment categories: (1) absolute return strategies and (2) directional strategies. In *absolute return strategies,* managers seek to capitalize on relatively small mispricings among closely related securities. They are not betting on the general direction of a stock, bond, or the broader markets. Instead, they can be seen as specialists who use their very specific knowledge and skills in statistics, valuation, financial modeling, and legal and regulatory issues, to profit from fully hedged, specialized strategies. In contrast, in *directional strategies,* investment managers use their skills and experience to make a bet, based on their view of stocks, bonds, or an entire asset class. They try to determine which stocks, bonds, or entire markets will go up and which will go down. They typically are not fully hedged, and they seek some degree of market correlation as the source of part of their returns. Figure 16.1 lays out the broad hedge fund categories and their subcategories.

Absolute Return	Directional
• Equity Market Neutral (aka: Statistical Arbitrage) • Convertible Arbitrage • Fixed Income Arbitrage • Merger Arbitrage (aka: Risk Arbitrage) • Distressed	• Equity Long/Short • Sector Long/Short • Short Sellers • Global Macro • Managed futures/CTAs

Figure 16.1 Hedge Fund Categories

ABSOLUTE RETURN STRATEGIES

Equity market neutral, sometimes referred to as *statistical arbitrage,* is a strategy that consists of equal weightings of offsetting long and short positions. The manager may rely on sophisticated models to identify securities that are undervalued for his or her long positions. Conversely, the manager seeks overvalued securities for his or her short positions. For example, a manager might be long Coke and short Pepsi at the same time. This seems somewhat counterintuitive. However, through a highly quantitative proprietary model the manager might have determined that Coke is undervalued specifically in its relationship to Pepsi. The manager believes that there is a better chance of being right about the movement of Coke and Pepsi with respect to one another than there is of attempting to make a bet on the next move in the broader market or industry. It is a strategy designed to limit market risk and to perform well in both up and down markets. Naturally, in a strong upward market cycle these strategies will inevitably leave money on the table due to the portfolio's short positions. However, in a declining market, the strategy should help to preserve and grow capital through these same short positions. This strategy is a good example of a nondirectional strategy because it is not dependent on the broader market to move up or down in order to generate investment returns. Also, because it is nondirectional, it naturally maintains a lower correlation with the equity indices, thereby providing additional overall portfolio diversification.

Convertible arbitrage is a strategy that simultaneously establishes long positions of convertible securities while selling short the underlying equities of the same issuer. The manager is most interested in the spread between the prices of these two instruments. The arbitrageurs are seeking to profit from mispricing of the convertible bond relative to the same company's common stock, and the ultimate convergence of the pricing relationship between the two securities. This is a hedged strategy designed to reduce volatility and avoid broad market exposure. The risks in this strategy are related to interest rates, credit quality, counterparty, and liquidity. It is an area of the hedge fund arena in which capacity issues are of concern because the issuance of convertible securities (and their aftermarket trading liquidity) is relatively limited. Since these strategies have generated attractive returns, particularly during the tough equity market years of 2001 and 2002, they have attracted large inflows of capital. As a result, there is concern about too much money chasing too few opportunities. At times, there may not be enough convertible securities, and it becomes difficult for the manager to put money to work efficiently.

Fixed-income arbitrage involves taking long and short positions in bonds or other fixed-income securities or derivatives. Managers are seeking to profit from small changes in the historical pricing relationships of different fixed-income securities. They seek a specific dislocation in a historical price relationship, and profit if they correctly anticipate this relationship returning to its historical norm. These managers are looking for minor dislocations; therefore, the profit from each move is small. This is an area of the hedge fund arena in which relatively large amounts of investment leverage are used. However, in these strategies, managers typically also establish offsetting positions throughout the fund to minimize potential negative effects of this leverage. Fixed income arbitrage is another example of a nondirectional strategy—the manager seeks to profit from the relationship between two securities, rather than the direction of the broader fixed-income markets.

Event-Driven Strategies

Event-driven managers focus on specific corporate events and the catalysts that drive these events. Event-driven strategies include distressed securities, merger arbitrage, and special situations. Managers seek to profit from their skills in valuing assets, understanding complex capital structures, the complex legal processes surrounding bankruptcy proceedings, or the regulatory issues involved in mergers and acquisitions. For example, recently a great deal of activity in event-driven investing has been focused on corporate restructuring in response to the difficult economic environment and accounting rule changes.

Distressed managers invest in companies experiencing varying degrees of financial difficulties. These include companies undergoing reorganizations, restructuring, and even bankruptcy. The hedge fund manager might purchase a company's corporate or bank debt, common stock, or warrants, depending on where in the company's capital structure he or she chooses to take positions. For example, profit might be generated by correctly anticipating a higher value for a company when it emerges from reorganization. Managers search for good underlying companies with specific financial problems and a valuation that has been artificially depressed by other investors who may have been forced to sell at distressed levels. For example, a distressed fund might invest in senior, secured debt of a particular company, and then, as a debt holder, take a seat at the negotiating table with the company's banks and other creditors.

It is a very hands-on, roll up your sleeves strategy. Good lawyers can be an important part of the investment team, particularly bankruptcy specialists. In this strategy the manager believes that he or she can focus on a few companies and be part of the solution to bring them back to life, again not relying on the general movement of the market.

Distressed investors typically do not employ investment leverage. The correlation of these strategies to the broader markets is low. However, distressed investing is by its very nature illiquid; the investment time frame is unknown and can be quite long. Also, the periodic valuation of distressed portfolios is an inexact science, more similar to private equity valuation than to public securities valuation, and this has been the source of controversy and several very public blowups. These strategies can do well in any economic environment but typically do best coming out of periods of economic slowdown or recession.

Merger arbitrage (risk arbitrage) involves investing in the securities of companies undergoing an acquisition or a merger. A common approach is for a merger arbitrage manager to establish a long position in the stock of a company being acquired when a deal is announced and sell short the stock of the acquiring company. The value of the target company's stock should trade at a discount to the ultimate value of the stock should the deal come to fruition. Typically, the purchase price is above the target company's price on the date of the announcement, and the probability of the deal closing is less than 100 percent. This discount can be seen as the result of the inherent "deal risk."

The time value of money also is important here, given the fact that the timing of deals is typically uncertain and will have an impact on investment returns. The primary risk in this type of strategy is specific transaction risk and not broad market risk. If the announced deal closes, then the pricing discrepancy should converge and the manager should make money on the trade. However, if the deal falls apart, the manager stands to lose money on the investment. The manager adds value through his judgment of whether or not a deal is likely to close and whether the market accurately reflects this likelihood.

DIRECTIONAL STRATEGIES

Equity long/short managers invest in individual companies and offset their positions with short sales of other individual stocks or with stock indices. The manager adjusts the ratio of long positions to short positions to reflect his or her outlook for the equity market or sector of the equity market in which the investment is made. Some managers' bias towards being more net long or net short may change over time, whereas other managers may keep their average net position (most long/short equity funds are on average in a net long position) fairly constant over time. For example, a long/short equity manager may believe that over the long term it is in everyone's best interest to have the portfolio always net long (more long positions than short positions). In contrast, another manager may be 75 percent net long during one period and net short the next. It may seem obvious, but it is important to understand that this is *not* equity market–neutral investing. These managers make directional bets on underlying companies as well as the broader equity markets—bullish (net long) and bearish (net short). Equity long/short managers may apply their strategy to domestic U.S. equities, non-U.S. equities, or even to industry sectors such as technology, biotechnology, or others.

Global macro represents the purest form of top-down hedge fund investing. The strategy is opportunistic in nature with investments based on potential shifts in the global economies. The manager tries to anticipate macroeconomic events throughout the world and capitalize based on how these events will impact financial instruments and financial markets. Macro managers may take positions based on anticipated changes in a specific country's economic situation, shifts in currency valuations or interest rates, and geopolitical events. These funds often take concentrated positions, use derivatives or futures, and employ investment leverage. Perhaps the most famous example of a global macro hedge fund trade was George Soros making a large profit in the 1990s by betting against the value of the British pound. His hedge fund squared off against the Bank of England and other huge players in the currency markets and won. Recently, global macro managers have focused on themes such as an expected rise in interest rates or the potential for dollar devaluation and concurrent global currency devaluation with its favorable impact on the price of gold. Clearly, these are directional strategies, and they are based on major global investment themes.

Short sellers seek to profit by selling securities that the manager believes are either fundamentally or technically overvalued. These hedge funds do not actually own the shares they sell. Rather, they borrow them from a broker-dealer and sell them short. The manager anticipates that the share price will fall, and he or she then will have the opportunity to buy back the shares later at a lower price to replace the borrowed shares. In short selling it is crucial to understand that going short a stock or the market is *not* the opposite of going long. If you own (are long) a stock and the price of the stock declines, your exposure to that stock is decreased—the most you can lose is the amount that was invested. However, when a short position goes against you, your exposure actually goes up—your potential loss is technically infinite.

The other risk peculiar to short sellers is a phenomenon known as a *short squeeze*. This occurs when the stock you have borrowed is "called" back by the lender, forcing you to sell at an inopportune time. Typically, this happens as the stock is rising, and the act of buying back the stock puts additional upward pressure on its price, further compounding your losses. Short sellers' returns may vary dramatically from year to year. It is possible for short sellers to be the hedge fund category with the highest return in one year and then be the lowest-return category the next year.

RISK-ADJUSTED RATES OF RETURN AMONG HEDGE FUND STRATEGIES

Figure 16.2 shows monthly returns for various hedge fund strategies and the monthly standard deviation of those returns. Standard deviation is used as a proxy for the risk inherent in an investment strategy. In basic terms, it measures the degree of variation of returns around the mean (average) return. The higher the volatility of investment returns, the higher the standard deviation will be. In the chart you can see that absolute return strategies such as arbitrage strategies have lower standard deviations—lower degrees of investment volatility—than more directional correlated strategies, such as long/short equity. Absolute return managers are seeking to extract volatility from their portfolios. Their goal is to earn less spectacular absolute rates of return, more in line with bond returns. They seek to generate reasonable positive rates of return during both good and bad market periods. In contrast, hedge fund managers who employ directional strategies like global macro and long/short equity use their talents to try to generate exceptional returns, albeit taking reasonable risk. Their returns over time should be higher than the absolute return strategies, but the volatility of their returns reflects these higher expected returns.

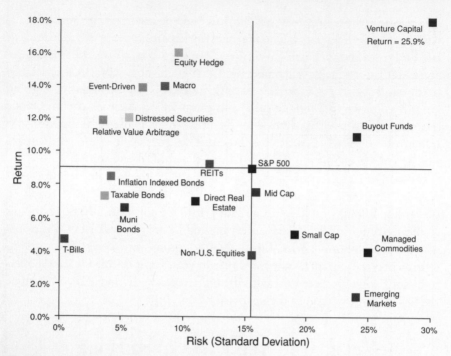

Figure 16.2   Hedge FundRisk/Return Scattergram
Note: Data from February 1992–January 2003.
Courtesy of SCS Financial; Data Sources: Salomon Smith Barney, Russell Investment Group,
Merrill Lynch, Standard & Poor's, Morgan Stanley, Venture Economics, NCREIF.

VARIABILITY OF RETURNS
AMONG HEDGE FUND STRATEGIES

Another way to illustrate volatility and the variation of returns among hedge
fund strategies from year to year is to look at their annual rankings. For example, in Figure 16.3, observe the number of times that short sellers were the top-
performing hedge fund style in one year only to be the worst-performing strategy
in the following year. Short selling is a rather extreme example of a directional
strategy. In 1994 short sellers were the top-performing hedge fund group with returns up over 18.5 percent. The next year, 1995, short sellers fell into last place,
down over 17 percent. This same pattern occurred again in 1999 and 2000,
only in reverse. You can observe how a strategy such as merger arbitrage takes
up more of the blocks across the middle of the chart. Anecdotally, this makes
sense since merger arbitrage is an example of an absolute return strategy with
less volatility than directional strategies. Figure 16.3 provides another way to illustrate the difference between absolute return strategies and directional strategies.

1991	1992	1993	1994	1995	1996	1997	1998	1999	2000	2001	2002
Macro 46.66%	Macro 27.17%	Macro 53.31%	Short Selling 18.53%	Equity Hedge 31.04%	Event-Driven 24.84%	Equity Hedge 23.41%	Equity Hedge 15.98%	Equity Hedge 44.22%	Short Selling 34.63%	Convertible Arbitrage 13.37%	Short Selling 29.16%
Equity Hedge 40.15%	Distressed 25.24%	Distressed 32.54%	Merger Arbitrage 8.88%	Macro 29.32%	Equity Hedge 21.75%	Event-Driven 21.23%	Equity Market Neutral 10.14%	Event-Driven 24.33%	Merger Arbitrage 18.02%	Distressed 13.28%	Convertible Arbitrage 9.07%
Distressed 35.66%	Equity Hedge 21.32%	Event-Driven 28.22%	Event Driven 6.00%	Event-Driven 25.11%	Distressed 20.77%	Equity Market Neutral 19.36%	Convertible Arbitrage 7.77%	Macro 17.62%	Convertible Arbitrage 14.50%	Event-Driven 12.18%	Macro 7.42%
Event-Driven 27.42%	Event-Driven 19.46%	Equity Hedge 27.94%	Equity Market Neutral 4.67%	Convertible Arbitrage 19.85%	Equity Market Neutral 19.63%	Macro 18.82%	Merger Arbitrage 7.23%	Distressed 16.94%	Equity Hedge 9.09%	Short-Selling 8.99%	Distressed 5.28%
Merger Arbitrage 17.86%	Convertible Arbitrage 16.35%	Merger Arbitrage 20.24%	Distressed 3.84%	Distressed 19.73%	Merger Arbitrage 16.61%	Merger Arbitrage 16.44%	Macro 6.19%	Convertible Arbitrage 14.41%	Equity Market Neutral 8.89%	Macro 6.87%	Merger Arbitrage -0.86%
Equity Market Neutral 17.84%	Equity Market Neutral 10.77%	Convertible Arbitrage 15.22%	Equity Hedge 2.61%	Merger Arbitrage 17.86%	Convertible Arbitrage 14.56%	Distressed 15.40%	Event-Driven 1.70%	Merger Arbitrage 14.34%	Event-Driven 6.74%	Merger Arbitrage 2.76%	Equity Market Neutral -3.16%
Convertible Arbitrage 17.60%	Short Selling 10.05%	Equity Market Neutral 12.62%	Convertible Arbitrage -3.73%	Equity Market Neutral 14.25%	Macro 9.32%	Convertible Arbitrage 12.72%	Short Selling -.54%	Equity Market Neutral -.17%	Distressed 2.78%	Equity Market Neutral 1.59%	Event-Driven -4.30%
Short Selling -16.96%	Merger Arbitrage 7.90%	Short Selling -7.50%	Macro -4.30%	Short Selling -17.14%	Short Selling -4.00%	Short Selling 3.86%	Distressed -4.23%	Short Selling -24.40%	Macro 1.97%	Equity Hedge 0.40%	Equity Hedge -4.70%

Figure 16.3 Variability of Returns Among Hedge Fund Strategies

Returns for the various hedge fund categories are represented by the returns of the HFR index for each category.

Courtesy of SCS Financial; Data Source: Hedge Fund Research, Inc. (HFR)

WHY INVEST IN HEDGE FUNDS?

The main attraction of hedge funds *should* be that by adding them to a traditional asset allocation portfolio of cash, traditional stocks, and bonds, even private equity and restricted stock investors can reduce the overall risk of their investment portfolio, while at the same time enhancing investment returns. The main attraction of hedge funds *should not* be to earn unreasonably high rates of return by way of the public equity markets. However, often this is still what investors believe hedge fund strategies should do. I suppose that in this way, hedge funds are not different from traditional strategies. In both traditional and hedge fund investing the market doesn't provide outsized rates of return without taking outsized risk and exposing the portfolio to the potential for large losses. However, by adding a reasonable percentage of appropriate hedge fund investments, perhaps 5 percent to 20 percent, to a portfolio, these lower-correlated hedged investments can reduce the volatility (standard deviation) of the overall portfolio. At the same time, the hedge fund manager, through his or her capacity to generate *alpha* (a measure of a manager's value added above a benchmark), can increase expected returns. The result actually can be to shift the investment industry's efficient frontier further towards its northwest quadrant, as Figure 16.4 shows.

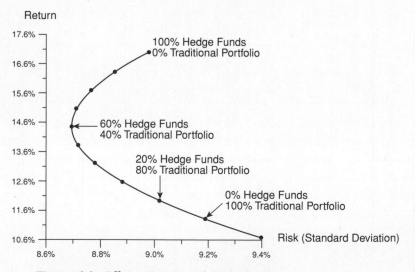

Figure 16.4   Efficient Frontier with Hedge Fund
Courtesy of SCS Financial.

Data Source: Van Hedge Fund Advisors International, Inc. Data from 1988–2001. Hedge Fund returns are based on the Van Hedge Fund Index. Traditional Portfolio consists of 60% S&P 500, 40% Lehman Aggregate Bond Index.

HOW TO THINK ABOUT INCORPORATING HEDGE FUNDS INTO A PORTFOLIO

The place to start might be to divide the hedge fund market into the two broad categories we have mentioned, absolute return and directional. Consider the absolute return strategies as a complement to (a partial substitute for) traditional fixed-income assets such as municipal bonds and U.S. Treasury securities. The various absolute return strategies (merger arbitrage, convertible arbitrage, equity market neutral, and others) are aligned more closely with the risk and return characteristics of a bond index, yet they are less correlated with the index than bonds so they add diversification value to a portfolio.

The directional strategies, such as hedged equity (not to be confused with equity market neutral) can be viewed as a complement to traditional long-only equity portfolios. The hedged equity category has generally performed in line with, or slightly better than, the S&P 500 and has done so with lower volatility. So rather than choose between these two categories, consider diversifying your overall hedge fund allocation between absolute return and directional strategies with a weighting toward the end of the spectrum that provides you with the level of risk you seek in your overall portfolio. This kind of approach will add to your overall portfolio diversification and give you a broad-based representation within the hedge fund category.

HOW TO INVEST IN HEDGE FUNDS: FUND OF FUNDS VERSUS INDIVIDUAL MANAGERS

The two most common means available for investing in hedge funds are individual hedge fund managers or a multimanager structure called a fund of funds. A fund of funds is structured, similar to hedge funds, as a limited partnership vehicle. Capital is pooled from many investors and then allocated by the general partner to the different underlying hedge fund managers. One benefit is that for a relatively small investment, perhaps as little as $500,000 to $1 million, an investor engages the services of an industry professional to select and monitor the managers and allocate the capital.

Remember, there are now over 6,000 hedge fund managers and selecting among this pool, particularly since transparency into their strategies is not always available, is a difficult job. This task is made more difficult by the fact that a number of the best hedge fund managers are closed to new investors. By investing through a fund of funds vehicle, investors may have an opportunity to invest in "closed" hedge fund managers. Also, by participating in a fund of funds, an investor is able to somewhat mitigate hedge fund manager risk. This is important. The major risk in the still unregulated world of hedge fund investing is manager risk, or blowup risk. As we have all read in the press, when a hedge fund manager has a problem, he or she may not simply underperform the S&P 500. Instead, the manager may actually go out of business, taking the investors' money with him. If you invest through a fund of funds and one manager of the 15 to 40 managers in the fund of funds blows up, the effect is not disastrous.

The argument most often heard against using a fund of funds structure is that the investor has to pay not only the underlying fees to the hedge fund managers themselves, but also the fee to the fund of funds manager. This creates the painful cry of "fees on top of fees!" This argument, however, only goes so far—mitigating manager risk, having a professional selecting and monitoring the underlying managers, and access to the best managers have value. As long as the investor is evaluating a fund of fund's performance net of fees, if it is achieving a reasonable rate of return, then there is value to the fund of funds structure. However, there are plenty of mediocre fund of funds managers simply chasing returns, and not adding value, but still collecting their additional fees.

Usually, I find that the decision between using a fund of funds versus individual managers comes down to the investor's personal preference, and is based on the investor's determination of just how involved he or she wants to be in the manager selection and monitoring process. Clearly, for an investor who is just getting started and investing $1 million or less in the hedge fund space, the fund of funds route should be considered.

WHAT TO LOOK FOR IN A HEDGE FUND MANAGER

There seems to be sufficient evidence that an allocation to hedge funds can make sense in an overall investment portfolio. However, identifying and gaining access to the best hedge fund managers is a real challenge. The hedge fund space was a cottage industry until the mid 1990s. Today, however, it is an industry unto itself. There is simply too much product—too many hedge funds. The sheer number of hedge fund managers and the ease with which these managers can start up a new fund is startling. In the words of Jim Rogers, a former partner of George Soros and author of *Investment Banker (Random House Trade Paperback, 2003),* "It is now too easy for people to get into the industry. When we started out it was a lot harder and there was nobody around to help us. Now there are brokerage firms, law firms, and accounting firms all specializing in hedge funds, which makes getting into the business easy." [quote from Strachman, *Getting Started in Hedge Funds* (Wiley, 2002)]. The ease of entry and the sheer number of funds make selecting the right manager all the more important.

Hedge fund search and selection have become an enormous industry with an army of consultants and new-found hedge fund experts anxious to assist the uninformed investor. There is one way in which the hedge fund world is quite similar to the world of traditional long-only investment strategies: Too often, investors end up simply chasing last year's great returns. Just as this is unwise in traditional strategies, it is potentially more dangerous in the unregulated and leveraged world of hedge funds. Figure 16.5 shows the dispersion of returns in the hedge fund universe relative to traditional investment management. Using 2002 as an example, you can see that the range of returns for hedge fund managers was much broader than for traditional large-cap equity managers. The most extreme example shown in the chart is the range of long/short hedged equity managers. The best-performing managers in this group achieved over 70 percent returns, while the worst lost over 50 percent of capital. Contrast this with the range of returns for large cap growth managers. In this group, the best managers lost approximately 10 percent while the worst lost close to 30 percent—a much narrower range.

In my opinion, the most important criterion to apply when evaluating potential hedge fund managers is the detailed story of the evolution of the manager and his firm. How did this manager and this fund get to where they

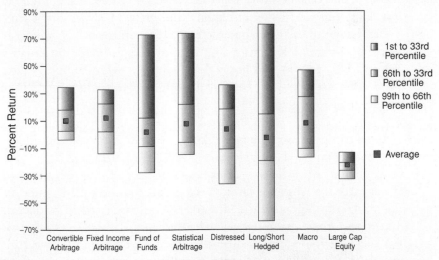

Figure 16.5   Range of Manager Returns in 2002
Courtesy of SCS Financial; Data Source: Hedgefund.net.

are today? Does that evolution follow a path that makes sense and gives me confidence? For example, one manager colleague utilizes a proprietary model of the global capital markets as the basis for his investment decisions. Of course, there are many quantitative models in the hedge fund space, but this manager has the following three key attributes:

1. He actually started working on this model 25 years ago as a math major at M.I.T. and during his MBA days at Wharton. Not only was the model well tested but also the manager had acquired a great deal of wisdom about the global capital markets through many market cycles over the last 25 years.

2. The manager spent time as a successful entrepreneur who has had a hand in building two successful companies before running a hedge fund business. This is important because many good money managers have no idea how to run, build, and grow a business. Running a hedge fund is a business, and at times what stalls out a hedge fund's growth or even brings it down is not performance but mismanagement of the business.

3. The manager had compiled an excellent 10-year track record, but the fund remained relatively small. Rather than being a negative, the assets under management were relatively small because he had always been more concerned with proving that his model worked and making money than with raising assets. He had no marketing staff and only met with potential new investors who called him through a referral. He was doing this for friends and family, and he was his own first client. Today, he continues to maintain almost 100 percent of his liquid net worth invested in his strategy. This kind of story is important because it is relatively easy to find hedge fund managers whose numbers look good. One needs to look beyond the numbers to understand if they will *continue* to be good.

In addition to a good story, there are some do's and don'ts you should follow when looking for good hedge fund managers. A partial list is:

- *Do demand a reasonably long track record.* If hedge funds are meant to deliver attractive absolute rates of return over an extended period of time during both good and bad markets, then you need to be able to observe performance through as many different market cycles as possible. There are too many good funds with at least three to five years of performance history. Do not risk allocating money to a hedge fund manager without a reasonable track record. Of course, the length of the track record is somewhat relative in the hedge fund industry because most funds are simply not that old. Fortunately, if a hedge fund has been around for the last five years, you get an excellent look at its performance in both a raging bull market and a devastating bear market.

- *Don't chase returns.* Don't make the same mistake that people make with traditional investment managers by chasing last year's hot hedge fund manager. As with traditional managers, most hedge fund strategies exhibit some kind of cyclicality. It is unusual to find hot performance three or more years in a row. Instead, if you are investing in directional strategies, look for a hedge fund manager who over time is able to deliver equity-like returns, perhaps 10 to 12 percent average annual rates of return after fees, but with much less volatility than a comparable equity benchmark. If you are looking for absolute return strategies, then target a 5 to 7 percent net return. It is more reasonable to work with hedge fund managers who target these kinds of returns. To seek returns that are two or three times the market averages generally requires employing excessive trading risk or portfolio leverage. It is speculation rather than investing.

- *Do focus on the* hedged *fund as a means to preserve capital in down markets more than a way to "knock the cover off the ball."* You should be much more interested in a hedge fund manager who preserves capital well when the traditional stock and bond markets are doing poorly. You should look for managers that perform well in down markets, and, in exchange for this, leave money on the table and underperform in a strong bull market. For example, you should be more comfortable with a long/short equity manager who uses his short positions as an offsetting hedge against his long positions. The manager focuses on making his returns on the long side of his portfolio but then hedges these positions to some extent through the use of short sales.

- *Do pay attention to leverage.* In my experience there is usually enough investment octane offered by the competitive edge a hedge fund manager may have in his investment strategy. Leverage may tilt the risk of a portfolio toward higher than acceptable potential volatility and drawdown. However, this rule is somewhat strategy-specific. For example, in fixed-income hedge funds, like fixed-income arbitrage, the use of leverage is common and acceptable because of the nature of the offsetting positions. Look for hedge funds that do not exceed their category's average portfolio leverage.

- *Do focus on after-tax returns.* Hedge fund strategies tend not to be tax-friendly. They generate a great deal of short-term capital gains, particularly through short positions, which tend not to be held for long periods of time. Also, even on the long side, most hedge funds tend to be trading-oriented. It is safe to assume that 100 percent of your return from most hedge fund strategies will be considered ordinary income. Offsetting some of the negative tax effect will be realized losses and any gains from futures contracts, which are considered for tax purposes to be 60 percent long-term gain and 40 percent short-term gain regardless of the holding period. Taxes are not a reason to avoid hedge funds altogether. Even net of fees and taxes, hedge funds generally will add material diversification benefits to a portfolio, but the investor should be aware of the impact of taxes at the outset.

- *Don't get too hung up on transparency.* Investors often complain about a lack of transparency, yet in my opinion, if the investor had complete transparency, position by position, what then would he or she do with this information? It is difficult to understand each specific investment and what risk each position represents. Rather, it makes more sense to understand the manager's risk in the aggregate—what factors will impact performance positively and what factors negatively and what the exposure is in dollar terms to these broad risk factors. As a general rule, "Know your manager" is a better solution than complete transparency.

CONCLUSION

It is likely that assets under management in the hedge fund industry will double again in the next five years. This asset growth will be fueled in part by institutional investors, including public and private retirement funds. In spite of this rapid growth or perhaps because of it, in 2002, approximately 15 percent of hedge fund managers closed their doors and went out of business because of poor investment performance, the inability to raise capital, or the inability to effectively run the day-to-day business. In the next few years we will find out how many of the remaining 6,000 plus hedge fund managers deserve to have investors give them money to invest.

Even with the influx of so many managers, the hedge fund world should remain a talent-driven industry in which the best and brightest can deliver excellent risk-adjusted rates of return through their skill, the flexibility of hedge fund structures, and the unregulated nature of the business. It is, however, the unregulated nature of the industry that also makes it a potentially more difficult and dangerous investment landscape.

Hedge funds can offer educated investors many benefits and should be considered seriously for inclusion in well-diversified public market portfolios.

Studies have consistently shown that by including a percentage of hedge fund investments as part of an overall asset allocation, investors should be able to both enhance expected rates of return as well as reduce the overall risk of a portfolio.

Note

1. The author would like to thank Susan Luvisi for her work on the graphics in this chapter.

Additional Reading and Resources

Lowenstein, Roger. *When Genius Failed: The Rise and Fall of Long-Term Capital Management.* New York: Random House, 2001.

McCrary, Stuart A. *How to Create and Manage a Hedge Fund.* New York: John Wiley & Sons, 2002.

Nicholas, Joseph G. *Investing in Hedge Funds: Strategies for the New Marketplace.* Princeton, NJ: Bloomberg Press, 1999.

Strachman, Donald A. *Getting Started in Hedge Funds.* New York: John Wiley & Sons, 2000.

Research Articles

Ineichen, Alexander M., "The Myth of Hedge Funds." London: UBS Warburg, October 24, 2001.

Schneeweis, Thomas, and George Martin. "The Benefits of Hedge Funds: Asset Allocation for the Institutional Investor." Center for International Securities and Derivatives Markets/Isenberg School of Management, University of Massachusetts, September 2002.

Schneeweis, Thomas, Hossein Kazemi, and George Martin. "Understanding Hedge Fund Performance: Research Results and Rules of Thumb for the Institutional Investor." Center for International Securities and Derivatives Markets/Isenberg School of Management, University of Massachusetts, September 2001.

Author Background

Fritz Folts is president and founder of Mettowee Capital Advisors, LLC, a Boston-based registered investment advisory firm. He has over 15 years of investment industry experience. Fritz previously spent three years as part of a private client team at Lehman Brothers, Inc. in Boston. Before joining Lehman Brothers, Fritz co-founded and served as president of Saugatuck Securities, Inc. of Westport, Connecticut—an NASD registered broker-dealer which provided private placement, and investment banking services on a global basis to investment management firms specializing in alternative investments. Fritz began his career at The Boston Company and later served as director of global funding for the Boston Safe Deposit & Trust Co. (UK) Ltd. in London, England.

Chapter 17

Performance

Robert E. Phillips

Nothing is ever as simple as it seems. Measuring investment performance is no different. Investors typically have very simple performance objectives that can be stated along the following lines:

"My goal is to achieve as high a return as possible with as little risk as possible."
"I'd like to preserve the purchasing power of these assets after fees and taxes."
"Please take these assets and invest them so that at some time in the future I will be able to meet my personal income needs."

Unfortunately, many professionals in the money management industry have found creative ways to sell their approaches through the manipulation of performance data so that it appears better than it is. By adjusting measurement time periods, benchmarks, and more subtle calculation methods, performance can be presented in its most favorable light. In order to know if the investment manager is meeting the performance objectives, investors must understand how to interpret and compare results in terms of both absolute and relative performance and in the context of the risk taken to achieve the performance. Return numbers outside the context of risk mean very little. In the sections that follow, the basics of performance and risk analysis are presented.

SINGLE-PERIOD RETURN CALCULATIONS

Most investment performance is reported in terms of a return. In its simplest form, a return is the ratio of the change in investment value to the initial asset value. Simply stated, this is a measure of how much was gained relative to how much was risked. The beauty of this measure of performance is that it allows comparison between different portfolios since it is independent of the size of the initial assets. For example, if the initial investment is \$100,000 and the value at the end of one year is \$110,000, then the return is calculated as:

Total Return = (110,000 − 100,000)/100,000 = 10,000/100,000 = 0.10 or 10%

If there are no cash flows into or out of the account, then the calculation of total return is a direct reflection of progress towards personal investment goals. As simple as this calculation is, the determination of the input values requires special consideration. In many cases, there are cash flows into or out of the account that will distort the return if not accounted for. When an account has cash flows, the return on investment (ROI) is calculated as:

ROI = ((EMV + Net Outflow) − (BMV + Net Inflow))/(BMV + Net Inflow)

where EMV is the ending market value of the assets and BMV is the value. Note that the treatment of inflows and outflows ensures that the return is not artificially inflated or deflated. In the ROI formula it is assumed that the inflows occur at the beginning of the period and the outflows occur at the end of the period. Generally, this is not the case so the return must be further adjusted for the amount of time cash is actually held in the account. There are two ways to calculate this return. The first is called the *dollar weighted return*. The dollar weighted return is calculated using the formula:

$$EMV = BMV(1 + IRR) + CF_1(1 + IRR)^{F_1} + \cdots + CF_n(1 + IRR)F_n$$

where IRR is the internal rate of return, CF is cash flow in the period, and F is the fraction of the period over which the cash flow has an effect. For example, if you invest \$100,000 at the beginning of a month, add \$1,000 on the fifth day of the month, remove \$2,000 on the twentieth day of the month, and the value of the assets is \$105,000 on the thirtieth day of the month (the last day), then the dollar weighted return is calculated by solving for IRR in the equation:

$$105,000 = 100,000 \times (1 + IRR) + 1,000(1 + IRR)^{0.9} - 2,000(1 + IRR)^{0.333}$$

In this case, IRR = 0.065 or 6.5 percent. Note that the total return without accounting for the cash flows would be 5 percent. The return must be larger to account for the withdrawal near the end of the period. This is a useful way to get a measure of the performance of an individual account. As pointed out, however, the dollar weighted return is strongly influenced by cash flow timing.

When comparing the performance of investment managers, it is important to remove the effect of cash flows. This is done using a *time weighted return* (TWR). The time weighted return is calculated as:

$$TWR = [(1 + R_1) \times (1 + R_2) \times \cdots (1 + R_N) - 1] \times 100$$

where R is the subperiod return calculated as:

$$R = \text{Ending Market Value} / $$
$$(\text{Beginning Market Value} + \text{Net Cash Flow During Period}) - 1$$

Using the example above, assume that the market value at the end of the fourth day of the month is $101,000, at the end of the fifth day the market value is $102,000, at the end of the nineteenth day the market value is $103,000, at the end of the twentieth day the market value is $101,000, and the final market value is $105,000. The subperiod returns are:

$$R_1 = 101000/100000 - 1 = 0.01$$

$$R_2 = 103000/(101000 + 1000) - 1 = 0.009804$$

$$R_3 = 105000/(103000 - 2000) - 1 = 0.039604$$

The time weighted return is then:

$$TWR = [(1.01) \times (1.009804) \times (1.039604) - 1] \times 100 = 6.03\%$$

It is useful to compare the dollar weighted and the time weighted returns. By removing the effect of the cash flows, the time weighted return presents a more direct performance measure attributed to the choice of investments rather than the timing of cash flows. In the example above, the effect of having the $1,000 inflow for nearly the full period and the withdrawal near the end of the period inflates the reported dollar weighted performance by 0.5 percent over the comparable time weighted return.

For the purpose of comparison the accepted global investment performance standard published by the Association for Investment Management and Research (AIMR) calls for investment managers to calculate performance using at least monthly subperiods accounting for daily cash flow. Acceptance of this standard by a money management firm will ensure that performance comparisons are based on a consistent calculation.

MULTIPERIOD RETURN CALCULATIONS

Studying returns calculated for a day or a month is interesting but not very useful for comparative investment analysis. Multiperiod returns are calculated based on the result of compounding the single-period returns over a fixed period of time. A cumulative total return is calculated as:

$$\text{Cumulative return} = [(1 - R_1) \times (1 - R_2) \times \cdots (1 - R_N) - 1] \times 100$$

Similarly, an annualized return can be calculated based on this cumulative return. For any period, if we have a cumulative return for that period and M is the number of periods per year, the annualized return is calculated as:

$$\text{Annualized return} = [(1 + \text{cumulative return}/100)^{M/N} - 1] \times 100$$

For example, if the three-year cumulative return is 15 percent then the annualized return is:

$$\text{Annualized return} = [(1.15)^{1/3} - 1] \times 100 = 4.77\%$$

COMPARING PORTFOLIO RETURNS

Comparison of portfolio returns requires a great deal of care. For example, most people understand the fundamental asymmetry of gains and losses that requires a 100 percent return to recover from a 50 percent loss. However, in comparing returns, there is often an assumption that average return and annualized return represent comparable quantities.

To understand the difference between average and annualized returns, consider the sequence of annual returns in Table 17.1. As can be seen, the average returns for portfolio 1 and portfolio 2 are similar, with portfolio 2 slightly better than portfolio 1. However, the volatility of portfolio 2 makes the annualized return roughly half that of portfolio 1. Most importantly, this

Table 17.1

	Portfolio 1	Portfolio 2
Year 1	3.0%	10.0%
Year 2	4.0%	−30.0%
Year 3	2.0%	5.0%
Year 4	3.0%	10.0%
Year 5	3.0%	−30.0%
Year 6	4.0%	8.0%
Year 7	3.0%	25.0%
Year 8	2.5%	20.0%
Year 9	3.0%	10.0%
Year 10	2.5%	5.0%
Average annual return	3.0%	3.3%
Annualized return	3.0%	1.5%

manifests itself as a dramatic difference in total returns. If $10,000 was invested at the beginning of year 1 in each portfolio, the amount in portfolio 1 at the end of year 10 would be $13,437, whereas the amount in portfolio 2 would be $11,648.

COMPOSITE PERFORMANCE

Most managers report performance for a particular investment style based on either a representative account or on the basis of composite performance of a complete set of portfolios. Calculation of composite performance requires some care and can be the source of confusion unless the standards for construction are met. The key requirement in composite construction is that all fee-paying discretionary portfolios must be included in at least one composite. This standard attempts to guard against selective inclusion of accounts to artificially inflate performance. This is not as black and white a consideration as one might imagine. The key word in the standard is "discretionary." If a client in any way constrains the investment decisions of the investment advisor, the portfolio must be excluded from the composite construction.

It may seem obvious, but the definition of a composite relies on the portfolios having similar investment objectives and/or strategies. Among the considerations in defining a composite are the asset classes used in the portfolio, the style or strategy, the benchmarks used for comparison, and the risk/return characteristics. It is also common to consider the type of client best suited for the strategy, the instruments used (including the use of derivatives, hedging, or leverage), the treatment of taxes, and the base currency. Once the basis for the composite is established, new accounts meeting the criteria must be added on a timely basis. Similarly, terminated portfolios must be included in the historical record of the appropriate composite.

A final consideration is the use of simulated portfolio performance. Combination of actual performance results with simulated or model performance must be clearly disclosed and should not be reported as composite performance.

ADJUSTING RETURNS FOR RISK

Most investors understand the importance of time in long-term investment. That explains the focus on returns when comparing investment manager performance. It is important to understand that past performance does not paint a complete picture as to whether or not a particular investment strategy will result in meeting an individual's investment goals. The other key consideration is the degree of risk associated with an investment manager's strategy. There are three typical measures of risk that can be used to compare investment managers. The first type of risk is *absolute risk*. Absolute risk is a statistical measure of the volatility of returns. Like total return, this is a historical measure. It is often used in conjunction with total return to determine the probability of achieving the historical returns. The most common measure of absolute risk is the standard deviation of returns, calculated as:

$$\text{Standard Deviation} = \sqrt{\Sigma(R_i - R_m)^2/N}$$

where R_m is the mean return over all N periods. For comparison between managers it is often useful to annualize the standard deviation where:

$$\text{Annualized standard deviation} = \text{Standard Deviation} \times \sqrt{P}$$

where P is the number of periods per year. The standard deviation is a basic measure of historical volatility. Although there is a strong relationship between volatility and the risk of achieving a particular return, the standard deviation represents a symmetric measure of volatility. In most cases, the investor is more concerned about downside volatility. This is often referred to as *downside risk*. The downside risk is often studied by examining historical drawdown of a portfolio. A drawdown is measured as:

$$\text{Drawdown} = (\text{Local Max Market Value} - \text{Local Min Market Value}) / \text{Local Max Market Value}$$

In many cases it is most useful to study the maximum drawdown over a long period of time for a given portfolio. Although this is still a historical measure, it is an indication of the worst case, (from the highest point to the lowest point), downside scenario for a given portfolio style.

ESTIMATING RISK-ADJUSTED RETURN

Information regarding the performance of a portfolio is often represented in the form of a ratio. Based on the Nobel Prize work of William Sharpe, one of the most common ways to compute a risk-adjusted return is through the Sharpe ratio. The components of the Sharpe ratio are built on the difference between the historical return of a portfolio and the return of a risk-free benchmark. In many cases the risk-free return is based on the interest rate on short-term Treasury bills. The Sharpe ratio is calculated as:

$$\text{Sharpe Ratio} = \text{Mean Differential Return} / \text{Standard Deviation of Differential Return}$$

The Sharpe Ratio is often annualized using the following relationship:

$$\text{Annualized Sharpe Ratio} = \text{Sharpe Ratio} \times \sqrt{P}$$

where P is the number of periods in a year. When comparing two different portfolios, or a portfolio to a benchmark, the Sharpe ratio measures the value added by the investment manager over a risk-free rate normalized by the volatility (risk). If two managers have the same differential return, the manager with the lower volatility will have a higher Sharpe ratio. This represents the increased probability that the manager with lower volatility will more likely achieve the historical returns.

COMPARATIVE EVALUATION OF INVESTMENT PERFORMANCE

Every investor is in search of a quantitative set of measures that will allow the comparison of an investment manager's ability to meet the investor's goals. The important thing to remember is that every measure described above is based on historical performance reported by the manager for a portfolio style. There is never any guarantee that future performance of a particular manager style will resemble past performance. Among the variables that are outside the scope of the measures described above are changes in style, future model risk, and future liquidity risk.

When comparing managers, it is best to request direct return data net of fees on at least a monthly basis so that the measures described above can be calculated using consistent approaches and benchmarks. Using the time weighted return will provide the best comparison of absolute total return performance. The downside risk defined as maximum drawdown will provide an estimate of the worst-case scenario at the point of withdrawal. Finally, the Sharpe ratio allows comparison of relative risk. Using these measures will provide a solid means of comparing portfolios and allow investors to evaluate managers on a level playing field.

Additional Reading and Resources

AIMR. *Global Investment Performance Standards Handbook*. Charlottesville, VA: AIMR, 2002.

Feibel, Bruce. *Investment Performance Measurement*. New York: Wiley Finance, 2003.

Author Background

Robert Phillips is President of R.E. Phillips Systems, Inc., a firm providing technology platforms and consulting to investment advisors. Bob is a recognized expert in configuration technology, customer relationship management systems and complex systems simulation and analysis. Most recently he was Executive Vice President and Chief Technology Officer at Windward Investment Management. There he was responsible for managing daily operations and technology used in investing and client service. Prior to Windward, he was the Chief Technology Officer for Whatifi Financial where he was responsible for building an innovative, fully automated mutual fund operation. Prior to joining Whatifi, he served as Vice President & Chief Architect with Oracle Corporation where he oversaw the integration of state-of-the-art configuration technology into Oracle's applications software and solutions. He also advised on product development for sales force automation. Bob served as Chief Technology Officer / Vice President Engineering for Concentra Corporation (previously named ICAD, Inc.) until the company's acquisition by Oracle. While at Concentra, he led the development effort for award-winning configuration-based customer relationship management systems.

Chapter 18

Ongoing Management and Accountability

Douglas Ederle and Todd Millay

The maxim "Trust but verify" applies equally well to wealth management services as it does to international diplomacy. The purpose of this chapter is to equip you with both the ability to strengthen the trust you have placed in your wealth managers and to verify that they are serving your best interests. In our opinion, the most trustworthy wealth managers are those whose incentives place them firmly on your side in all of the situations you and your family likely will face. Verifying this is crucial to ensure that your wealth manager will do the right thing for you and your family when it really counts —even after you may no longer be able to supervise them personally.

As a successful entrepreneur, you likely will have a bias to be more hands-on in both the selection and oversight of your wealth manager than would the average high-net-worth individual. You also will be more likely to demand a higher level of service and technical know-how than simply the industry standard. The good news is that, with the right tools, these attitudes put you in a good position to hold your wealth manager accountable for delivering a high level of service.

The bad news, however, is that you are at risk of mistaking a high degree of involvement with true insight into how well your interests are being served and your needs met. We hope that the ideas discussed in this chapter will prevent this from happening, and help you to stay on top of your wealth management solution. In addition, if you are no longer able to supervise your affairs (whether because you are incapacitated, deceased, or simply immersed in a new business venture), these tools should help to empower and protect your loved ones as well. Make sure that those who will come after you are comfortable with and trust your wealth manager.

Selecting and monitoring a wealth management solution is a highly personal and family-specific event. High-level advice on managing your financial affairs can be useful, but it only goes so far. Some of the tools described below will be more important than others, depending on your family's circumstances and needs. Usually, there will be one or two issues that rise above all others in importance for you and your family.

In particular, you should think about how you view the purpose, or meaning, of your wealth. For example, you could view your wealth as primarily working capital for future projects, as a source of ongoing security for your family, or as a family legacy in which each generation serves as steward for the next. By clearly defining what is most important to you, you will simplify the task of monitoring ongoing performance, and will ensure that the wealth manager is focused on serving your most pressing needs.

In the end, some level of trust is not only desirable; it is *essential*. We emphasize, therefore, that the single most important thing you can do is to ensure that you have found a wealth management solution in which all of your advisors face no incentives other than to give you the best possible service and advice. Having a truly *independent* and *objective* wealth manager monitoring your situation, and cutting through all of the industry's smoke and mirrors, can go a long way to ensuring that your trust will be well placed.

RANGE OF STRUCTURES
FOR ONGOING MANAGEMENT

As you know, many options exist for structuring the array of service providers that will meet your wealth management needs. Each of these different structures brings its own advantages and challenges in ongoing management and accountability. The following classifications include most of the major types of service providers, and provide a useful backdrop to our discussion. The right solution for you may well depend upon the level of family wealth.

These solutions are not mutually exclusive, and many entrepreneurs have found a combination or variant of them to be the right answer for their needs:

- *Do it yourself.* With surprising regularity, this is often the first choice of entrepreneurs who have created significant wealth. The rationale seems to be, "If I created my wealth, why should I not manage it?" In this case, the primary challenge is managing yourself and honestly assessing your own performance across a range of wealth management disciplines (investment management, tax strategy, estate planning, etc.).
- *Single professional.* Many entrepreneurs employ a single trusted individual to manage their affairs. This person is often a CPA or lawyer who started working for the entrepreneur in a narrow professional capacity, and then gradually assumed ever greater responsibilities beyond his or her area of primary expertise. Interestingly, although it is not clear why, this solution seems to be particularly prevalent in the venture capital community.
- *Administrative family office.* In this situation, the entrepreneur hires one or more people to look after his or her administrative needs (e.g., bill paying, travel arrangements, insurance summaries) and relies on others (e.g., law firms, accounting firms, investment management companies) for professional services.
- *Full-fledged family office.* In some cases, usually involving substantial wealth (e.g., over $200 million), the entrepreneur decides to create a private office capable of providing a full range of services, rather than just administrative help. A dedicated family office will employ a number of professionals who work only for the family.
- *Multifamily office.*[1] The idea of a multifamily office is to combine the intimacy and responsiveness of a dedicated family office with the ability to attract very high caliber talent covering the spectrum of necessary services. Multifamily offices usually consist of a small group of professionals who serve a limited number of client families.
- *Multifamily cooperative.* Multifamily cooperatives bring groups of wealthy individuals and families together for the purpose of knowledge exchange and pooling of buying power, and to consider unique investment opportunities.
- *Major financial institution.* A final category of solutions is the private client distribution arms of many large financial institutions. This is also a popular port of call for entrepreneurs because they offer the comfort of a recognized brand name and also may have participated in the cre-

ation of the entrepreneur's wealth. Indeed, the bulk of the clients of many of these firms are often the result of cross-selling from other services (such as investment banking or lending).

In closing this brief overview of the providers available to meet your needs (singly or in combination), we would like to let you in on the dirty little secret of the private wealth management business. It is a secret that all of the above players know, and we hope that bringing it to your attention will heighten your interest in our advice on managing and holding these providers accountable for their recommendations.

The secret is this: Your assets are widely believed to be very "sticky." This means that, once you have decided on your wealth management solution, even if the decision is made during a very busy time of your life when you cannot conduct a thorough due diligence (e.g., during your company's IPO), you are highly unlikely to change it unless you are absolutely fed up. Many studies have shown that this is indeed true, even for entrepreneurs like you. The pursuit of large pools of sticky assets continues to lure all kinds of players to pursue the wealth management market for high-net-worth individuals.

Assets are sticky for good reason. A lot of effort by you is involved in establishing and setting up a relationship. In addition, you expect the quality of service to improve over time as your advisor gets to know you better and is more attuned to your family's needs. In the wealth management business, inertia is a powerful force, and it takes considerable effort to uproot and move. This means two things: (1) Choose carefully and (2) watch carefully— do not allow your providers to think that they have you for life. By regularly evaluating your wealth management solution, you can avoid falling into the sticky assets trap.

BASIC MONITORING CRITERIA
FOR EXTERNAL PROVIDERS

Many of the basic criteria that you should monitor in any group or person with whom you work are, to large degree, the same as those you most likely looked for as you assembled employees and partners to build your business. Even though these base criteria seem intuitive, it is important to highlight them explicitly:

- *Competence.* Those who advise you on any wealth management topic should be experts in their fields. They must demonstrate that they are thoroughly familiar with all the tools available to them, and know how to use them. For example, an asset manager should be well versed in all kinds of investment vehicles, including alternative investments, such as hedge funds and private equity, and tax-advantaged index replication strategies. The most competent, best professionals continuously keep themselves abreast of the latest developments in their fields.

- *Experience.* Competence usually comes from relevant experience. Check to see whether a wealth manager has experience with people like *you* and situations like *yours*. Long experience in serving multigenerational families may not translate directly to your situation as an entrepreneur (potentially first generation). Ask for examples of how the wealth manager has helped people in a similar position to your own.
- *Commitment.* Wealth management is a profession that, like all professions, requires a high degree of commitment. Long experience is often evidence of a deep commitment, but you also should look for examples of where a wealth manager has gone "beyond the call of duty" to help you. The best wealth managers enjoy and are passionate about what they do, and this commitment should be easy to see over time.
- *Teamwork skills.* Because of the complexities involved in managing private client wealth, it is very hard for one person to have all of the answers. It is not enough to have great individuals working for you; they also must be well integrated as a team. This teamwork should extend beyond the wealth management firm to include your other providers (accountants, insurance advisors, attorneys, and others). Be sure that you are also viewed as a part of the team, rather than as a passive recipient of prescribed answers. Any successful entrepreneur living in a good-size metropolitan area should be able to choose from a wide range of competent service providers. Be sure that those you select add up to a team that is greater than the sum of the parts.

These baseline criteria are essential to evaluate and reconsider over time, to be sure you remain comfortable with your initial assessment. In addition to these general criteria, there are a number of specific traits to monitor and evaluate that are essential in wealth management. As you will see from the comments below, monitoring these criteria depends as much on your overall feel for the situation as it does on any well-defined metrics:

- *Trust.* Trust is the foundation of any successful, sustained relationship with a wealth manager. Listen to your instincts. If you ever have doubts about the trustworthiness of the people working for you, even if you cannot say why, reconsider the relationship.

- *Sensitivity.* Wealth management is deeply personal. You need to work with someone you can talk to openly and honestly about personal family issues. If you are not comfortable opening up in this way, then your wealth manager will not get the information he or she needs to help you. Equally important, if your wealth manager is not sensitive to your needs, and a good listener, then the value of this personal information will be lost. Trust your instincts as to whether your wealth manager really "gets it" when it comes to your family's needs.

- *Confidentiality.* Your information should be treated with absolute discretion, period. Do not settle for anything less. It is an environment of true confidentiality that makes the frank exchange of information possible. Avoid wealth managers who are too free with information about other clients that they serve. If you sense at all that you could be the topic of conversation at the ballgame or an after work happy hour, it is time to move on.

- *Value.* By any measure, wealth management services cost a lot of money. The people you employ are (or should be) skilled professionals who charge a premium for their services. At the end of the day, you need to be sure that the tangible returns (investment returns, tax savings, etc.) and intangible benefits (peace of mind, advice on philanthropy, etc.) of your wealth management solution more than justify this expense. Your wealth manager should give you a periodic accounting of the value that he or she is delivering to you, as we discuss in the next section of this chapter. This accounting of the value delivered should contain a clear summary and as much detail as you need to make an evaluation.

You should apply the above criteria to all of your dealings with your wealth manager, from your initial meeting to periodic updates on your family's current situation. Be sure that, over time, you are actively asking yourself whether you are comfortable that all of the above criteria are being met.

The following section discusses the mechanics of how to review your provider's performance over time. As we said at the outset, this kind of continuing oversight is necessary to ensure that the trust you have placed in your wealth manager (trust will always be necessary to some degree) is well founded.

REVIEWING YOUR PROVIDER'S PERFORMANCE OVER TIME

Because it is such an attractive industry for financial services providers (remember the "sticky assets"), private wealth management has become increasingly competitive over time. This is good news for you, because it means that all wealth managers should be holding themselves to ever higher standards. For example, 10 years ago just about all wealth managers only would sell their own investment products. Today, open architecture is increasingly common, with far greater choice among higher-quality investment solutions and products for the client.

Unfortunately, however, the evolution of the wealth management industry still has a long way to go. Wealth management continues to be a very highly fragmented industry with thousands of providers. This means that, for now, innovative business models that are finely attuned to the client's interests coexist with antiquated practices that are mostly geared to the financial benefit and preferred working style of the provider.

Unfortunately, many still feel that there is a lot more hay than needles in the wealth management industry. To monitor and evaluate your provider, we recommend the best practices below.

UNDERSTAND THE ECONOMICS OF THE BUSINESS

You always should be comfortable asking your wealth manager any questions you have about his or her business model. In particular, you should be sure to drill down into the economics of the business. Be sure you understand all the ways that your wealth manager makes money, both at the outset of your relationship and over time. To do so, be sure you know the answer to questions such as:

- What have I been charged, *all-in,* in fees, commissions, markups, and other costs? Be aware that some advisers make money beyond their basic wealth management fee. If you have questions or cannot fully understand how much you are paying, get it in writing.
- Do the fees that I pay vary depending upon the performance of my wealth manager?[2]
- Am I being charged any hidden fees or markups? For example, some players claim to manage their clients' bonds "for free." In reality, these play-

ers often are capturing a substantial spread over what you would pay for the exact same, or similar, bonds in a competitive bidding process. This spread can amount to tens (perhaps, even hundreds) of lost basis points in performance (and therefore extra fees) to you, the client. Who picks up these dollars at your expense? The person managing your bonds "for free."

- How much of what I am being sold is off the shelf and proprietary to the provider versus a best-in-breed, competitively priced solution? For example, are you being sold marked-up bonds from inventory, or a "custom" solution that is in fact a standardized package?

- How does the total cost of this solution compare with that of other comparable quality wealth managers in the marketplace?

- Have I paid more for certain investment strategies than others? If so, does the firm or individual making those recommendations earn more from me by recommending one versus the other? Does this skew the advice that I receive?

- How does the organization value and compensate its professionals? If sales are valued over advice, integration, and client service skills, you will be treated more like a distribution outlet than a valued wealth management client.

UNDERSTAND YOUR WEALTH MANAGEMENT PERFORMANCE

Your providers should explain to you your level of investment performance *after fees and taxes*, to the extent it can be readily calculated, and how this compares to the appropriate benchmark. There are several important elements to the preceding sentence.

First, be sure that your wealth manager is focused on performance net of fees and taxes—otherwise he or she is missing a large and essential part of the equation. This perspective on performance will help to ensure that your solution is being integrated (e.g., by harmonizing tax and investment decision making) and not solved piecemeal. Although computing after fees is, or should be, straightforward, precise estimates of after-tax performance are often difficult to make. The point is not that your wealth manager should present you with a precise after-tax figure, but that he or she adopts a mindset that focuses on the performance that is actually of value to you. You can't spend or even save pre-tax performance.

Second, be sure that the benchmark your provider is trying to beat is the right one. Does it have approximately the same risk profile as your portfolio?

Is it transparent (you can easily access information about it, e.g., the S&P 500)? Can you actually invest in the benchmark (you could actually choose to put money into the benchmark, e.g., a Vanguard index fund)?

Third, you should also understand how and why your provider either over- or underperformed the benchmark. Was it only because he or she took on more risk? We have seen wealth managers who delivered exceptional returns in the heyday of the late 1990s deliver equally stunning underperformance in the early 2000s. Which investments performed the best, and which performed the worst? What does your wealth manager intend to do as a result of this performance record? Do you sense a real investment strategy for the portfolio? Be extremely cautious with any manager who seems to chase whatever new hot investment product that comes along. As the past few years have graphically demonstrated, past returns are no guarantee for the future—chasing them usually ends in buying at the top of a cycle.

Finally, we emphasize that you should take a holistic view of performance. The quality of a wealth management firm's client service and measurable benefits attained beyond investment performance (e.g., designing an investment plan within your comfort zone, advice leading to income tax or estate/gift tax savings, and/or unlocking value by integrating all wealth components) should be taken into account. How you weigh such factors relative to pure investment performance is up to you, but be sure you are looking at all the value your wealth manager is supposed to deliver.

HOLD YOUR PROVIDER ACCOUNTABLE

In our view, wealth managers can truly serve your interests only when they are directly accountable for the consequences of their advice. When accountability is fragmented among several providers, or when you are given general advice rather than specific recommendations, the buck will always be passed back to you. We like to see a single person or firm on the hook for integrating the total solution, and not just for each separate piece (investment management, tax, estate planning, etc.) because of the huge amount of value that is at stake from this integration.

The best way to ensure accountability is through regular review sessions that cover your situation, and by extension, all aspects of your wealth manager's performance. Because of the value of integration, these sessions should be a comprehensive wealth management review rather than simply an analysis of how your investment portfolio did last quarter. We think that periodic reviews are important, but the frequency of these sessions should be up to you—our recommendation is quarterly, and annually at the very least. The quarterly meetings often will focus on investments, and current wealth management concerns, whereas the annual meeting is often a more comprehensive, holistic view.

At each review session, come prepared with questions for your wealth manager. Do not simply go over a questionnaire, as this can be impersonal and often off the point, but prepare in advance to cover all the topics that you would like to address. Example topic areas and questions you may wish to ask include:

- *Personnel.* Has there been any turnover of key people? If so, why did they leave, and where did they go?
- *Portfolio strategy.* Are you still following the investment process you explained to me in the beginning? Are there any additions to my portfolio that might be outside the range of what I might have expected? What scenarios are favorable to the way we have invested, and which are not favorable? What is your view of the economy and the capital markets today, and how is my portfolio positioned in light of your view and my personal situation?
- *Investment performance.* Why do you use this benchmark to measure my investment performance? What is the risk/volatility level of the benchmark vs. my portfolio? How does recent performance affect planning for my long-term goals?

Even though it may be seem tedious, you should be sure to understand the details that underlie the reports your wealth manager gives you. Review items such as trade confirmations and tax returns to be sure you understand them—if you do not, you may inadvertently waive your right to a claim even if something truly has gone meaningfully wrong.

WATCH OUT FOR WARNING SIGNS

Just because your wealth management solution is performing well and seems right for you at the outset does not guarantee that it will remain high quality over time. Luckily, there are a number of warning signs that you can watch out for that should alert you to the potential for problems:

- *Organizational turnover.* Look out for changes in your relationship manager and other key personnel, especially at higher client service/investment levels. This can signal internal turmoil. Once a few of the key people are gone, especially at a smaller, more personal wealth management organization, the result can be a rapid collapse.

- *Organizational change.* Mergers, acquisitions, and even rapid growth, all which seem to be increasingly common occurrences, can lead to shifts in a firm's values. Following such an event, it is common for a best advice approach to erode over time and be replaced with product pushing and/or for a different investment philosophy to emerge. Even more problematic, a firm's long-term positive culture can disappear, followed soon thereafter by key personnel. Pay attention to these potential cultural shifts any time there is a major corporate event or change at your wealth manager—despite the fact that internally the employees may be in turmoil or looking to leave following the event, you will be the last to know unless your radar is up.

- *Fee changes.* Be sure that explicit and underlying fees are not being altered covertly or changed on you without a good reason. This can be a signal that the wealth manager is struggling with its economic model. It also goes to the basic requirement of trust in your relationship.

- *Poor reporting.* Your monthly and quarterly reports are an important signal of overall quality. Check them for errors—most reports require some degree of manual data entry, and mistakes can happen. Any mistake that you do find should be rectified swiftly, and not recur in the future.

- *Poor investment results of shifting investment strategy.* Although the wealth manager should be shifting your assets around over time to try to take advantage of market conditions and deliver you a better return, all these changes should be grounded in a consistent underlying investment philosophy that is stated clearly to you in writing. Radical changes to this underlying approach can be a signal of underlying internal turmoil or deep uncertainty. Be sure your investment management firm explains its market thesis and investment outlook to you in clear terms—don't hold back from asking even basic questions if you need to. Make sure that your plan is in synch with your needs and long-term goals. Usually, such shifts start to occur when there has been a sustained period of poor investment performance. If poor investment performance extends over a multiyear period, you should dig deeper to determine the reasons, and decide whether they can be corrected.

As several of the above warning signs demonstrate, thorough, regular reporting from your wealth manager is essential. However, this reporting is a backstop and foundation for the ongoing dialogue that you should be having with your wealth manager. You should ask the firm as many questions as you need answers, and never be hesitant to push for greater clarity. Although wealth management does require a high degree of skill and training, the best practitioners are those who can explain it clearly. Any successful entrepreneur should be able to understand how the wealth manager is addressing his or her needs.

There is a significant degree of turmoil around having to switch wealth managers once a team has gotten to know you and your family well over a number of years. When you find a team that provides the service and results you require, a willingness to fairly compensate that team, recognizing the importance of a high-level wealth management solution, can be critical. Positive results require some investment on your part—enough time to be a team player with your wealth manager, and a willingness to pay a fair fee for exceptional service, which makes sense to support the continuity of your team.

PROVIDER-SPECIFIC ISSUES TO WATCH

With the foregoing general caveats in mind, this section provides some final, more targeted advice to you that is specific to each of the types of providers that exist in the marketplace[3]:

- *Do it yourself.* As we have said, in this case, the primary challenge is managing yourself. Certainly, you know yourself well, but ask yourself some hard questions. Do you have the necessary expertise in investment management, trust, estate and tax planning, philanthropy, and insurance? If not, how much time and effort will you devote to acquiring this specialized knowledge? Do you understand the true opportunities and risks concerning the integration of these various disciplines, where much of the value lies, as opposed to understanding the basics of each in a vacuum? Just like the field in which you made your wealth as an entrepreneur, the field of wealth management is complex and laden with traps for the unwary. Some level of guidance is essential. We are all familiar with the old adage that "the lawyer who represents himself has a fool for a client."
- *Single professional.* It is comforting to rely on a single trusted advisor. If the advisor is skilled, even better. Even the most trusted advisor or individual CFO, however, may be reluctant to admit when he or she is in over his or her head. We have experienced several cases in which the

individual CFO has disclosed privately that he or she feels significantly "out of their league" in certain critical areas, especially investments; it is unlikely that the client knows this. With this arrangement, you must be on your guard whenever this person strays from his or her true expertise. This is not a question of bad intentions (usually) but rather of a good person getting out of depth in an unfamiliar field. Neophyte investment advisors can make truly regrettable mistakes with their clients' money. Investment professionals can make spectacular tax blunders as well. In the field of wealth management, it is very difficult for one person to do everything well.

- *Administrative family office.* An administrative family office can be a major source of convenience. The main concern in this case is that the right hand will not know what the left hand is doing. Administrative family offices often lack the skills to truly integrate all aspects of an entrepreneur's financial life. As with the single professional, it is important to ensure that this solution does not stray beyond its core competency. Integration of the overall big picture will likely be up to you. In addition, some have found that overreliance on the family office can make their children less self-sufficient individuals.

- *Full-fledged family office.* A dedicated family office is usually responsive and dedicated to the needs of your family. Although this kind of family office can provide excellent integration and focus on your needs, you will need to be careful to find the best talent possible. Unfortunately, with notable exceptions, the best talent in the wealth management industry, especially concerning investments, may not gravitate to serving the needs of a single family. This solution can also be very difficult to unwind if it does not work out over time, putting an even greater premium on selective hiring and continuing oversight. One wealthy individual recently remarked that he has seen several poorly supervised family offices quickly turn into "rat's nests," where more time and energy is being devoted to managing the office rather than the assets of the family.

- *Multifamily office.* With a multifamily office, the main consideration is the quality, skill-set, and incentives of the partnership group. How will they assure you that, in every situation, they truly will be on your side? Ideally all of this firm's revenues should accrue from client advisory fees, without any hidden sales commissions or fees on in-house products. Is the firm willing to judge its performance on an after-fee basis, and willing to tie a portion of its advisory fees to its clients' investment performance? These kinds of structures are the best way to align the firm's interests with those of its clients, and should be expected from any multifamily office. In addition to incentives, you should watch to be sure that the multifamily office does not grow too large, or take on so many clients that it is unable to focus enough time on your needs. Finally, be sure that the office has all of the skills you require under its roof, with multiple, quality individuals covering the wealth management spectrum, and is not really just a glorified single professional firm with only one or two top-caliber people.

- *Multifamily cooperative.* A multifamily cooperative can be an excellent supplement to your overall wealth management solution. If you join a cooperative, be sure that it is designed around the interests of its members, rather than as a way to aggregate attractive customers for its sponsors. For example, the CCC Alliance, which is based in Boston, has no corporate sponsors and membership is meaningfully limited to families only. The CCC Alliance's only source of revenue is an annual membership fee. This kind of model may be the best way to ensure that you are getting truly objective advice.
- *Major financial institution.* With this solution, you get a larger organization with multiple lines of business, which can be appealing. However, you need to be extremely vigilant to ensure that you are not being sold quantities of (potentially inferior) in-house products and that you understand all the ways that the institution is making money from your account (e.g., by charging meaningful spreads on bond trades). Make sure that the institution's sales motive is directed toward creating a good long-term solution for you, and not just putting you into as many proprietary products as possible. If the sales incentive is too great, you can end up with a hodge-podge of investment products instead of what you need—a comprehensive, long-term investment strategy. From time to time, you also want to think hard about whether tangible benefits actually show up in your portfolio from the "global" reach and "deep, talented bench" that likely were touted in the marketing phase.

SUMMARY

Choosing a wealth management provider is just the beginning of your journey; managing your provider and checking performance are equally important. Finding a trustworthy objective wealth manager to monitor and coordinate your affairs will take a lot of the burden of monitoring off you, but be sure that your trust is well founded. True peace of mind can come only from being, and staying, well informed about how your wealth manager is serving the needs of your family.

Notes

1. We should disclose that SCS Financial falls into this category.
2. The answer is almost always no, but some wealth managers, such as SCS Financial, have introduced performance-based fees.
3. Again, SCS Financial is a multifamily office, so we are, of course, somewhat partial to that model.

Additional Reading and Resources

Aldrich, Nelson Jr. *Old Money*. New York: Allworth Press, 1996.

Boorstin, Daniel J. *The Creators*. New York: Vintage Books, 1993.

Brenner, Lynn. *Smart Questions to Ask Your Financial Advisors*. Berkeley Publishing Group, 1999.

Bruehl, Brian H. *Staying Wealthy: Strategies for Protecting Your Assets*. Princeton: Bloomberg Press, 1998.

Hausner, Lee. *Children of Paradise: Successful Parenting for Prosperous Families*. Los Angeles: Jeremy P. Tarcher, 1990.

Hughes, James E. Jr. *Family Wealth: Keeping it in the Family*. Princeton: Hughes and Whitaker, 1997.

Kleberg, Sally. *Private Wealth*. New York: McGraw-Hill, 1997.

Rosenberg, Claude Jr. *Wealthy and Wise*. Boston: Little, Brown, 1994.

Tracy, John A. *How to Read a Financial Report: Wringing Vital Signs Out of the Numbers*, 5th ed. New York: John Wiley and Sons, 1999.

Trone, Donald B, et al. *The Management of Investment Decisions*. Irwin Professional Publishing, 1995.

Williams, Arthur. *Managing Your Investment Manager: Complete Guide to Selection, Measurement, and Control*. Irwin Professional Publishing, 1992.

CCC Alliance, 121 High Street, Suite 400, Boston, MA 02110 (617-457-8368).

Author Background

Doug Ederle is a Managing Director at SCS Financial. He is a senior wealth management investment advisor to high-net-worth families. Most recently, he was a Senior Vice President at Atlantic Trust Company, N.A. (formerly Pell Rudman), and an Associate Partner of its parent company, AMVESCAP plc. He was Chair of the Management Committee prior to Pell Rudman's acquisition by AMVESCAP. At

Atlantic Trust, Doug was a senior client relationship manager advising many of the firm's most sophisticated and substantial clients. Doug previously was a Partner at Testa, Hurwitz & Thibeault in the Trust and Estates Group, where he was active in the firm's Fiduciary Investment Group. Earlier in his legal career at Testa he practiced corporate and securities law.

Todd Millay is a Partner at CCC Alliance, a global consortium of wealthy families. CCC Alliance was built "by families, for families," and offers its members a dynamic peer network, collaborative purchasing power, and a source of insight and opportunities. Prior to CCC, Todd was a Senior Engagement Manager at McKinsey & Company, where he specialized in serving financial institutions, particularly asset managers. During his five-year career at McKinsey, Todd worked with senior management at a wide variety of major financial services companies in both the United States and Europe, providing strategic advice on a investment opportunities and operational improvements.

Philanthropy

Chapter 19

Philanthropy and
the Venturesome Donor

Stephen P. Johnson

Most of those donors with whom The Philanthropic Initiative (TPI) has worked over the years have been entrepreneurs of one sort or another at some point in their lives. Even those who made their money in conventional, relatively risk-averse careers (e.g., securities, law, or manufacturing) typically have shown an entrepreneurial flair in life.

This common denominator is not surprising. Those men and women who are creative, adventuresome, prudent risk takers in the "getting," often bring those same qualities to the "giving." Indeed, many years ago we coined the label "the venturesome donor" to describe our most enterprising clients.

One client frequently tells us that making the money was easy—the natural consequence of doing those things at which he was good. In contrast, giving it away *well*, was less intuitive and more difficult. Supporting his alma mater, the United Way, and his regional hospital's capital campaign were obvious charitable choices and important ones. But figuring out how to make a difference in society, how to align his values and his passions with his charitable giving, and how to create giving strategies that leveraged his charitable gifts, how to determine the impact of his giving, and how and when to involve his family, was a much more difficult challenge for him. It was at that crossroads that he first appeared at TPI.

Why do those who give so well, who seek to change the world or their communities, decide to become venturesome donors? How and from whom do they learn the ropes of giving well? How important is a philanthropic mission, goals, and strategies? What are the risks and opportunities posed by involving spouses and children on one's philanthropic voyage? What is the right medium for giving? Is it a private foundation (in 1992 infamously predicted by Silicon Valley futurist, Paul Saffo, to be "the BMW of the '90's") or is it a donor-advised fund at the local community foundation, a simpler and more connected vehicle for giving? What is "Social Venture Partners," and why are the "giving circles" emerging around the country so popular among high-tech entrepreneurs? Finally, where does one seek and find the advice and support necessary to create and advance giving programs that are both satisfying and effective?

Much has been written about such questions, but as with most subjects in the Information Age, the challenge in acquiring the knowledge and skills to become a high-impact donor is not a shortage of information, but often just the opposite. What many donors who are embarking on the odyssey of effective giving really need are charts—or at least good compasses—to guide them on the seas of venturesome giving.

This chapter provides the venturesome donor with the rudiments of such navigational tools. Like those that guided the mariners of the fifteenth century, such maps have their limitations. At some point some donors—the greatest of the adventurers—may well sail right off the edge of the known philanthropic world. And that is where the adventure really begins.

WHY GIVE?

The answer is unique to each and every donor. Sometimes the calculus is quite simple: "My wife died of breast cancer, and I want to help find the cure and memorialize her extraordinary life." But more often it is complex, a rich mix of motives, dreams, and objectives.

In TPI's 14 years of working with high-wealth individuals and families, we have seen almost as many motives for giving as we have seen donors. Some of the more frequent motivations include:

- *Legacy.* Among some donors, the desire to create a spiritual legacy as a balance or a complement to their material legacy is strong.
- *Community.* Many donors rightly feel blessed—by intelligence, education, caring families, supportive communities, hard work, success, and fate. Some may feel privileged to be able to support their communities with a portion of their wealth. Others may feel morally obliged to "give back." Some feel both.
- *Healing.* In Hebrew there is a lovely phrase, *tikkun olan,* which means "to heal the broken world." There is much to heal—hunger, homelessness, disease, child neglect, environmental degradation—and sadly, the list goes on and on.
- *Challenge.* Among entrepreneurs, the challenge of solving a vexing, seemingly intractable social problem can be the motivator for creative philanthropy.
- *Family.* Now that the family business has been sold, what are the opportunities for working with the family? For many, philanthropy can provide that platform.
- *Honor.* Those who endow symphony halls, libraries, and research laboratories in memory of family and friends do so to honor those loved ones.
- *Recognition.* For some, the desire to be recognized by society, or to rub shoulders with "the right people," is an important reason to give.
- *Tradition.* In some families, philanthropy is a long-standing tradition.
- *Satisfaction.* Perhaps the most primal motive for giving is just "feeling good." Giving feels good. It is satisfying to rise to a challenge, to make an impact, and to change the world (and sometimes oneself) for the better.

Understanding one's motives for giving is important. Absent a clear understanding of what is driving one's giving, choosing a giving vehicle, finding a focus, and deciding on a strategy are nothing so much as a random walk.

GETTING STARTED—SOME DEFINITIONS

Getting started in philanthropy is not about choosing between a charitable remainder trust and a donor-advised fund at the neighborhood community foundation, although some skilled and well-intended legal and financial advisors will wish to begin there. Long before the issue of the appropriate vehicle presents itself, the wise social investor will ask:

- What can I achieve with my charitable capital?
- What are the issues about which I care deeply?
- What is my vision of a world changed for the better through strategic giving?
- What is philanthropy, anyway? Is it different than charity?

Before one can answer these questions, some understanding of the words themselves may be in order.

To begin with, in its most literal sense *philanthropy* means "love of human-kind." Implicit in that meaning are two of philanthropy's great motivators and inspirations: compassion for and concern about one's fellow man. Peter Goldmark, a TPI Senior Fellow and a past president of the Rockefeller Foundation, once described philanthropy this way: "Philanthropy is the practice of applying assets of knowledge, passion and wealth to bring about constructive change."

Passion? What does passion have to do with high-impact giving? Passion is a subject with that not all our clients are comfortable, but one that we talk about a lot nonetheless. Personal passions are something givers are urged to explore deeply and thoughtfully before making a single gift. What are those things about which you care deeply, that will motivate you to give not only wisely, but with heart, as well as mind?

In a 1996 study that TPI conducted for Bankers Trust Private Bank, although 40 percent of the bank's ultra-high-net-worth clients said additional tax incentives would lead to increased giving, 65 percent said they would give more when they found "a passion." This is consistent with our experience with donors across the entire income spectrum.

And then there is *vision*. Some of our clients are initially perplexed by vision, inclined to ask, as George Bush Sr. once did, what's with this "vision thing"? Like passion, vision can be a powerful motivator and guide for giving.

In the world of high-performance institutions, "vision" is usually thought of as a compelling image of that better organization the institution seeks to become. A shared vision among family members about what they hope to achieve with their giving can be a powerful bond and inspiration. Similarly, a shared vision between donors and the nonprofit institutions they support can give rise to a sense of shared mission, agreed-upon goals, and common purpose.

GETTING STARTED—THE ADVISOR'S ROLE

Your money manager is the indispensable partner in the growth and preservation of your financial and social capital. Your estate planner is the professional to turn to in planning for the careful conveyance of your wealth to future generations. Private bankers, accountants, and life insurance planners also may be valued members of your wealth advisory team. Unfortunately, by their own admission, few among these professionals do the work of philanthropy planning well. No less than in the purchase of other services, when creating a plan for one's philanthropy it pays to be an informed consumer.

For almost 10 years TPI has been seeking to better understand how legal and financial advisors do and don't support their clients' charitable giving. In major studies involving almost 1,000 advisors nationwide we have been surprised to find that:

- Few advisors routinely ask their clients about their philanthropic interests.
- Many only discuss philanthropy when the client raises the issue.
- Discussions regarding philanthropy between client and advisor focus largely on the tax consequences of charitable giving.
- Many advisors feel that any inquiry into a client's philanthropic interests is unprofessional—possibly even unethical—and can result in the loss of the client's trust, or even his or her business.

The reasons for this ambivalence among advisors about philanthropy counseling are many and complex, but in the main can be reduced to two: lack of training in the art of philanthropy counseling, and lack of personal experience with philanthropy planning, at least beyond introducing clients to the mechanics of giving.

The reasons aside, among the consequences of well-intended advisors finding themselves out of their depth in such matters are donors who (1) are equipped with the wrong giving vehicles, (2) have no compass for their giving, (3) have little or no understanding of how to go about identifying the right organizations to which to give, and (4) have no idea how to identify the resources needed to avoid such pitfalls.

Thus, a word to the wise. When getting started with a philanthropic plan, make sure your advisor understands the values that ground your philanthropic vision, as well as your philanthropic objectives. Also, take the time to understand the fundamentals of the different giving vehicles available to you (see the discussion below). A nominal investment in time and preparedness can head off unforeseen and unwanted consequences down the road.

CHOOSE YOUR ADVISORS CAREFULLY

After launching and operating a successful venture capital firm for many years, Dana Tabbor had recently sold the controlling interest. Before starting the next venture, Dana and her husband Joe had decided to invest some time in creating a charitable fund to address the issues immigrants confront in coming to the United States. In addition, as successful children of immigrants, they wanted to create a legacy for their own children, one that would further anchor their children in this country.

In a conversation with their estate planner, Dana and Joe were advised to create a charitable remainder trust to benefit unspecified charities. On their trip home from their lawyer's office, Dana remarked how peculiar it was that their lawyer had never asked them about their values, their philanthropic dreams, or the role of family legacy in their philanthropic future. Joe agreed that there appeared to be a disconnect between their objectives and their lawyer's approach to creating what was in fact a very important part of their total wealth landscape.

The next day the Tabbors called their financial advisor, a woman well versed in the art and method of wealth and philanthropy planning. With her help they quickly realized that because of their desire to create a legacy for their children and lack of need for current income from their charitable gift, they would be far better served by a supporting organization at their local community foundation, or even a private foundation. They called their estate planner and told him so.

GETTING STARTED—SOME QUESTIONS

In working with individual and family clients who are ramping up their giving or considering a new level of philanthropy, TPI often interviews the donor and asks questions such as:

WHY GIVE?

- Why are you interested in philanthropy?
- What are your values? Your philanthropic goals? Your passions about society and the world in which we live?

- What do you hope to accomplish with your giving?
- Is it important that your family be involved in your philanthropy? Why? How would you like them involved?

FINANCIAL CONSIDERATIONS

- How much can you afford to give?
- How much do you want to give now? How much later? How much at death?
- Is the decision of how to give time-sensitive?
- Do you need income now, but would like to benefit a charitable organization at your death?

HOW MUCH TIME CAN YOU INVEST IN YOUR PHILANTHROPY?

- Do you imagine that your philanthropy will be primarily or exclusively the gift of money, or do you imagine investing significant amounts of time as well?
- Are you at a point in your life where you can afford to invest considerable amounts of time in your giving?
- If you were to start a private foundation, would you be willing to put in the time to conduct regular site visits, and attend and manage regular board meetings?
- Do you believe in the "venture philanthropy" model of giving, bringing your professional skills as well as your financial assets to the governance and operations of an organization.

HOW HANDS-ON DO YOU WISH TO BE?

- Do you want to give to nonprofit organizations and be able to direct the programs to which your dollars go?
- Do you want to get to know the people who work for the organizations to which you give? To meet with them on an ongoing basis?
- Do you have a low tolerance for administration and paperwork? Do you prefer to delegate that work to others?

WHAT DO YOU WISH TO GIVE?

Almost any type of asset may find a grateful charitable recipient. Tax implications will vary, however, and you should consult with your financial or legal advisor in seeking answers to such questions. Among the assets you may donate are:

- Cash and cash equivalents
- Publicly traded securities including restricted stock
- Stock in a closely held corporation
- Life insurance policies
- Real estate
- Mutual funds
- Personal property
- Retirement assets
- Artwork
- In-kind gifts and pro bono services
- Volunteer time

GIVING WELL—QUALITIES OF EFFECTIVE PHILANTHROPY

In the course of working with hundreds of clients over the years, TPI has found that those donors who have the most impact and derive the most satisfaction from their giving practice philanthropy that is characterized by some—and for a very rare few, *all*—of the following qualities.[1]

VALUES-DRIVEN

Effective philanthropy is usually driven by strong personal or family values, beliefs about what is important in life. Those values, and the personal or family passions that often accompany them, provide the compass for giving. In working with families and trying to help them identify their values, TPI often asks questions such as:

- What are your personal/family values? What do you and/or your family stand for?
- What values guide the choices you make in life?
- How do the values you hold dear speak to the kind of donor you wish to be?
- What are the stories you tell in your family about your family and ancestors? What values do they represent?
- What values do your past gift decisions exemplify?

PROACTIVE

Effective donors are often proactive donors. Their giving is driven by their vision and passions, not in response to the requests of others. Such philanthropists decide what they are interested in, what issues and causes they wish to tackle, and then design approaches to address those objectives.

FOCUSED

TPI was once described by one of its own board members as being "propagandists for focus." Whether or not it is propaganda, it *is* an article of faith. A focus for giving creates the ability to concentrate resources. It helps define and clarify philanthropic goals. Focus enables the donor to build knowledge and intelligence about a particular issue, and to evaluate funding opportunities against the backdrop of that knowledge. Moreover, focus also provides donors with a rationale for saying "no" to requests that are outside their area of interest. Focus comes in many forms. It can be:

- Programmatic—eradicating disease, ending homelessness, or preserving wetlands
- Geographic—the community that was home to the family business for generations
- Population-specific—women and girls, single mothers
- Value-specific—organizations committed to preserving families
- Strategic—building infrastructure and capacity of nonprofits

GOAL/OUTCOME-DIRECTED

Many effective donors are clear about their desired goals and outcomes, and ask their grantee-partners to be the same. Where possible, the philanthropist develops concrete, measurable indicators of success for the philanthropy. For example, a funder interested in providing economic opportunity for inner city populations might assess the impact of a grant by looking at new job creation, wage increases, or, less concrete but still measurable, new skill development among residents of the community.

RESEARCH- AND REALITY-BASED

The most effective philanthropy involves a combination of both head and heart. Although the issue areas and goals may be driven by vision and values, strategic philanthropy involves rigorous research and analysis of, for example, service/funding gaps, needs, opportunities, best practices, and effective approaches. Equipped with such a studied understanding, the donor can then determine how most effectively to target philanthropic resources to make important differences.

CLEARLY DEFINED STRATEGIES AND ROLES

Once the vision is clear and the focus and goals defined, the next step is selecting the strategies that are most likely to achieve the donor's philanthropic goals. In addition, what roles does the donor wish to play in his or her philanthropy? Some roles include:

- Capacity builder (of organizations, neighborhoods, or even a field of interest)
- Innovator/incubator (of new ideas, programs, or organizations)
- Disseminator/replicator (of effective models and best practices)
- Change agent (of cultural, social, and legal structures, or of expectations, addressing underlying causes and systems)
- Community builder (developing human, social, or physical capital in an area)
- Critic or advocate (of public or social policies)
- Venture philanthropist (supporting social entrepreneurs who are starting up or building the capacity of organizations, or trying new approaches)
- Developer of leaders (of organizations, schools, or communities)

The roles that funders choose influence the types of charitable gifts they make, the structure and mix of gifts, and whether they choose to use tools other than grants, such as technical assistance, convening like-minded donors, program-related investments (charitable loans), and/or media outreach.

DUE DILIGENCE

Just like a financial investor, the prudent donor typically conditions any significant gift on appropriate due diligence, that is, assessing the capabilities of the organization to which the gift will be made, as well as the design and management of the specific program to be funded. Philanthropic due diligence may include careful proposal reviews, site visits, and reference checks.

VEHICLES FOR GIVING

Now that you, the venturesome donor, have decided *why* you wish to give, *what* you hope to achieve, the *focus* for your giving, and the *strategies* you wish to employ, you need to decide what tools and vehicles are most likely to enable you to achieve your goals. Multiple tools are available, and you need not be stingy in choosing among them—many effective donors use multiple vehicles to achieve numerous and sometimes very different philanthropic objectives.[2]

> *Note:* An important and emphatic *caveat emptor* is appropriate here. The choice, creation, and application of charitable vehicles moves the giving experience from the realm of art to that of law. What follows is a rough and necessarily summary overview of the primary tools for giving. The law of charitable giving is in constant flux, and the reader is urged not to rely on the following menu of giving options as more than a very large-scale road map. As in any other serious investment matter, we urge you, the prudent donor, to consult with a professional advisor in choosing and creating the appropriate legal vehicle to achieve both your philanthropic and wealth-preservation goals.

DIRECT GIFTS

With the possible exception of volunteering, the direct gift is the simplest way to give. A tax deduction is available for most direct gifts, so long as they are to recognized, tax-exempt organizations. Such organizations include private nonprofit organizations that address social, cultural, environmental, religious, and other issues. You also may make qualifying tax-deductible gifts to a public agency, for example, a public school.

As a general rule, an income tax deduction is allowed for the amount of a direct gift, and such a deduction is available for gifts that in the aggregate do not exceed 50 percent of annual adjusted gross income (AGI). Gifts of stock and real estate are typically capped at 30 percent of annual AGI.

What are the principal resources that will help you learn about (1) the nonprofit status of an organization to which you may wish to give, and/or (2) the quality of such an organization? The charitable status of a nonprofit organization can be verified at Guidestar (www.guidestar.org), which provides information about the nation's roughly 800,000 nonprofits in the form of their annual IRS tax filings. For additional on-line information you can also check the Better Business Bureau's Wise Giving Alliance *www.give.org,* which includes information on the nation's larger nonprofits and rates them according to a limited set of criteria. If you seek a more personal or local point of view, your community foundation and/or United Way may be a useful source of information.

PLANNED GIFTS

Planned gifts allow donors to give during their lifetime or after their death, while in some cases providing current income to the donors and in others, depending on the form of the planned gift, providing for their heirs. A planned gift can be created to take effect either at death or during the donor's lifetime. Among the most common planned giving tools are:

- *Charitable bequest.* Charitable bequests are probably the oldest of the many planned giving options. A charitable bequest is essentially anything that a donor leaves to a charity from his or her estate through a will or *intervivos* trust. A donor can leave a bequest to charity that specifies a specific dollar amount, that specifies a percentage of his or her estate, or leaves any assets after the family has been provided for. A paid life insurance policy or appreciated securities also can be the subject of a charitable bequest and net the donor considerable tax savings.
- *Charitable gift annuity.* This tool provides the donor with lifetime income. To establish a gift annuity, the donor contributes cash or other assets to a nonprofit organization, which in turn agrees to make fixed annuity payments to the donor for the rest of his or her life. The donor can take an immediate income tax deduction for a portion of the gift, and a portion of each annuity payment is treated as a tax-free return on investment. The nonprofit organization that receives the gift benefits from the portion of the gift not used for payments.
- *Charitable remainder trust.* A CRT is a planned giving device that pays income to beneficiaries named by the donor for a specified period of years. At the end of that period, the balance of the trust is transferred to one or more charitable organizations selected by the donor. The creator of the trust can take an income tax deduction—for the actuarially determined value of the portion of the gift that will ultimately pass to a charity—in the year in which the trust is created.

- *Charitable lead trust.* A CLT allows the donor to select a nonprofit organization or organizations to receive income from the trust for a period of years, with the remainder typically passing to the donor's beneficiaries at a reduced rate of taxation.

PRIVATE AND FAMILY FOUNDATIONS

For certain families and individuals, a private foundation provides the ideal vehicle for philanthropic investment. Unique in the constellation of vehicles for charitable giving, a private foundation provides personal control over and unequalled flexibility in charitable giving. But those benefits have trade-offs, namely, the costs—both financial and time- and energy-related—of creating and managing the foundation.

For families that seek a forum in which family members can work toward common goals, a private or family foundation has no peer. It can perform this function over multiple generations and indeed, most are established with the expectation that they will be "perpetual."

A *private foundation* receives most of its funds from and is usually subject to the control of an individual or a family. Created as either a not-for-profit corporation or a charitable trust (the former is more common), a private foundation must receive tax-exempt status from the Internal Revenue Service (IRS). Once it has done so, a private foundation confers certain tax advantages, for example, a donor may deduct up to 30 percent of AGI for cash donations to the fund. (Gifts to public charities provide deductions of up to 50 percent of AGI.)

As this book goes to press (2004), private foundations must make charitable expenditures of at least 5 percent of the market value of their net investment assets (referred to as the *minimum distributable amount*) each year in order to avoid penalty. They also must pay a 1 to 2 percent excise tax on net investment income. Congress is currently considering legislation to increase the minimum payout or reduce or eliminate the ability of foundations to count administrative costs against the minimum distribution, proposals that have been criticized by the nonprofit community as calling into question the ability of foundations to preserve principal.

A *family foundation* is not a distinct legal entity, but merely a private foundation that is strongly influenced by the original donor family through board membership. Family foundations provide the opportunity for family members to learn about family governance, money management, communications, and other life skills. Although rules against self-dealing apply to private foundations, they do not preclude family members from serving as compensated staff and compensated board members, so long as that compensation is reasonable.

There are three common types of private or family foundations:

- *Private endowed foundations.* The most common form of private foundation; described above.
- *Private operating foundations.* Nonpublicly supported organizations that devote most of their resources and energies to operating charitable programs, rather than making grants to other organizations. Examples include operating a historic property or research facility or museum.
- *Pass-through foundations.* Nonoperating foundations that distribute all the contributions the foundation receives in a given year. The pass-through option may be declared or revoked on a year-by-year basis.

This question is often heard: How much principal do I need to make it economically sensible to create a private foundation? Although there is no right or wrong answer, for endowed foundations $2 million is sometimes cited as a threshold that justifies the administrative burdens of creating a foundation (notwithstanding the fact that the great majority of private foundations in the United States have endowments of less than $1 million). A $2 million foundation will typically make grants in the range of $100,000 a year.

Creating a private or family foundation is neither complicated nor particularly costly, but it requires a qualified attorney to do so. The management and administration of a private foundation, however, entail relatively complex annual tax filings with both the IRS and a state's attorney general.

For those considering creating a private foundation, a first step should be obtaining a good comprehensive overview, (see "First Steps in Starting a Foundation" in the Additional Reading Section at the end of this chapter).

COMMUNITY FOUNDATIONS

Many donors are strongly committed to their communities and wish to invest and/or give back to them. Community foundations provide a flexible, supportive, and administratively convenient means for doing so.

Community foundations are tax-exempt public charities. They typically receive charitable gifts from a broad base of private sources and manage them under community control for charitable purposes, primarily focused on local needs. A community foundation's raison d'etre is to address community or regional issues, and to improve the lives of people in its geographic area.

There are roughly 700 community foundations in the United States today. While a few are statewide in their reach, most serve cities, regions, or towns. They are typically governed by a board of involved citizens from the community they serve, and are managed by professionals with expertise about community needs.

A community foundation's endowment usually consists of (1) numerous donor-advised funds (see below), (2) a general fund over which the foundation has full discretion in giving, and (3) other funds that are restricted to use for specific charities or for support of charitable efforts in a particular field (e.g., education or youth programs).

In addition to providing administrative support to the "donor advisor," a community foundation can provide advice to the donor on community needs and effective organizations. This often occurs within the scope of the financial relationship between the donor and the community foundation; more comprehensive advice will sometimes entail an additional fee. Donors may make gifts to community foundations in the following ways:

- By creating a donor-advised fund, over which the donor has advisory authority in recommending gifts both within and outside the community.
- Through a gift to a field-of-interest fund, a fund dedicated to supporting organizations that address issues relating to, for example, the environment, children, women, or education.
- Through an unrestricted gift, the principal or income from which will be put to use in the community in the ways the trustees deem most needed.

Because community foundations are public charities supported by donors from across the community, all contributions enjoy the maximum tax benefit—up to 50 percent of AGI.

DONOR-ADVISED FUNDS

Donor-advised funds may be created at virtually any public charity, but they are still most commonly found at community foundations. In the last 10 years, a number of other public charities such as universities, local United Ways, Combined Jewish Philanthropies, women's funds, and others have begun offering donor-advised funds. Such host organizations typically offer the benefit of their expertise on specific populations and/or issue areas.

In the last decade, donor-advised funds have also become common at public charity subsidiaries of major mutual fund companies. More recently, enterprising, smaller, client-oriented institutions have created boutique donor-advised funds for specialized purposes.

In a donor-advised fund, donors recommend gifts, subject to the public charity's formal approval. As a matter of practice, the host organization's board almost always will approve the recommended gift, on the condition that it is to a legitimate charity. Although there are rumblings at the IRS that this virtual "rubber stamp" does not constitute adequate due diligence, the status quo seems secure for now.

Although minimum gift requirements vary from host organization to host organization, the minimum gift required to establish such a fund is often $10,000. In most cases, there is no prescribed timetable for gifting from such funds; some donor advisors will make significant gifts in one year and very few in the next. Unlike in a private foundation, from which a 5 percent annual payout is typically required, there is no minimum payout required from a donor-advised fund. In most cases, there is a right to appoint successors (usually family and/or friends) to advise the host organization at such time as the original donor specifies—often at death, but sometimes before.

Why choose a donor-advised fund over other philanthropic vehicles? First, because of its convenience. The public charity that is home to the fund assumes all the administrative responsibilities that would fall to family or staff at a private foundation. Second, like family foundations, a donor-advised fund can provide a platform for the practice of charitable family enterprise, an opportunity to articulate family values, practice family democracy, and invest in the family's community. Third, a donor-advised fund allows the donor to participate in a larger community of donors in support of a common cause.

The benefits of the donor-advised fund notwithstanding, for the donor or family that wishes to create a long-lived philanthropic enterprise, one over which they can exercise complete control and one that offers the opportunity to teach children money management and administrative skills, the private or family foundation may offer the superior vehicle.

Investing in Vermont

Sam and Susannah Patrick had enjoyed successful careers in Burlington, Vermont, and wanted to invest in the community that had supported their various enterprises. Because of their limited interest in (and truth be told, tolerance for) administration and management chores, they established a donor-advised fund—the Patrick Family Fund—at the Vermont Community Foundation (VCF).

The Patricks' objective was to be involved in the operation of the fund for their lifetimes, with their children as equal partners. At the death of the founders, their intent was to have their children succeed them as donor advisors to the fund. Over that two-generation period—which they projected would be 50 years—Sam and Susannah and their children will use the family fund as an opportunity to give together and to make that giving an expression of what the Patrick family "stands for." Their gifts will largely target economic development and education in Vermont's poorer communities.

Although the Patricks could have specified that the family retain effective control over the fund's charitable assets for succeeding generations, they decided instead to "sunset" their advisory rights, effective upon the death of the last of their children, believing their objectives to have been met at that point. At that time, control over the fund will pass to VCF's board and become subject to the board's discretion. However, the Patrick Family Fund will retain its name indefinitely, thereby affording the family a small measure of "posterity in action."

SUPPORTING ORGANIZATIONS

Imagine that you seek a measure of control over your philanthropy that is greater than that available via a donor-advised fund, but you also want the administrative convenience and the higher annual contribution levels permitted by the Internal Revenue Code for gifts to a public charity. A *supporting organization* may be the right vehicle.

Once relatively rare, supporting organizations are increasingly common at community foundations and are beginning to appear at some universities. As their name suggests, supporting organizations are closely associated with a public charity in a way that supports its purposes. For instance, a donor who wished to support his or her alma mater through the creation of a scholarship fund might create a supporting organization over which the donor and his or her family could exercise considerable control.

Supporting organizations offer important advantages over the alternatives. Because the organization is attached to a public charity, the donor enjoys the superior tax benefits of a gift to a public charity. In addition, supporting organizations are typically governed by a board that comprises members of the family, as well as outside members identified by the donor. It will also include members appointed by the public charity. Typically, the public charity has the right to make the majority of board appointments.

As suggested above, the supporting organization may be an especially appropriate vehicle for the donor who (1) wishes to involve his or her family in grant-making decisions, (2) seeks grant-making assistance from the host organization's staff, and (3) wants the more liberal tax contribution allowances afforded to donors for gifts to public charities.

Supporting and Supported

Rachel Lansford went to work for Microsoft in the late 1970s, and, through the vesting of generous stock options, had made a fortune. She now sought to make the preservation of the meadows, marshes, and summits of Washington's Cascades her philanthropic mission in life. She also was determined to involve her children and grandchildren in the enterprise.

It was clear to Lansford that a planned giving vehicle such as a charitable remainder trust to benefit a local land trust would not give her the hands-on involvement she was seeking. Nor did she want the responsibilities of a private foundation, or the arm's-length limitations of a donor-advised fund.

After talking with her advisors, Lansford arrived at the solution of creating a supporting organization at the Cascades Land Trust. This choice would allow her to (1) significantly involve the children in the organization's grant decisions and governance, (2) make a more permanent statement than would a donor-advised fund at the local community foundation, and (3) create a relationship with the premier land trust in the region, one that would support her and her descendants in generations of creative, intelligent investment in the environment.

GIVING CIRCLES

Giving circles are among the oldest and the newest of giving vehicles. With roots in ancient Jewish, Christian, and Muslim traditions, giving circles are essentially social investment clubs.

In their simplest form, giving circles are an alliance of like-minded donors who pool some charitable resources, learn together about issues and causes that interest them, and make collective social investment decisions. As the circle evolves and becomes more sophisticated, members of the circle sometimes choose to adopt a style common to venture philanthropists, bringing to the circle and its investments contributions of time, skills, in-kind resources, and contacts. This serves to leverage the impact of the monetary contributions.

Some giving circles are sponsored and staffed by a public or private foundation and operate over a predetermined period of time. Others may be created for a specific purpose, be quite short-lived, and operate outside of any formal structure or sponsorship.

Finding a Donor Community

Emile Poncet was a gifted donor. He had a clear vision of the better community he wished to create in West Palm Beach, and the roles that affordable child care and early-childhood education played in that vision. Moreover, he had the skills and the time to attend to his small private foundation and to contribute substantial volunteer time as well.

But Emile felt isolated, unsure of his judgments about the best nonprofits in his areas of interest, unsure about his ability to conduct the best due diligence, and somewhat distant from the larger donor community.

By chance, in talking with the West Palm United Way, Emile learned about a new giving circle in town called Small Wonders. Begun five years earlier by four donors passionately committed to offering disadvantaged pre-K-aged children the same educational opportunities as their wealthier peers, the circle had by now grown to 60 members and was supporting two pre-K education programs. The circle recently also had begun to consider the related issue of affordable day care, hoping to support economically challenged parents at the same time that it was contributing to the education of their children.

Emile attended the next meeting of Small Wonders. He was pleasantly surprised at the modest level of the required contribution—$5,000 a year for two years, which Emile chose to double—and to learn that private foundations were welcome as members of the circle. He signed on the dotted line, and was soon the *eminence grise* and a regular presence at the Small Wonders Nursery School, a creative learning environment for children aged 2 through 5 of poor working parents.

CONCLUSION

Making good decisions about giving is, like making good decisions about any other investment decision, part art, part science. There is no off-the-shelf process that will ensure success with every gift or grant. But for those donors who successfully marry their vision and values with thoughtful inquiry, research, and due diligence, the impact of their giving can be virtually unlimited.

Becoming a skilled donor can take time. It takes hard work, persistence, patience, a willingness to experiment, and a willingness sometimes to fail. But it can and should also be fun—not in a frivolous sense, but as in enjoyable and capable of bringing joy. Philanthropy, while serious work, should not be so serious that it becomes a burden. If it seems overwhelming at times, don't be reluctant to seek out peers, partners, and outside help.

Perhaps most important of all, remember the endgame: the venturesome donor's opportunity to dream big dreams about what is important, about the future we seek for our children and our children's children. Those dreams, thoughtfully and creatively pursued, are philanthropy's real opportunity, and arguably its mandate. Money given well can change the world, if sometimes only one life at a time.

Notes

1. Thanks are due my colleagues Leslie Pine, Melinda Marble, and Joe Breiteneicher, who prepared earlier versions of this menu.
2. Portions of this chapter were developed for Citigroup's Private Bank. The author is grateful to Citigroup for permission to publish this material here.

Additional Reading and Resources

Publications

Alda, Alan. "Giving Well," TPI Newsletter *Initiatives.* Volume Four, Number 1, Winter 1996. Text of a speech given to the Council on Foundations' 1995 Family Foundation Conference.

Breiteneicher, Joe, Ellen Remmer, and Amy Zell Elssworth. *Philanthropy for the Wise Donor-Investor.* The Philantrophic Initiative, Boston: 2001. An introductory primer for families on strategic giving with examples and family stores.

Edie, John A. *First Steps in Starting a Foundation.* Washington DC: Council on Foundations, 1998. Guide for the creation of foundations, including a list of references and sample documents.

Esposito, Virginia M., ed. *Family Foundation Library.* Washington, DC: Council on Foundations, 1997. Comprehensive four-volume series: *Family Issues, Governance, Grantmaking, and Management.*

Esposito, Virginia M., ed. *Resources for Family Philanthropy.* Washington DC:, National Center for Family Philanthropy, 1999. Essays offering family philanthropies guidance for reviewing and evaluating available resources for giving programs.

Gersick, Kelin. *The Succession Workbook: Continuity Planning for Family Foundations.* Washington, DC: Council on Foundations, 2000. Workbook with exercises, discussion points, and tips for planning the future involvement in the family foundation.

Johnson, Stephen P. "Advancing Philanthropy: Tapping the Potential of Legal and Financial Advisors," *Trusts and Estates,* Summer 2000.

Johnson, Stephen P., ed. *Doing Well by Doing Good—Improving Client Service, Increasing Philanthropic Capital: The Legal and Financial Advisor's Role.* Boston; TIP, June 2000.

Price, Susan Crites. *The Giving Family: Raising Our Children to Help Others.* Washington DC: Council on Foundations, 2001. Inspired ideas and real stories that can help parents, teachers, and other adults instill the spirit of giving and volunteering in children.

Organizations

The following organizations provide materials, education, and networking services to a wide range of independent, corporate, community, and family foundations.

- *Council on Foundations.* Publishes a wide variety of very useful materials for family foundations, as well as conducts an annual Family Foundation Conference and period Next Generation Retreats. www.cof.org; telephone 202-466-6512.
- *Regional Associations of Grantmakers.* Regional, state, or community associations of grantmaking members, many of which conduct roundtables for family foundations. http://www.rag.org/; telephone 202-466-6512.
- *National Center for Family Philanthropy.* Conducts research and develops educational materials and programs for families and individuals. www.ncfp.org; telephone 202-293-3424.
- *Association of Small Foundations.* Assists foundations with few or no staff, runs a colleague to colleague program, and organizes regional meetings. www.smallfoundations.org; telephone 301-907-3337.
- *Guidestar.* A source of online information about operations and finances of nonprofit organizations. http://www.guidestar.com/.

Author Background

Stephen P. Johnson, is a Vice President at The Philanthropic Initiative, Inc. (TPI), a nonprofit consulting firm that provides planning, program design, and management services to individual and family donors and corporate, private, and community foundations. Steve works with families, individuals, and foundations in creating and managing effective giving programs. He also leads TPI's efforts to enhance the professional advisor's role in promoting philanthropy.

In addition to his work at TPI, Steve has for many years served as the managing trustee of his family's foundation, which focuses its giving in the Lake Champlain Basin. Prior to joining TPI, he spent 20 years in law, public policy, education, and strategic planning. He has been a corporate litigator and a counsel to the U.S. Senate, a government-relations professional, and a strategic and long-range planner for the courts and the organized bar. Steve has taught both undergraduates and law students, and written and spoken extensively on public policy and the future of the justice system. He is a regular speaker and writer on philanthropy.

Conclusion—Getting It Right:
The Key Decisions You Will Make

Louis P. Crosier

Many people focus time and energy on decisions that will have a small impact on their financial lives, yet they spend little time on the key decisions that will have a great impact. An important example of this is the asset allocation decision. Despite the widely accepted view that asset allocation drives around 90 percent of investment returns, most people spend most of their time on manager and security selection instead of deciding how much to have in stocks versus bonds versus other broad asset categories. In college, I remember a young woman who spent two hours each day running, stretching, and lifting weights so that she could make the varsity tennis team. She worked much harder than the other players, yet she never moved up the ladder. Although she was in great physical condition, she had lousy shots. If she had spent time improving her forehand and backhand, I suspect she would have made the team. She simply was not focused on the variable that had the most power to impact her performance.

In this Conclusion, I have tried to distill the key insights from the book into bite-sized "take-aways." I also make suggestions with regard to where I think you should spend your resources—time and money. I find people get this wrong all the time, and, ironically, it is very costly. These take-aways are based on my experience working with entrepreneurs and are general in nature. They should be a catalyst for you to review the corresponding sections of this book as you see fit, rather than as specific directives. As with the advice in every chapter of the book, you should not act upon the recommendations without obtaining specific legal, tax, and investment counsel from a licensed professional as it applies to your situation.

Here are, in my view, the most important take-aways:

1. *Lay the groundwork early.* Some decisions should be made early on when your company's valuation is low. A nicely laid foundation can be of great benefit down the road, even if it appears costly at the time the work is done. I would spend the money to put a good team in place for advice with regard to exercising stock options, making 83(b) elections, signing employment agreements, and creating trusts for wealth protection and transfer. Be vigilant of tax-related issues, especially as they relate to the alternative minimum tax.

2. *Negotiate well.* In an effort to go public or to get purchased, people often focus too much on making sure the transaction does not fall through, and they neglect to push for certain important deal terms.

If your company is purchased for cash, avoid earn-outs and escrows. If there is an escrow, it should be attached only to an audit of accurate representation of what has happened in the past, not future performance when you may have less decision-making impact and accounting control than you did before selling the company.

If your company is purchased for stock, you want the right to sell the stock immediately, subject to few or no restrictions. For this reason you want registered shares, and, if possible, you want to avoid affiliate status. Furthermore, try to be outside the material nonpublic information loop and minimally subject to employee "blackout" periods. Most people are offered executive positions in the company that acquires theirs. Although this can be flattering and allow for some control over corporate affairs, it materially impacts your ability to achieve liquidity in a sale. From this perspective you are better off in a lower position or leaving the company altogether. It is worth hiring experienced M&A legal counsel to help you negotiate the most favorable deal terms.

3. *Focus on the people not the brand.* When selecting advisors, don't overemphasize the name of the firm you choose. In the service industry

brands are often developed by great people and maintained by mediocre people. Success in services is difficult to scale. The brand name of the firm should
be secondary to the person you work with. Whether it is a law firm, accounting firm, investment advisor, or other professional, do not take the brand
of the firm to mean quality control. Unlike a branded commodity product,
produced and checked by a machine, wealth management is a people business. The intelligence, training, experience, and ethics of individuals vary.
As a basic rule of thumb, I would apply the good doctor theory to selection
of advisors. How many years out of medical school is the person, under
whom did he train, how frequently does he perform this operation, and is
he well supported by his institution? Great sales people are not necessarily
great advisors.

   4. *Sell the stock.* Large single-stock positions provide one of the greatest
opportunities in life for mind games. You can approach the decision of
whether or not to sell a single-stock position from many perspectives. Of
those who do not want to sell their stock, most are reluctant to pay the tax;
others have a price target in mind that is higher than the current price; and
others have so much faith in the company, frequently because it is an industry giant, that they just will not sell it. Yet these reasons often blind people to
the reality that single-stock risk is the highest order of investment risk one
can take.

   I usually ask people if they had all the proceeds from their sale in cash,
how much of their stock would they buy with it. The answer is almost always
less than 100 percent. I have seen smart people who sold their business for
stock to well-known firms in "stable" industries lose fortunes by not diversifying. Stock prices do come down, and you can see the proceeds from your
life's work quickly vanish. When your business gets acquired, you have
already won the game.

   Consider a possible solution:
   a. Decide how much you want to have as a nest egg, an amount
      that you never want to have at risk, and then sell as much stock
      as it takes to get that amount and pay the taxes on the sale.
   b. Include in the nest-egg capital enough of a cushion so that if
      you earned 1.5 percent of the value of the nest egg each year, it
      would give you enough annual income to maintain the lifestyle
      you desire. (After taking fees, taxes, and inflation into account,
      1.5 percent is a fairly good ballpark for an investment return
      obtainable from a moderate-risk portfolio.)

c. With the rest of the stock, do as you like because this is your "risk capital." However, I would suggest it is prudent to sell out of your *entire* single-stock position in a reasonable time frame, pay the tax, and reinvest it in a broadly diversified portfolio that has the risk/ return characteristics with which you are comfortable. In my view this will allow you to live well (and sleep well) into the future.

If you are in top management of a public company a selling program (10b5-1) makes sense. As a general guide, aim to sell 1 to 5 percent of your equity each year, but get professional legal advice because the amount you sell will vary depending on the trading liquidity of the company shares, the anticipated market impact of your selling on the stock price, and regulatory issues related to your status within the company. Exchange funds can be a good second choice. If your company allows it, hedging and prepaid forward sale contracts can provide some insurance for you, but be careful of the tax implications of these more complex strategies.

5. *Do not reinvest immediately.* If being wealthy is new to you, experience what it feels like. You will not know immediately how it feels to see your portfolio move up and down by hundreds of thousands of dollars each day. Even if you have $100 million, it might feel uncomfortable to see your portfolio down $5 million in a short period of time, but this equates approximately to an average month's volatility of the U.S. stock market. It takes a while to understand how big a nest egg you want to set aside. You will be bombarded with people who want to invest your money. They will be well paid for doing so, whereas, if there is no action taken, they typically will not make money. Once you are in cash (T-bills or the tax-free equivalent), there really is no rush. The chances are you will not be losing much to inflation, so why hurry into an investment plan that you might want to undo once you understand your wealth management alternatives and yourself better.

6. *Seek out objectivity, integrity, and transparency.* It is important to understand how firms make their money and how individuals within those firms are compensated. For example, salespeople generally receive higher compensation for recommending that you invest in riskier assets like small-capitalization and international equities, hedge funds, and other alternative investments. They are compensated more for selling you actively managed investments than index funds. In short, they are compensated differently for each type of investment product they sell. How then can you know whether the advice you receive is based on what they believe is truly in your best interest, or whether they are trying maximize their compensation.

Within wealth management firms themselves, different layers of conflict exist. Firms that select and monitor investment managers for you also might have those managers as clients, either for trading or consulting work. In this case, it is hard to know if the investment manager has been selected for you because it is an outstanding money manager or because it is a good client of the firm recommending it. Ask the firms you are considering for their sources of revenue. And ask individuals within these firms how they are compensated.

7. *Cordinate your tax, trust and estate, insurance, and investment decisions.* You can accomplish this by using a firm that does everything, you can get all of your advisors in the same room on a regular basis, or you can hire an individual to coordinate it all for you. Look for advisors you really trust. It takes considerable homework and time to find and cultivate good advisors. Generally, this requires interviewing many firms and checking references carefully. Once you find a good advisor, nurture the relationship. Switching costs—trading and taxes—are high. If you think of advisors as partners in managing your wealth, you likely will have a more successful relationship than if you think of them as vendors. In the same way that you would like them to be committed enough to you to take personal pride in the work they do for you, make the same commitment to them. I believe strongly in independent advisors who do not benefit from any of the decisions of the other advisors. If you have a large amount of money, this generally means a dedicated family office or a relationship with an investment consulting firm that works with families as a core part of its business. If you have less money, you might seek out this kind of relationship through a multifamily office or an individual with a strong background in multiple areas of wealth management.

8. *Spend time and money on asset allocation.* Fortunes are made by concentration of risk; fortunes are maintained by diversification, good governance structures, and a well-thought-out spending policy. You likely made your money through a single company or a series of companies. You probably knew the industry well and ran a smart business. Whether or not you spent time thinking about it, you were taking very high company-specific risk. You also had industry risk and broad economic risk. If the company, the industry, or the economy had trouble, there is a good chance you had trouble, too.

Once you sell your business, you have the opportunity to diversify away the vast majority of all three of these types of risk, even economic risk. You can invest in a full range of assets that do well at different times in the economic cycle and that all do well over long periods of time. The myth that you must own equities to make attractive returns over the long term has been exposed as false. International government bonds, commodities, REITs, and other assets all have done as well as stocks, but their performance zigs and zags at different times so that the overall volatility of your portfolio is reduced. You can get the same attractive return as equities with less risk by using a broadly diversified portfolio.

Your allocation should include exposure to U.S. and non-U.S. public and private equity, U.S. and international government bonds, inflation-protected securities, hard assets such as gold and commodities, hybrid assets such as commercial real estate and, uncorrelated assets such as certain types of hedge funds and managed futures. Each of these has its own risk, return, liquidity, and expense characteristics, and you will need help understanding how they all interact together. But, to the extent that they are accessible to you, you should have some of each. The amount in each asset category should vary depending on the degree of risk you are seeking, but I would urge you to adopt an allocation that includes many asset categories. You will have to think in terms of the risk of the overall portfolio rather than its individual components because at any one time, one or more of these asset classes will have gut-wrenchingly negative performance, while others will be flying high, and that is what true diversification provides *by design*.

For your asset allocation work, engage a firm that has the ability to model as broad a range of asset classes as possible. The firm should be able to provide you with its views of expected risk, return, and correlation between these asset classes and should run simulations to show you the possible range of outcomes of different kinds of portfolios you might consider. All this should be done on an after-tax, after-fee basis. The exercise of going over the different scenarios seems frivolous in good economic times when stocks reach new highs each day, but in difficult times, you will be glad you went through a thorough asset allocation process.

9. *Write an investment policy statement.* Although at one time only endowments and foundations wrote investment policy guidelines, it has now become very fashionable for individuals and families to undertake the exercise. And for good reason. An investment policy statement helps you clarify your investment goals, risk and return expectations, and parameters surrounding the implementation of your investment plan. It helps you remain disciplined when you have the urge to move in or out of asset classes at inopportune times. And importantly, it serves as a working document to keep your advisors on track and accountable for their work.

10. *Understand risk.* Recognize that there will always be a trade-off between inflation risk (maintaining purchasing power) and the risk of losing capital. If the goal is to never have the principal value of your assets decline, then you want all your assets in cash instruments. This almost guarantees you will lose purchasing power over time. If, in contrast, you never want your purchasing power to decline, you would want all your assets in investments that match or outpace the rate of inflation. And this will expose you to the potential for loss of capital as market values fluctuate. Inherently, there is risk in either scenario.

Some investors can be fooled into thinking that they have no risk when they are all in cash. In fact, the long-term inflation rate as measured by the Consumer Price Index (CPI) is close to 3 percent. Many of us believe this is too low a hurdle, since the things we care about—education, medical care, and other services—rise at a faster rate. So, by being in cash, an asset class that will not lose principal value, you risk losing purchasing power. If inflation averages 3 percent, then you can lose approximately half of your purchasing power in 25 years. This is what happens when retirees maintain a stable income but realize over time that they don't have enough to live on.

When you consider how much capital you want to risk, think about risk in terms of maximum drawdown—the worst-case scenario. Ask investment managers you are considering what their maximum drawdown has been since the inception of their track record and what they would anticipate it to be in the worst-case scenario going forward. It's nice to get this in writing if you can.

11. *Do not chase performance.* Many people switch investment managers at the worst time, thinking they have been using a bad manager. Sometimes that is true, but generally they just have been invested in an asset category that is out of favor. Most managers neither outperform nor underperform their respective asset class benchmarks by very much. Therefore, if you have done a good job with the asset allocation decision, you will have some investments that are doing very well and some that are doing poorly. It is unlikely the same ones will do well or badly consistently over long periods of time. As long as you have the right categories represented in the overall pie, you will do fine. It is tempting, and generally a mistake, to move money out of poorly performing categories into ones that have been doing particularly well. In fact, evidence suggests that you should do just the opposite. If you are going to use active managers, evaluate them based primarily on their process, experience, references, and ability to understand and control risk.

12. *Evaluate performance net of taxes and fees (and risk).* In many cases, this will predispose you to favor index funds and shy away from hedge funds. For many asset classes this makes sense, but for some, active management will likely add value after all these considerations are taken into account. Generally, asset classes in which the range of investment manager returns is very wide make good candidates for active management. These include emerging markets, long/short equity hedge funds, commodities, and microcapitalization equities, among others. As a general rule, the smaller you go in market capitalization and the less developed the market, the more opportunity there is for good investment managers, typically with highly specialized and local market skills, to add value.

Although it may be appealing to compare returns at cocktail parties, it is essentially meaningless for people to do so without taking into account taxes, fees, and risk. So the next time someone tells you about a "great" investment manager, ask them three questions:

a. What is the Sharpe ratio (measure of risk-adjusted return) associated with the strategy net of fees and taxes?
b. What benchmark are they using, and what is its Sharpe ratio over the same time period?
c. How long is the track record? (as a general rule, less than three years of data makes it hard to establish whether chance or skill drove the return).

If you consider investing money in the manager, it is the track record going forward that matters. You will want someone experienced to evaluate the firm's process, its people, and its viability as a business. These criteria, and others, rather than past performance, likely will be more meaningful in helping you establish whether or not the track record can continue.

13. *Seek second opinions.* The audit function is important. Use the money you would have spent on active management of efficient asset categories (which you have decided to index) to hire an independent "second set of eyes" who can cut through the smoke and mirrors of the business to tell you how your overall portfolio is really doing and raise any red flags. Putting firms in competition can facilitate this because they will point out each other's mistakes, but it is better to hire someone impartial to analyze the data. Once you have selected this person, come up with a list of questions that will help you evaluate and hold advisors accountable (see Chapters 10 and 18) and incorporate these questions into the ongoing monitoring process you have outlined in your investment policy statement.

14. *Do not take the emotional side of your transition for granted.* Spend time talking as a family, take time to reevaluate what is important to you, and pick your friends based on whom you enjoy spending time with—then you never have to worry about people's motivations for being with you.
Once all the pieces are in place, if you haven't been doing it along the way, think deeply about what you really enjoy doing and do more of it.

Author Background

Louis P. Crosier is a Principal at Windward Investment Management and serves as a member of Windward's Investment Committee. His responsibilities include managing client portfolios and overseeing the firm's investment consulting practice.

Prior to joining Windward, Mr. Crosier worked in the investment management and consulting industries, most recently as a Vice President in the Wealth Management Division of Goldman Sachs. At Goldman Sachs, his clients included high-net-worth individuals and private foundations. His experience includes advising clients with regard to single-stock risk management, asset allocation, portfolio construction, and manager selection. He has helped clients invest in equities, fixed-income investments or, private equity, hedge funds, and derivative instruments. Prior to Goldman Sachs, he worked as a Manager of Business Development and Product Manager at Cambridge Energy Research Associates, an international energy research and consulting firm. During his time at business school, he spent two summers as an analyst at Cursitor-Eaton, an institutional investment advisor specializing in global asset allocation. Mr. Crosier earned a BA in French Literature and Psychology at Dartmouth College, a Master of Education degree from Harvard University, and an MBA from the Amos Tuck School.

His philanthropic activity includes work with Tenacity, the Youth Tennis Foundation, and Roxbury Preparatory Charter School.

Index